Protest,
Policy, and the
Problem of

Violence
Against
Women

A CROSS-NATIONAL COMPARISON

S. Laurel Weldon

UNIVERSITY OF PITTSBURGH PRESS

Published by the University of Pittsburgh Press, Pittsburgh, Pa., 15260
Copyright © 2002, University of Pittsburgh Press
All rights reserved
Manufactured in the United States of America
Printed on acid-free paper
10 9 8 7 6 5 4 3 2 1

Library of Congress Cataloging-in-Publication Data

Weldon, S. Laurel.
    Protest, policy, and the problem of violence against women : a
cross-national comparison / S. Laurel Weldon.
        p.   cm.
    Includes bibliographical references and index.
    ISBN 0-8229-4171-6 (cloth) — ISBN 0-8229-5774-4 (paper)
        1. Women—Violence against—Government policy—Cross-cultural
studies. 2. Women—Abuse of—Government policy—Cross-cultural
studies. 3. Protest movements—Cross-cultural studies. 4.
Feminism—Cross-cultural studies.   I. Title.
    HQ1236 .W425 2002
    362.83 — dc21

                                                    2001005281

PROTEST, POLICY, AND
THE PROBLEM OF VIOLENCE
AGAINST WOMEN

For my mother, Sirje Weldon
my father, Larry Weldon
and my grandmother, Audrey Mundell
with love

Contents

Tables and Figures

Preface

On a gray day in 1989, an activist from a Vancouver women's shelter stood outside the pub at Simon Fraser University, handing out fact sheets and taking donations. I remember picking up one of those fact sheets on violence against women, reading it, and putting all the money in my pocket (which wasn't much) into the can. Unfortunately, the facts about the prevalence of violence against women that disturbed me more than a decade ago don't seem to have changed much. This book is intended to help those committed to understanding and improving our collective response to this persistent and pervasive problem. It is also intended to demonstrate that studying violence against women provides important insights into the reasons for women's continued political marginalization and into the dynamics of policymaking in general.

I have not always focused on violence against women in my scholarly work. As a master's student at the University of British Columbia, I studied Indian politics. As a graduate student at the University of Pittsburgh, I studied group rights and social policy. But the importance of violence against women nagged at me as I explored these other subjects. While studying Indian politics, I became interested in the way culture was invoked to justify so-called traditional practices such as suttee and "dowry deaths." Later, as I studied social policy in the "woman-friendly" Scandinavian welfare states, I wondered why the governments there seemed to be doing so little to address violence against women. In fact, the more I thought about it, the more I realized that policies on violence against women in the countries I knew best (Canada, the United States, India, and Norway) did not seem to follow the patterns one would expect from studying other areas of social policy. Was that true? Why?

This book is the result of my puzzling through these issues. In it, I compare government responsiveness to violence against women across thirty-six countries, and I draw out the lessons for social scientists, activists, and policymakers. I find that the form and strength of social movements and political institutions determine government responsiveness to violence against women. More generally, I find that examining the development of government responses to this issue reveals the impact of social structures on the policy process. Accordingly, I propose that we take what I call a structural approach to the study of public policy. On the basis of these findings, the final chapter suggests a number of ways of improving government responsiveness to violence against women, and to women more generally. It also suggests some ways to make policymaking more democratic and inclusive.

The good thing about writing a preface is that you finally get to thank all the people who helped you with a book. The bad thing is that it is hard to thank them all properly. Let me try.

I am exceptionally fortunate to have Iris Young as a mentor and friend. When I first met Iris at the University of Pittsburgh where I was a graduate student, she nurtured my hopes and ambitions. To a degree that I had never before experienced, Iris made me feel that I had good ideas, worthy of scholarly attention. Of course, as students and junior scholars who have worked with Iris know, Iris's mentoring includes tough but constructive criticism. I'm sure this book reflects her careful criticism and suggestions, and I hope it vindicates her faith in me. I cannot thank her enough for all her help and support.

Lisa Brush read and commented on the book manuscript at several stages, saving me from some critical errors. She also provided moral support, delicious food, and good laughs as needed. Bert Rockman was always a demanding but helpful critic. His encouragement to "be bold" echoed in my head as I wrote this book. I hope he is not sorry! Susan Hansen had lifesaving comments and suggestions on a number of occasions, and kept me running to the library with her expansive knowledge of the literature. Bill Dunn asked me hard questions and held my feet to the fire on a variety of issues. All of these people made detailed comments on the entire manuscript. I hope this book reflects the care and thoughtful attention I received from them.

I would also like to thank Amy Elman, who encouraged me to work on violence against women when I was first struggling to frame my project. When others said it couldn't be done, Amy said it could. She read and commented in detail upon the entire manuscript. Most importantly, perhaps, she blazed the trail for me, by writing what seems to me to be the first political science book focusing on violence against women. My debt to her is evident.

Amy Mazur also spent time discussing the project with me and made many helpful suggestions. When I first contacted her for help, out of the blue, she was happy to help, and promptly sent me data and publications for my research. Over the past five years, she has been very generous with her time and expertise. Her detailed comments and queries greatly improved the book. She is a model colleague and mentor.

A professor once told me that for any scholarly project that requires serious commitment and hard work over a long period, one should pick a topic about which one cares passionately, since there would be days when no one but one's mother would be interested in the project (and sometimes not even she would care). Although I still think that was good advice, I am fortunate that he was wrong in this case. Many people, from academics to civil servants to activists, were interested enough to help me gather the data for my ambitious study. Thanks specifically to Joyce Outshoorn in the Netherlands, Jane Connors at the United Nations, Sara Conwell at the Violence Against Women Office in the United States, Charlotte Von Redlich in Sweden, Mari Niki-Koutsileou in Greece, Jukka Lindstedt in Finland, Helen Klonaris in the Bahamas, Marva Alleyne of Barbados, Jytte Mejnholt of Denmark, M. P. Paternottre of Belgium, and Lori Heise of Washington, D.C. To all the other activists, scholars, and civil servants whom I have missed, thank you for your selfless efforts.

In general, Purdue University, and especially my colleagues in the Political Science Department, have provided institutional and intellectual support for my work. This project benefited from the support of a 2000 Purdue Research Foundation Summer Faculty Grant. Several of my colleagues at Purdue, including Pat Boling, Jay McCann, Bob Bartlett, Bill Shaffer, Ann Clark, and Mike Weinstein, read and commented on chapters or related conference papers. Colleagues at other institutions also helped. Ralph Bangs aided me with the original research design. Doug Dion read the entire manuscript and made many useful comments. Presentations of this work at the University of Pittsburgh, University of Toronto, University of California at Irvine, University of Victoria in British Columbia, and Purdue University, as well as at meetings of the Midwest Political Science Association and the American Political Science Association, have also produced suggestions and criticism. In these contexts, I received helpful comments from Aaron Hoffman, Don Kerchis, Rita Mae Kelly, Virginia Sapiro, Jane Mansbridge, Carol Swain, Joyce Gelb, Chris Hunold, Jyl Josephson, Melissa Williams, Jenny Nedelsky, and Sylvia Bashevkin. Carol Bohmer, Phyllis Coontz, Guy Peters, and Mark Peterson helped me with related work on public policy that contributed to making this work better.

I would also like to thank John Wood, my master's advisor, and Avigail Eisenberg, my second reader for the M.A., for all they taught me about political science. Thanks also to Niels Aaboe at the University of Pittsburgh

Press for his interest in the book and his assistance with the process of publication. Deborah Meade and Nancy Trotic provided thorough editorial assistance.

Finally, I would like to thank all my family (Hoffmans, Walkers, and
Weldons!) and friends for helping me get through the stressful parts of the
work. Rosie Clawson, Keith Shimko, Bill Scheuerman, Julia Roos, Cathy
Lu, Dave Taylor, Jessica Gelberg, Ximena Arriaga, and Chris Agnew provided encouragement and humorous comments on my travails. Laura
Barker, my friend for fifteen years, has been unwaveringly supportive.
Thanks to my brother Kaljo for reminding me to keep the book accessible
and clear. I hope it is. I would like to give a special thanks to my mother,
Sirje Weldon, and to my father, Larry Weldon, as well as to their respective
partners, Don and Jill, for their love and support. My mother and father,
each in their own way, exemplify commitment to principle and to inquiry. I
hope this book makes them proud. Thanks also to my grandmother, Audrey
Mundell, who is always with me through thick and thin. Last but not least,
I thank Aaron, my partner in life, for reading my work, for arguing with me
about every little detail, for having fun with me when I needed a break, for
cooking, for cleaning, for listening—in short, for everything.

Given all the help I have received, there really should not be any errors
in this book. Nevertheless, I take full responsibility for the ones that in-
evitably remain.

PROTEST, POLICY, AND
THE PROBLEM OF VIOLENCE
AGAINST WOMEN

1

Introduction:
From Protest to Policy

■In 1979 in a small town in Maharashtra, India, protests erupted in response to the gang rape of a fourteen-year-old girl, Mathura, by local police. The case made its way through the Indian criminal justice system, and the High Court convicted the rapists. However, the Supreme Court reversed the High Court judgment and suggested that Mathura was of loose morals. The resultant outrage spawned a nationwide antirape movement, which demanded the reopening of the case and amendments in the rape law (Patel 1991). In Canada, in 1991, the Supreme Court struck down the 1983 "rape shield law" that had protected women reporting rapes from having their sexual history reviewed in court. Women's groups mobilized to demand government action to restore the law. Within a year, after consultations with feminist groups, Minister of Justice Kim Campbell introduced legislation replacing the original law.[1] The legislation met with widespread approval from feminists (Gotell 1998; Sproule 1998). In Italy, women's movement activists lobbied the government on the issue of violence against women for twenty years without success. In the mid-1990s, activists took to the streets

1

in frustration, circulating a nationwide petition to demand government action (Hellman 1996).

In all of these instances, social movements responded with outrage to state treatment of women victims of violence. They demanded change. Indeed, women's groups in countries from Trinidad and Tobago to Norway make surprisingly similar demands for an improved government response to violence against women: they demand legal reforms that recognize violent acts against women as serious crimes that should not be relegated to the private sphere; they demand government funding for services for victims; they demand government action in recognizing and promoting public awareness of violence against women; and they demand increased sensitivity on the part of police, judges, and other criminal justice officials.

In some cases, these movements have transformed government response. As recently as 1982, a discussion of wife battering provoked public snickers from legislators in the Canadian parliament (Begin 1997). Now the Canadian government spends millions of dollars responding to violence against women (Gotell 1998). In the United States in the early 1980s, Republican president Ronald Reagan canceled the limited federal funding available for shelters for women victims of violence, claiming it was a private problem and that domestic violence shelters were hostile to traditional families (Gelb 1998, 7). In 1981 Republicans unsuccessfully sought to prohibit funding for shelters through the Family Protection Act (which was introduced but not passed). However, by 1994, conservative Republican Orrin Hatch was co-sponsor of (and even at times a "key advocate" for) the Violence Against Women Act, which provided hundreds of millions of dollars to fund shelters and crisis centers, public education, training for police, and other programs (Gelb 1998, 13, 20). In 1998, the Republican-controlled House of Representatives surprised feminist activists by *unanimously* voting to approve extensions of the Violence Against Women Act and authorizing nearly a billion dollars for antiviolence programs (Erickson 1998).[2]

These transformations of government response, however incomplete or imperfect, are remarkable instances of how social movements can provoke official action on previously unrecognized, even taboo, issues. Of course, women's movements have had widely varying degrees of success across countries, and spectacular failures as well. The governments of Canada and Australia, for example, have worldwide reputations for introducing the most innovative programs in police training and specialized research. These governments were among the first to introduce legal reforms to encourage reporting and prosecuting of rape and domestic violence, and to provide funding for shelters and crisis centers. Meanwhile, national governments in countries such as Italy and Spain undertook none of these activities. Even after twenty years of women's movement activity on the issue, the Italian government remained unmoved. Why are some governments quick to respond to such demands by women's movements while others resist even mere symbolic gestures, such as official recognition of violence against women as a problem?

In this book, I find that certain types of institutional reforms, coupled with independent social movement activity, can dramatically improve government responsiveness to violence against women. I argue that our current models of the politics of policymaking (both feminist and otherwise) cannot adequately capture the dynamic relationship between social movements, political institutions, and public policy. A better understanding of democratic policymaking can be achieved, I suggest, by theorizing the policy process as being fundamentally shaped by social structures that systematically disadvantage some groups and advantage others. I propose a structural account of political institutions and social movements and show how this understanding improves on current conceptualizations in feminist scholarship and policy studies. I also suggest some concrete steps that democratic governments and social activists can undertake to improve policy responsiveness to violence against women and other issues of concern to disadvantaged groups. In the sections below, I outline the book's argument and how it relates to the existing body of scholarship on policies on violence against women, social policy, and comparative public policy more generally.

POLICY ACTION, SCHOLARLY SILENCE

Over the past two decades, some governments have adopted a wide range of measures to address violence against women, while others have done little or nothing. Yet there has been little scholarly attention to cross-national variation in this area of policy. The paucity of systematic cross-national studies of policies on violence against women stands in contrast to the vast literature comparing government action in the area of social welfare policy or family policy. Violence against women is rarely considered in discussions of the welfare state or social policy, even in feminist political science and political sociology circles. Yet the cross-national pattern of government response to violence, which often involves considerable expenditures and substantial legislative change, is quite unlike the patterns scholars discern in relation to women and employment or in the area of family policy. This suggests that studying violence against women may reveal aspects of social policymaking that are obscured in examining other issue areas. Moreover, violence against women creates barriers to many other goals of democratic governments, such as economic development, welfare reform, public health, pay equity, and the well-being of children.[3] Government responsiveness to violence against women may affect policy effectiveness in these other areas. Thus, government response to violence against women is an important but understudied area of public policy.

The relative silence on issues of violence should be particularly worrying to researchers who seek to understand gender dynamics, since many feminist scholars argue that violence is central to women's subordination (MacKinnon 1989; Elman 1996a; Brownmiller 1975; Martin 1976). Barely a handful of comparative studies of national violence-against-women policy seek to investigate and explain variation in government response to violence against women (Elman 1996a; Busch 1992; Heise, Raikes, Watts, and Zwi 1994).[4]

WHAT EXPLAINS RESPONSIVENESS TO VIOLENCE AGAINST WOMEN?

All of these studies identify the mobilization of a women's movement, and especially a women's movement with some organizational independence from government, as a key catalyst to policy change in this area. In addition, the number of women in political office is identified as a possible determinant of government response (Heise 1994). One study finds that federal, pluralist institutional structures create more points of access for women's movements than do corporatist, unitary structures (Elman 1996a). Although these studies provide a good starting point for understanding cross-national variation in government responsiveness, they leave many questions unanswered.

In this book, I seek to further our understanding of this policy issue by providing a global overview of government response to violence against women in countries that have been continuously democratic from 1974–1994. I also examine the process of policy development in the eight most responsive countries in order to better understand the dynamics of policy change. The results are puzzling: the cross-national patterns of government responsiveness to violence against women that I identify in this study confound conventional explanations offered by feminist scholars and comparative policy scholars alike. Political culture explanations might suggest that the more egalitarian Scandinavian countries would be the most responsive, and that countries commonly thought of as having "macho" political cultures (such as Latin American countries and Australia) would have the laggard governments. In fact, the Swedish government is far behind others in addressing this problem, while Costa Rica is among the most responsive governments. Nor does the entrenchment of the Catholic Church explain much of the difference: Ireland has had one of the most responsive governments, while Italy is one of the least responsive democratic governments in the world. I present this evidence in chapter 2.

Furthermore, as I show in chapter 3, although the presence of a strong women's movement is important, it is far from determinative: in the United States, activists demanded national government action on violence for decades without result. In other "Anglo" federal states, such as Canada and Australia, on the other hand, similar women's movement demands were met more than a decade earlier than in the United States. But perhaps the most puzzling finding of this study is the fact that the most responsive governments include many that have very few women in government (such as the United States, Australia, and France), while some governments with a large proportion of women in government (such as Finland) have been among the least responsive. The analyses I present in chapter 4 support these observations.

What, then, determines government responsiveness to violence against women? It appears to be determined to a large degree by the presence of a strong, autonomous women's movement that draws on and reinforces state institutions designed to promote the status of women. When these "women's policy agencies" (as they have come to be called) have considerable material and institutional resources, and when they maintain consultative relations with activists, they greatly improve government responsiveness to violence against women.

In chapter 5, I argue that the impact political institutions have on policies on violence suggests that "institutions matter" for comparative social policy. It also suggests that analysts of gender politics should focus more attention on variation in the structure of public administration. More generally, the study of gender and politics should focus less on women as policymakers and more on social and institutional structures and processes.

The finding that women's policy agencies affect policymaking on violence against women also has important implications for neoinstitutionalist approaches to policy analysis. It appears that women's policy machineries improve government responsiveness to violence against women because they correct for an institutional gender bias: political institutions tend to be organized around the priorities and perspectives of historically powerful groups of men. This suggests that institutional capacities (such as information gathering or innovation) are not always group-neutral: institutions may function differently depending on the substantive issues at stake, *systematically* underperforming on issues of concern to particular marginalized groups.

But political-institutional factors alone do not explain variation in policies on violence: women's policy agencies improve government responsiveness to violence against women only when they operate in the context of a strong, autonomous women's movement. In chapter 6, I examine the impact of the interaction between social movements and political institutions on policies on violence against women. I find that women's policy agencies and strong, autonomous women's movements have a mutually reinforcing, interactive effect.

This interaction is best explained by a structural approach to policy analysis. In chapter 7, I argue that the dominant models of the policy process are inadequate for conceptualizing the interaction between political institutions and social movements and for understanding their joint impact on policies to address violence against women. A better conceptualization can be achieved if we theorize the policy process as being fundamentally shaped by social structures that systematically disadvantage some groups and advantage others. I offer a structural account of political institutions and social movements. Political institutions are components of social structures, both reflecting and shaping social norms, while social movements seek to change social structures. A structural approach, I contend, best captures the interactive effect of political institutions and social movements on policies on violence against women. Moreover, I suggest, a theoretical approach to public policy that acknowledges such social structures improves our understanding of democratic policymaking in general. It also makes policy analysis more useful in confronting important public policy issues in contemporary democracies.

In chapter 8, I make some concrete recommendations for policymakers and activists working to eliminate violence against women and other problems confronting marginalized groups. I also suggest some potential ways to improve government responsiveness to marginalized groups more generally. Before turning to the argument, however, I outline some details of conceptualization, measurement, and method.

THE DESIGN OF THE STUDY

In this study, I seek to explain why some democratic governments are more responsive to the problem of violence against women than others.

Specifically, I ask why some stable democratic governments undertake broad, multifaceted initiatives to address violence against women while other governments do not even recognize the problem, or respond only partially or belatedly.

Defining Government Responsiveness

In the policy literature, *responsiveness* can refer to bureaucratic responsiveness (whether bureaucracies respond to complaints or requests) or to government responsiveness in general (whether government acts in response to problems or citizen demands) (Bachelor 1986; Chaney and Salzstein 1998; Powell 1982; Putnam 1993; Meyer and Baker 1993; Rodrik and Zeckhauser 1988; Dye 1998). In this study, I focus on government responsiveness to violence against women in the latter sense: I ask whether governments are taking action to address violence against women or whether they are avoiding such action.

This definition may seem to conflate two types of responsiveness: responsiveness to problems and responsiveness to citizen demands for action on a problem.[5] One of these types of responsiveness involves responsiveness to citizen articulations, while the other involves identifying and addressing problems. In this book, I want to examine the claim that women's movement activity improves government responsiveness to violence against women. For this reason, I focus on government responsiveness to the problem of violence against women and ask whether and how policy responsiveness to the problem is increased by women's movement activities. In this way, the book examines both the question of responsiveness to citizen articulations and government responsiveness to violence against women itself. This approach allows me to investigate (rather than make assumptions about) the role that women's movements play in the development of government response to violence against women.

Note that responsiveness does not necessarily imply effectiveness. *Effectiveness* refers to policy impacts, such as whether government actions mitigate a particular problem. In this case, measures of effectiveness might include victims' reports about their experiences in shelters and crisis centers and about the treatment they received in the criminal justice system and hospitals; changes in public attitudes toward violence against women; and reduced incidence of such violence. A study of effectiveness would require much more detailed analysis of particular programs than is undertaken here. Given the problems of measurement and the lack of data on this policy area, it is at present unfeasible to carry out this type of study for most countries.

It is important to distinguish policy responsiveness from effectiveness for a number of reasons. Policies may be rendered ineffective at many stages. In some cases, the problem is not in the design of the particular policy or in the intentions of lawmakers, but in the policy process itself. If we want to identify the barriers to addressing a policy problem, it is critical to know whether it is a problem of political will or ignorance among the leadership (politicians are unwilling to take on a problem), institutional barriers to adopting a policy, a problem of poor policy design, a problem of inadequate implementation of a sound policy, and the like. Effectiveness can be blocked at any of these stages, but responsiveness relates primarily to the quality and timeliness of the policy response, rather than to its implementation or impact.

Some scholars have noted that responsiveness and effectiveness may be conflicting goals (Rodrik and Zeckhauser 1988). For example, many women's groups demanded mandatory arrest policies as a way of getting around police reluctance to arrest male batterers in their own homes. The police responded to the enactment of these policies by arresting both parties (claiming they didn't know who the aggressor was), thereby deterring abused women from calling the police—not the intention of the reformers (Martin 1997). Now, after learning of this and other problems, many women's groups oppose mandatory arrest policies (Mills 1998; Saunders 1995). Should we say that governments that adopted and then amended these policies were less responsive to violence against women because the policy they first adopted failed? I think not. When a government is making an effort to address a problem, it is responsive.

Policy responsiveness is at least as important as policy effectiveness. As Powell (1982, 186) notes, "The most important identifying characteristic of a democratic system is the assertion that the government is doing what the citizens want it to do." The concept of responsiveness captures whether governments are on the cutting edge of efforts to address a problem or whether they are slow to respond to problems and citizen demands. When problems are pressing, governments are sometimes willing to risk resources in order to do something about the problem in the absence of data about likely effectiveness. This impulse can reflect concern, and a willingness to act out of a legitimate sense of urgency. This willingness to act may be very important to citizens, regardless of the ultimate effectiveness of the government action. For example, it is estimated that five million women in Canada are suffering the consequences of violence (Johnson 1998). Surely, there is some urgency to the question of government response.

Responsiveness is not only about speed; quality of response is also an issue. Are governments just doing something to make it seem as if they are responding to the problem, or are they trying to do as much as they can to address violence against women? Women's groups and international experts have developed a set of policy initiatives that national governments can undertake to address violence against women (Heise, Pitanguy, and Germain 1994; Connors 1994; United Nations 1998b, 1998c). While this set is not exhaustive, it provides a benchmark for the scope of government response. How broad is the response to violence against women? Is it focused only on domestic or "family" violence, or does it also include sexual assault? Is it primarily a criminal justice response aimed at punishment? Is it a narrow social service response aimed solely at after-the-fact treatment of victims? Or is it a broad effort, encompassing more than one form of violence and taking on treatment of victims, punishment of offenders, and prevention of future violence? Why do some governments do all of these things, while others do none? This is an important question, because exploring it will tell us what makes democratic governments more or less disposed to address an issue of critical importance for women, and for society at large.

Violence Against Women

Violence against women takes a number of forms, including female genital mutilation, rape, wife battering, incest, stalking, sexual harassment, and psychological harassment. These categories of violence are referred to as "violence against women" because this violence happens to women at least partly *because* they are women. In its declaration on this subject, the United Nations (1993) defined violence against women as "any act of gender-based violence that results in, or is likely to result in, physical, sexual or psychological harm or suffering to women, including threats of such acts, coercion, or arbitrary deprivations of liberty, whether occurring in public or private life."

The available evidence suggests that violence against women is a widespread problem with appalling consequences. In 1993, a comprehensive national study (using random sampling techniques and legal definitions of crimes) found that about half of all Canadian women were victims of violence; 39 percent reported sexual assault and 34 percent reported physical assault (some women had experienced both forms of violence) (Johnson 1998). National studies in the United States and Belgium revealed similar levels of violence (Tjaden and Thoennes 1998; Belgian Coordinating Committee 1994). Although we need better information about the level and extent of violence against women, there are sufficient data to establish that such violence is a serious public policy problem in all stable democracies (see appendix A). Among particularly vulnerable categories of women, such as poor women in both developed and developing countries, low-caste women in India, or African American women in the United States, the rates of violence appear to be even higher.

Violence against women has effects that go beyond the harms to the immediate victims. Even women who never become victims of sexual assault or wife beating are expected to alter their behavior to minimize risk: they oughtn't stay late at the office alone, or walk unescorted after dark, or draw public attention to themselves, or be in private spaces with men—even men they know well. Thus, violence against women restricts the ability of all women to take advantage of their rights as citizens of a democratic public.

As governments and women's groups from 180 countries have affirmed, violence against women constitutes a violation of women's human rights (U.S. Department of Labor 1996; Nelson 1996). Governments that claim to be democratic must make defending the human rights and physical security of their citizens a priority. Indeed, most democratic governments have now promised in one public forum or another to address violence against women.

This study focuses on policies that address the victimization of women. This should not be taken to imply that violence against men is nonexistent or unimportant. The violence that afflicts men, however, is a different phenomenon from violence against women and must be analyzed as such. Men and women tend to be victims or perpetrators of different kinds of violence, under different circumstances. Men are more likely to be assaulted by strangers (usually men), while women are more likely to be assaulted by intimates or people they know, also usually men. This is because violence against women is largely a result of women's economic and social dependence on men, as cross-cultural studies have demonstrated (Levinson 1989; Sanday 1981). The phenomenon of violence against women is part of a network of social practices that devalue women and render them dependent on, and thus vulnerable to, men in a wide range of situations (home, employment, traveling in public spaces). Gang wars or bar fights, for example, are not the result of one group's being economically and socially dependent on, and therefore vulnerable to, another. The point is not that violence against men is less serious, or the effects on the victims less harmful, but that violence against women is fruitfully analyzed as distinct from these other forms of violence.[6]

In this study, I focus on the categories of sexual assault of women by men and battering of intimate female partners by males. Focusing on these two categories facilitates cross-national comparison because violence against women, rape, and wife beating are concepts used by activist groups and governments in all stable democratic countries. Information on the incidence of and activism around these two types of violence is thus available for all thirty-six countries studied here.

Comparing Government Response

This study does not attempt to explain variance in violence against women itself, but rather variation in government responsiveness to this problem. What makes some governments undertake a broad, multifaceted policy on violence against women while other governments pursue a course of inaction?

Policy refers to "a course of action or inaction pursued under the authority of government" (Heclo 1974, 4). Note that "policy silences" or "non-decisions" can be considered policy outcomes (Conway, Ahern, and Steuernagel 1995; Bachrach and Baratz 1962). *Action* includes statements by government officials, legislation, executive orders, and other activities of government and its representatives.

Government is used here to mean the agencies of highest public authority for a particular territorial unit, as in "the government of India." Government in this sense is continuous across particular administrations (such as the Carter and Reagan administrations). Governments commit themselves to international treaties that are binding for future administrations, and they often take on the legal responsibilities (such as debts) accumulated over previous administrations. In this sense, the government of Canada is a corporate (if not unified) entity. Governments act through but are not identical to political institutions or administrative structures. Thus, it is possible that constitutional reform would transform administrative structures under the auspices of the same national government. So government is not equivalent to public administrative structures.

This distinction is important for arguments I want to make later in the book. The concept of the state, as I shall demonstrate in chapter 5, is often used to refer to policy, administrative structures, legal codes, and governments at all levels. Because I want to distinguish between national government actions and the structure of public administration, I shall usually use the concept of government, as defined above, rather than state. However, I should say at the outset that I take government, policy, and public administration to be aspects of the broader concept of the state.

A Common Standard for Comparison

Ethnocentrism is always a danger when Westerners seek to develop standards for cross-cultural comparison. It is sometimes assumed that avoiding generalizations across cultures is a guard against ethnocentrism, and this is one reason that both comparativists and feminists prefer to focus on particular contexts in their analyses. This way of dealing with ethnocentrism, however, assumes that no cross-cultural comparison is possible. But we all know of many useful cross-cultural studies, even studies using large numbers of countries or settings, that have furthered our thinking (see, for example, Esping-Andersen 1990; Gornick, Meyers, and Ross 1997; Halperin 1997; Sanday 1981; and Levinson 1989). Moreover, assuming that others are different and that generalizations do *not* apply to them can be as dangerous as assuming that they do (Narayan 1997; Reinharz 1992). Narayan (1998), for example, joins other Indian feminists in criticizing Western feminists for not seeing dowry deaths as a form of domestic violence. Jane Jacquette points out that ignoring other countries is a form of ethnocentrism particularly virulent among feminists in the United States (cited in Reinharz 1992).

One way to mitigate this problem is to ask whether the standards one is creating would be agreeable to women's movements in the contexts in question. As I have noted, in every country in this study where women's movements are organized (which is all but one—the tiny island nation of Nauru, where there appears to be no mobilization of women as women), they have identified violence against women as an important issue. Indeed, in Beijing in 1995, women's groups from 180 countries signed an agreement stating that violence against women is a problem that demands top priority, and concluding that "violence in all its forms must be stopped" (U.S. Department of Labor 1996).[7]

This agreement reinforced the mounting evidence that violence against women in the form of sexual assault and wife battering is a serious problem everywhere in the world.[8] For example, standardized victimization surveys, carried out in both developed and developing countries in the early 1990s, showed an alarming prevalence of sexual assault in at least thirty countries (UNICRI 1996). Numerous other studies establish the existence and seriousness of domestic violence in countries as diverse as Norway and Japan, Papua New Guinea and Poland.[9] Violence against women is a problem in every country considered here.

Despite the diversity of institutional arrangements and legal traditions in the countries included in this study, a common standard can be developed to compare the scope of national government response to violence against women. Similar features of the problem and of the existing policy structure across these countries make it possible to identify a common set of areas in which actions or reforms are needed to address violence against women. International experts find that it is a large-scale, deeply rooted problem, not easily attributed to isolated factors such as alcohol use or mental illness (Heise, Pitanguy, and Germain 1994; UN, CEDAW 1998b).

The UN Declaration on the Elimination of Violence Against Women (UN 1993) argues that "violence against women is a manifestation of historically unequal power relations between men and women" and that violence against women "is one of the crucial social mechanisms by which women are forced into a subordinate position compared with men." Indeed, cross-cultural studies of violence against women have found that economic inequality between women and men, cultural patterns of conflict resolution through violence, cultural norms of male dominance, toughness, and honor, and male economic and decision-making authority in the family are the best predictors of high levels of violence against women (Levinson 1989; Sanday 1981). As research on this topic has progressed, the relationship between violence against women and male dominance has become increasingly well established.

Governments can undertake to address violence against women in general, and sexual assault and domestic violence in particular, in several different areas of policy action.[10] A government that addresses more of these areas is more responsive, because the scope of the response is broader. Seven aspects of national government response to violence against women can be meaningfully observed for each of the countries in this study:

(1) Has there been legal reform dealing with wife battering?

(2) Has there been legal reform dealing with sexual assault?

(3) Are there shelters or other forms of emergency housing provision for victims of wife battering? Are they government-funded?

(4) Are there crisis centers for victims of sexual assault? Are they government-funded?

(5) Are there government-sponsored programs to train service providers and other professionals who deal with violence against women, such as police, judges, and social workers?

(6) Are there government-sponsored initiatives to educate the public about violence against women?

(7) Is there a central agency for coordinating national policies on violence against women?

Each of these elements of government response is explained in more detail below.

(1) and (2) Legal Reform for Wife Battering and Sexual Assault
Regardless of national context, attempts to address violence against women under the rubric of more general laws against violence or assault have generally been unsuccessful. Law enforcement officials have tended to

see the sexual assault and beating of wives as a private affair or a male prerogative that is not covered by general laws against sexual assault or assault
more generally. Moreover, female victims of sexual assaults have been
viewed with suspicion and have been stigmatized. For these reasons, obtaining an effective response from the law enforcement bureaucracy has
generally required both legal reform and training of law enforcement officials from police officers to judges. Legal reform can greatly improve the
legal and criminal justice response to sexual assault and domestic violence.
For example, language detailing that rape within marriage is a crime is often
required before courts will consider rape a possibility in such an intimate relationship. Similarly, "rape shield" provisions protecting victims of sexual
assault from a "second violation" as defense attorneys probe their sexual
history can greatly improve the likelihood that rape victims will prosecute
their assailants (Connors 1989; Dutton 1984; UN, CEDAW, 1994, *Experts
at Committee on Elimination of Gender Discrimination*; Elman 1996a;
Greece, General Secretariat for Equality 1998; Krishnaraj 1991; Rhode
1989; Women's Research Center [Canada] 1982).

Criminal justice response can be made more effective through coordination with shelters and other service providers. For example, mandatory arrest policies have been much more effective in increasing arrests in those
jurisdictions in Britain where such coordination has been undertaken
(Canada, House of Commons 1982, 5:63). Similarly, a recent national evaluation of responses to domestic violence in the United States found that when
community intervention projects coordinated police, judicial, and social
service responses, they had "a significant impact on both police and judicial
responses to woman battering" (Chalk and King 1998, 113). This underlines
the importance of coupling legal reform with social policy initiatives.

(3) and (4) Funding for Emergency Housing and Crisis Centers

Emergency housing and financial assistance are of particular importance. In addition to providing women with an emergency escape, shelters
appear to play a pivotal role in helping them seek appropriate support services (Gondolf and Fisher 1988). As the U.S. National Research Council
notes, "Housing, education or job training and acquisition, economic self-
sufficiency, child care, safety and other issues need to be resolved before a
woman can completely separate from an abusive partner on whom she has
been emotionally or financially dependent" (Chalk and King 1998, 113).
Many women must leave their homes with their children at a moment's notice to escape a violent partner. These women must be assured that they will
be able to go someplace where they will be safe and can get food, clothing,

and assistance with protection-from-abuse orders where applicable. Material provision is especially important, because many battered women are economically dependent on their male assailants. Counseling for children who witness domestic violence may also be provided through shelters, and such counseling can have a significant effect on children's attitudes toward the acceptability of domestic violence (Jaffe et al. 1986; Wagar and Rodway 1995; Chalk and King 1998, 293). Some observers also suggest that shelters provide battered women with a community in which they can discuss their situation with other women seeking refuge, and that this opportunity for shared analysis creates a sense of empowerment and a better understanding of the power dynamics behind intimate-partner violence.

Although there are few formal evaluations of shelters in terms of their impact on violence, one well-designed study did find that they can reduce the risk of violence for a woman who is taking control of her life in other ways (Berk, Newton, and Berk 1986). Similarly, counseling and advocacy for victims of sexual assault can facilitate their negotiation of the criminal justice system and make it more likely that they will report abuse and prosecute the offender (Elman 1996a; Krishnaraj 1991; Sullivan and Davidson 1991; Tan et al. 1995). Thus, provision of aid to victims helps both to decrease their distress and prevent further violence.

Government funding for women's shelters and crisis centers is particularly important. Initially established by autonomous women's collectives, these facilities were soon overwhelmed by demand. In retrospect, this is not surprising; a handful of shelters and crisis centers could hardly be expected to handle the millions of women affected in each country. Recall that national studies in Canada, the United States, and Belgium have found that about half of all women have, in their lifetime, been the victim of some form of violence at the hands of men. The scale of need in this area and the pressing nature of the problem suggest that government funding is needed in order to provide adequate services.

(5) Training for Police, Social Workers, and Other Service Providers

Activists worry that victims of sexual assault and domestic violence are not adequately protected from further physical and emotional violations through the legal process or from retaliatory attacks by their original abusers. One former shelter worker recently told me, "Policymakers just don't understand the danger that these women are in if they attempt to solve their problems through the criminal justice system" (U.S. Department of Justice 1998). Some women are even vulnerable to a second violation from the very police who are supposed to protect them: custodial rape is a serious problem in many countries, such as India and Brazil. Some countries, including Canada and Israel, have developed special training packages for police. Costa Rica, Colombia, and India have established women's police stations or special units of women police officers.

Social workers, lawyers, judges, and others who interact with victims are also more effective when they are more knowledgeable about the dynamics of violence against women. Training these service providers can mean important improvements for victims of violence when they seek help (see, for example, Heise, Pitanguy, and Germain 1994; Krishnaraj 1991).

(6) Public Education Programs

In order to help identify and stop violence against women and to prevent it before it starts, governments can initiate public education programs, both broadly based media campaigns and workplace and school programs. National public education programs (such as those in Australia in the early 1980s) appear to have some effect in influencing both men and women to think that wife battering is unacceptable. Similarly, violence-prevention programs in schools have succeeded in changing the attitudes of children and young adults toward the acceptability of violence (Jaffe et al. 1986; Jones 1991; Krajewski et al. 1996; Lavoie et al. 1995). Whether public education programs translate into an actual reduction in violence is not known (Chalk and King 1998, 114). In any event, they are important in sending abused women the message that they should not tolerate abuse and that the community as a whole does not condone it.

(7) A Coordinating Authority

A comprehensive government response to violence against women will attend to the immediate needs of victims (such as shelter, police protocols for dealing with victims, rape crisis services, and protection from further abuse) as well as to long-term, preventative efforts such as public education programs (Connors 1989, 1994; Bunch 1991; Davies 1994; Dobash and Dobash 1992; Heise, Pitanguy, and Germain 1994; Heise, Raikes, Watts, and Zwi 1994; Krishnaraj 1991; Japan, Office of Gender Equality 1998a, 1998b; UN 1993; Botswana, Women's Affairs Division 1995). The wide range of policy action required for an effective response to violence against women suggests that an interdepartmental coordinating authority is in order (Hague 1998). Such an office can, for example, ensure that efforts to provide victim services are linked to law enforcement responses to calls by women in distress. Some countries, such as Canada and Australia, have already created such a coordinating body. Germany, Sweden, and Norway have recently introduced coordinating centers on a pilot basis. Thus, an official body to oversee implementation and coordination of policies is an important part of government response to violence against women.

It might be assumed that more decentralized governments, such as federal states, are less likely to have a centralized agency to coordinate national policy. Federalism does raise questions about the validity of focusing on national government response, questions that I address below. However, if we stipulate that we are focusing on policies enacted at a national level, then whether these policies are coordinated or work at cross-purposes is an important question with respect to the quality of government response. Empirically, it does not appear that federal governments are any less likely to have such coordinating mechanisms.

These seven areas of government response to violence against women are consistent with the main recommendations for national action developed by the UN Convention on the Elimination of All Forms of Discrimination Against Women (CEDAW) at Beijing and updated in committee discussion of the reports of the UN Special Rapporteur on Violence Against Women, (UN, CEDAW 1998b, paras. 26–44).[11]

Scope of National Policy

Among the thirty-six countries considered here, I rank national policies on violence against women as better or worse based on their scope (how many of these seven areas are addressed?) and their leadership among stable democratic nations (was this government the first or the last to implement a policy?)(Putnam 1993). A government that addresses more areas is enacting a broader, more multifaceted response, and a government that addresses an area earlier is more responsive to the problem. Ranking government response on these two dimensions (scope and timing) provides a picture of which governments are doing more to address violence against women and which governments are lagging. These measures appear accurately to reflect the consensus of international experts as to which countries are aggressively and comprehensively attacking the problem at a national level and which countries entered this policy arena later on and less thoroughly. For example, Canada and Australia have addressed more issues over the study period, and addressed them earlier, than any other country. Similarly, these measures identify Costa Rica and Israel as leaders among developing countries.

All seven policy areas are important for addressing violence against women, both symbolically and substantively. Note that I am not trying to

find out which governments enact policies that result in the greatest reduc
tion of violence. Many of the policy measures considered here are aimed a
serving victims or raising awareness, rather than at directly reducing th
overall incidence of violence. Instead, I am asking which governments d
more types of important things to address violence against women, an
which of them do so sooner. What spurs governments to take more actior
on violence against women, and which factors appear to block governmen
action? This question can be distinguished from whether the policie
adopted actually reduce levels of violence.

Although I am not focusing on effectiveness, this is not a study of re
sponsiveness in purely symbolic terms. For example, in examining whethe
a government funds shelters, I asked first whether shelters in fact existe
and whether they received funding from the government. In many cases
spoke directly with shelter representatives, who viewed financial assistanc
from government as critical to their operations. In other words, I aske
about whether shelters actually received money from government, no
whether governments promised to spend money. Similarly, in studying public education and training programs, I was able to obtain materials dissem-
inated by these programs or to confirm with independent parties (such a
scholars or activists) that the government was in fact undertaking educatior
programs. So although the measure does not focus on implementation, it i
not a measure of purely symbolic governmental activity.

Some readers will want to disaggregate the legal reforms from the redistributive aspects of government response, since the former seem like purely
symbolic reforms that involve little cost to government and are therefore
easier to undertake. I dispute this interpretation. Legal reforms may not put
food on a woman's table, but they can have an important effect on her treatment in the criminal justice system. The women agitating for such reforms
certainly do not view their efforts as merely symbolic politics. Legal reforms
that specifically recognize rape and physical abuse in marriage as crimes
have made it more difficult (although not impossible) for judges to conclude
that such incidents are matters of private concern. Rape shield laws, in spite
of their flaws and imperfect implementation, have been viewed as providing
important protections for women victims of violence seeking redress. Indeed, mandatory arrest policies, rape shield laws, and other criminal justice
reforms in the United States and Canada have been much more controversial politically than funding for domestic violence shelters and rape crisis
centers.

It is not always the case that spending state money indicates a greater
commitment to addressing a problem than does "mere" legal reform. In dis-

ussing violence against women with officials in Norway, for example, I ound that they were quite amenable to speaking about redistributive policies for shelters and crisis centers but resisted using language that singled women out for special treatment, and that they viewed the concept of violence against women with disdain. I was told that such a focus on women was inferior to a gender-neutral stance, which "treated all citizens equally." Elman (1996a) tells a similar story about Sweden: efforts to raise the issue of violence against women were characterized as "shrill" and "divisive." This insistence on gender neutrality may be one reason that the Nordic countries lagged behind others in efforts to address violence against women. In this case, the seemingly lower-cost policies of public education, training, and legal reform likely met with the greatest resistance.

I contend that all of the seven types of policy initiatives identified above are important in addressing violence against women, and that no one policy can be assumed to be more important than the others. We can say that the more policies out of the seven that a government adopts, the more committed it is to addressing violence against women. Thus, we can ask about the number of policy initiatives as an indicator of the scope of a government's response, regardless of which particular elements are included. An examination of patterns involving the specific elements of the response and the relationships among them is left for future research.

The question at hand concerns the overall structure (specifically, the scope) of the policy response to violence. Focusing on the overall structure of government response, as opposed to particular programs, involves a trade-off. As Esping-Andersen (1990, 2) notes, "Since our intention is to understand the 'big picture', we shall not be able to dwell on the detailed characteristics of the various social programs." Nevertheless, understanding government response to violence against women more generally should ultimately provide insights into why, when, and how particular programs are adopted.

Temporal Focus

This study focuses on the responsiveness of democratic governments in the late twentieth century. Although some national governments reformed rape laws or began funding shelters in the mid-1970s, many countries did not begin to address the problem of violence against women until the latter half of the 1980s, and many more only in the first half of the 1990s. Thus, I study the development of government response since 1974. The most recent year for which I gathered data is 1994, the last year before the Beijing conference.

Focus on National-Level Policies

In examining the seven aspects of government response to violence against women, I focus on national government response for a variety of reasons. National government action has important symbolic and practical consequences, even in very decentralized states. It often indicates the importance of an issue area to the political community. For example, in the United States, although state and local governments have been responding to violence against women for more than twenty years, the amount of public attention and legitimacy the issue has received in both scholarly and mainstream political circles increased after the passage by Congress of the Violence Against Women Act in 1994. This act served to recognize violence against women as a category of national government action and reinforced the growing international consensus that dealing with rape and wife battering is an issue of basic human rights—fundamental to the functioning of the democratic polity and too important to be left to the discretion of state and local governments. In general, action by the central government, even if it consists only of providing funding to local areas, is a key symbolic indicator that the political community is seriously addressing a problem.

This focus on national government action is meaningful even in federal systems when responsibility for the issue in question belongs to the unit (state or province). For example, in both Canada and the United States, the federal government frequently buys its way into areas such as health care policy or legal drinking age—which are understood to be constitutionally allocated as a provincial or state responsibility—by tying federal funding to policy changes. In the area of violence against women, funding from the federal government for shelters, crisis centers, education, and training have galvanized state and local governments into action as they endeavor to secure and spend this money. Similarly, in Australia, although legal reforms with respect to rape and domestic violence tend to be criminal justice reforms that are state-level responsibilities, the national government has undertaken to develop model legislation in both areas, which it recommends to state governments. These actions indicate that federal governments can and often do take action on legal reform, funding for shelters, and the like even when these are formally the responsibility of the units.

Scholars of gender and public policy have emphasized the importance of regional and local variation in the impact of national policies (Duncan 1995; Haney 1996; Sabatier 1999). Certainly, the study of state and local governments and subgovernments is critical to a complete understanding of gender and public policy. It is estimated that in the United States there are more than 86,700 local governments (Peters 1998). International institutions have also become more important for domestic policymaking. The interconnection between these different levels makes understanding policy outcomes and processes extremely challenging.

Pragmatically, of course, cross-national comparison, even on a smaller scale than I undertake here, requires simplification. Even in one national context, and even leaving aside international influences, it is impossible to study policy at all levels of government in any comprehensive fashion. Focusing on national government response is one way to make cross-national comparison feasible.

More importantly, however, this study concentrates on the determinants of national policy outputs because this still seems to me to be the most important level of government for setting the national agenda and responding to large-scale problems. I do consider (briefly) local and international influences as possible determinants of national government response, and it is certainly true that state and local governments are often important in implementing policies or in determining policy outcomes. However, in this study I maintain an analytic focus on the responsiveness of national government, not the outcomes of national policies. This helps to simplify the analytic task at hand: local and regional governments are considered only as possible determinants of national government response, not as an aspect of that response itself.

Variation Across Different Groups of Women

The policies considered here have differing levels of importance for different groups of women. In the United States, for example, women of color have often felt alienated from shelters run by white feminists, for a variety of reasons (Matthews 1993). In multilingual states such as India, Canada, and Belgium (and increasingly the United States), the language in which services are provided can determine how accessible they are to minority women. This raises the question of whether the seven-item indicator measures government responsiveness to all women or just to middle-class women of the dominant racial or ethnic group. There may be different dynamics behind responsiveness to women of privileged classes and attention to the needs of women from marginalized groups. As one observer has noted, it may be that women of privileged classes are more effective in eliciting government response precisely because they speak the language (literally or figuratively) of governing elites.[12]

One might be able to get at this question empirically by asking whether any of the shelters and other outreach services funded by the national government are targeted to women of vulnerable or disadvantaged groups, such as immigrant women, women of color, or poor women.[13] The existing data on policies to address violence against women did not permit such an investigation for the entire data set. However, I was able to consider this question through an examination of policies to address violence against indigenous, immigrant, and minority women as part of my analysis of policy development in Canada and Australia. This discussion is presented in chapter 6.[14]

Focus on Democratic Countries

Policymaking as it affects violence against women is likely to involve different dynamics in democratic and nondemocratic countries. First, in democratic policymaking, we expect governments to respond to publicly articulated problems. Second, where there is a minimum degree of respect for civil rights and freedom of association, one can expect that women's groups will be able to organize peaceful demonstrations and put pressure on government without facing the threat of torture or incarceration. The degree of latitude afforded women's organizations, or whether they are permitted at all, can vary greatly among nondemocratic regimes. Third, in democratic countries, one might expect women legislators to have an effect on public policy, since they are in principle free to engage in deliberation within and without their parties and may raise new issues or insights previously excluded from the legislative arena. In nondemocratic countries, women legislators may not have the freedom to dissent from a male majority, and so one might not expect to see an effect. Analytically, then, in order to explore the hypotheses offered in this book, it makes sense to focus on democratic governments.

A very thin definition of democracy is necessary here. I am examining countries in which, at a minimal level, basic civil liberties (freedom of association, freedom of speech, freedom of the press) are respected and in which free and fair elections are regularly held. I selected countries using data from the Comparative Survey of Freedom, which has been conducted by Freedom House since the 1970s and aims to "provide an annual evaluation of political rights and civil liberties everywhere in the world" (Freedom House 1997). Freedom House data have been used to distinguish democracies from nondemocracies by a number of other scholars of comparative and international politics (LeDuc, Niemi, and Norris 1996; Bremer 1992; Maoz and Abdollali 1989). The survey evaluates the freedoms enjoyed by people in practice, not merely the rights formally guaranteed to them. Political rights include free and fair election of government authorities, freedom to organize in political groupings or parties, the presence of an organized opposition, and a reasonable degree of self-determination for minorities. Thirteen civil liberties, encompassing freedom of expression, association, rule of law, and some degree of personal autonomy from the state, are examined. I view democracy as a continuum, and this operationalization reflects the minimal level of democracy required for the purposes of this study. Many of the countries I consider have a long way to go before they approximate an *ideal* democracy.

I have also used Freedom House classifications of countries to determine which ones were continuously democratic over the twenty-year period covered by this study. Some degree of continuity over time in a country's respect for minimal democratic rights and procedures is important in order for political movements and organizations to develop and for processes of accountability, such as elections, to take effect. States that were continuously democratic from 1974 to 1994 were included in the study.[15] Based on these decision rules, the total number of countries in the study is thirty-six (see table 1-1).

Some will object that while all these countries meet minimal criteria for democracy, it is absurd to include countries such as India and Venezuela in the same category as European nations with long histories of stability and democracy. I disagree that these countries are obviously in a different category of democratic government. Many developing countries have been

Table 1-1: 36 Countries Continuously Democratic from 1974 to 1994

Australia	Greece	New Zealand
Austria	Iceland	Norway
Bahamas	India*	Papua New Guinea*
Barbados	Ireland	Portugal*
Belgium	Israel	Spain*
Botswana	Italy	Sweden
Canada	Jamaica	Switzerland
Colombia*	Japan	Trinidad & Tobago
Costa Rica	Luxembourg*	U.K.
Denmark	Mauritius*	U.S.
Finland	Nauru	Venezuela*
France	Netherlands	West Germany

Source: Freedom House, 1991, 1997
* Countries classified as "partially free" for less than three years of the study period and "free" for the remainder of it.

democratic longer than some European ones: India has been an independent democracy since 1947, while Spain and Portugal were controlled by fascists until the mid-1970s. Costa Rica has been independent since 1820 and Venezuela since 1821, which means they have been independent longer than Australia, New Zealand, and Canada. The literacy rate in Costa Rica and Jamaica (94 percent) is higher than in Portugal (84 percent) (Russett and Starr 1989). Women didn't get the national vote in Switzerland until 1971 (Norris 1987, 131), while they could vote in all the developing countries considered here long before that. For our present purposes, then, these thirty-six countries constitute a set of continuously democratic countries that are roughly comparable—not because they are similar in all respects, but because they are sufficiently similar in the relevant respects (Sartori 1991).

Sources of Data

Data on government response to violence against women have been compiled for this study from a variety of primary and secondary sources, including published articles and studies of government response to violence against women; CEDAW documents, including shadow reports, committee conclusions, and country reports to CEDAW; U.S. Department of State human rights reports; Human Rights Watch reports; publications of women's organizations and other activist groups; and my personal communications with activists and government representatives in the countries.

There are multiple sources for every country, including at least one government source and one source independent of the national government. For a list of sources by country, see appendix C.

Method and Methodology

This book is a global study that combines qualitative and quantitative methods.[16] In comparing a large number of countries, the study is somewhat unusual for both the field of comparative politics and policy and the field of feminist scholarship. Single-country case studies may be the most common form of analysis in comparative politics (Peters 1998). In addition, many scholars associate feminist approaches with qualitative, interpretive, and historical methods.

However, there is growing acknowledgment that quantitative studies may also make a contribution to both comparative and feminist work. There are ever more works in comparative feminist policy studies and in comparative politics more generally that employ a large number of cross-national comparisons (for example, Gornick, Meyers, and Ross 1997;

Gough 1997; Bradshaw et al. 1993; Siaroff 2000; and Silver and Dowley 2000).[17] In addition, as Dobash and Dobash (1998, 9) note with respect to feminist scholarship:

> Until recently, many (although certainly not all) feminist scholars have stated a clear preference for qualitative methods, believing them to be more humane and more likely to produce valid results about sensitive issues. This orthodoxy has now been challenged, and examples of different methods, including the strongly quantitative and a combination of quantitative and qualitative, have now joined the once exclusive domain of qualitative research among such scholars.

Harding (1987) argues that feminist methodology means asking questions about the purpose or aim of research and about the relationship between the researcher and the research, as well as drawing on women's experiences or perspectives for new theoretical and empirical insights. Thus, it is not a particular method or technique that is feminist, but rather the end to which it is put. Methodologies may be feminist, but methods or techniques are just tools that can be used for a variety of feminist or nonfeminist ends. Many of the qualitative methods that feminist scholars prize, such as ethnography and participant observation, have traditionally been used for nonfeminist research and have not protected the investigators against male bias or ethnocentrism. Quantitative methods, depending on how they are used, may be historical, interpretive, or feminist methods. Like participant observation or discourse analysis, statistical methods can be more or less historically informed or grounded, and more or less ethnocentric.

If there is one principle that should guide selection of feminist research methods, it is the same as that which should guide all good research: to use the method of analysis best suited to the question and the data. As Dobash and Dobash (1998, 3) note, "many different methods can and must be employed in seeking to expand empirical knowledge and theoretical insights, and . . . there is no 'perfect' method nor one which is always the 'best'. Instead, there is a wide array of methods that suit the different tasks necessary to make up the whole area of study." (See also Reinharz 1992; and Neilson 1990.)

For these reasons, I employ both quantitative and qualitative methods.

The Quantitative Analysis

In the quantitative part of the analysis, I summarize the patterns of government responsiveness that I observe cross-nationally, and I ask which factors appear to be the most strongly associated with a better government response to violence against women. I compare policy development across all thirty-six countries that were continuously democratic between 1974 and 1994. In order to identify the factors that might explain differing outcomes across countries, I employ a commonly used statistical technique, multiple regression. Multiple regression is a form of analysis that helps in sorting out *how much* of the variance in one variable or factor (the dependent variable) can be reasonably attributed to changes in one of several possible explanatory factors (independent variables). Strictly speaking, such analysis examines how strongly the dependent variable is associated with each independent variable. Multivariate analysis is very useful for evaluating the relative importance of a number of closely intertwined variables.

Often, statistical methods are used to make generalizations about a wider population on the basis of a sample. In this study, I am considering the countries in table 1-1 to be the complete set, or population, of stable democracies in the late twentieth century. For this reason, I am not employing sampling techniques. I am using statistical methods to describe and assess the strength of the relationships I see in the countries under study. For a fuller explanation of these methods, see appendix B.

The Qualitative Analysis

In this study, I employ some analysis of particular cases of policy development as a sort of "plausibility probe." Does the general argument I am making about government responsiveness capture the dynamic of policy development in particular countries over time? Claims about causality must include a convincing story about why the cause would have the observed effect. What is the process by which the cause exerts its influence? The case-study method of process tracing is useful for answering this question.

Process tracing is a method for assembling bits of evidence into a story of what happened, a detailing of a sequence of events leading up to the event of interest. In studies of foreign policy decision-making, for example, process tracing

> is intended to investigate and explain the decision process by which various initial conditions are translated into outcomes. A process-tracing approach entails abandonment of the strategy of "black-boxing" the decision process; instead, this decision-making process is the center of investigation. The process-tracing approach attempts to uncover what stimuli the actors attend to; the decision process that makes use of these stimuli to arrive at decisions; the actual be-

havior that then occurs; the effect of various institutional arrangements on attention, processing, and behavior; and the effect of other variables of interest on attention, processing, and behavior. (George and McKeown 1985, 35)

Throughout the book, but mostly in chapter 6, I attempt to show how the argument I advance makes sense in particular cases. I pay special attention to whether my argument captures the dynamics of policy development in the eight most responsive countries (Australia, Canada, the United States, France, Ireland, Costa Rica, Israel, and New Zealand). I focus most of my attention in chapter 5 on Canada and Australia, because these countries have responded more quickly and comprehensively to violence against women than any other democratic national government. Examining these eight cases, I ask whether the general story I develop through statistical analysis seems to describe the development of policies on violence against women in these countries. Thus, the statistical analysis is combined with a series of narrative accounts in order to develop a model of the policymaking process as it plays out in national government response to violence against women in stable democracies.

The Comparative Method

All comparative studies must strike a balance between paying attention to the details of each case and describing overall patterns across cases (Sartori 1991). Global studies and so-called large-N studies—those involving more than twenty countries—are often criticized as superficial or misleading (Peters 1998; Blomquist 1999). In order to create measures that "travel," it may be necessary to define categories so vague that they are meaningless. "Conceptual stretching" to accommodate cross-national differences may result in concepts so vague that they include phenomena that are fundamentally different (Sartori 1991). Peters (1998), for example, argues that global studies simplify relationships so much that they cease to be relevant to "real countries" and real-world settings. After all, he argues, we aren't interested in the distributions of data themselves, we are interested in particular political settings.

These concerns about oversimplification and superficiality are important. We must confront the question: Have I created a "dog-bat" (Sartori's example of a nonsense category), or some other conceptual category that is meaningless? Does the focus on a large number of countries render this study irrelevant to scholars who seek to understand one or a few national contexts?

The measure of government response that I have developed here is certainly a rough one, and one that permits considerable variation in actual policy. However, it has "face validity"—that is, it seems to make sense given our intuitions and existing knowledge about the subject. The measure correctly identifies those countries that experts acknowledge to be the leading nations in this policy area. Similarly, nations that are doing nothing are clearly and correctly identified. Moreover, this study depends to a large degree on exactly the rich national accounts of the type that many comparativists advocate: country case studies made this study possible. Thus, although it is true that the richness and depth of country (or city) case studies is sacrificed to some degree in this analysis, the measures used are still meaningful. If this study can speak in turn to the country-specific research on which it draws—and I think it can—the study of comparative feminist policy will be advanced.

Culture, Development, Parties, and Policies on Violence Against Women

> The dimension of 'culture' is important in explanations of cross-national differences but it has usually been excluded or only marginally integrated in theoretical explanations. Instead, culture is often treated as the residual explanatory variable.
>
> BIRGIT PFAU-EFFINGER, 1998

> Only comparative empirical research will adequately disclose the fundamental properties that unite or divide modern welfare states.
>
> GØSTA ESPING-ANDERSEN, 1990

■Which governments do the most to address violence against women, and which do the least? In this chapter I provide a global overview of government responsiveness to violence against women and explore the utility of some common explanations for cross-national policy differences. Most comparative studies attempt to control for cultural differences and level of development by avoiding cross-national and especially cross-regional studies (Peters 1998). Cultural differences are thought to be especially important in explaining policies that affect women (Conway, Ahern, and Steuernagel 1995). This is one reason that most comparative studies of women and public policy avoid comparisons across what are assumed to be differing *national* cultures (Duncan 1996).[1] Comparisons that include countries at different levels of development are also rare, since level of development is assumed to be a fundamental determinant of policy variation.[2] This is most commonly conceptualized as the difference between advanced industrialized countries and less developed countries (see, for example, Stetson and Mazur 1995). If level of development and cultural factors are really

29

as important as most comparative studies assume, then a regional or national focus allows greater refinement in the hypothesis by controlling for these factors.

One advantage of taking a global comparative approach is that one is able to examine the impact of these differences empirically. In this chapter I first summarize the pattern of variation in government responsiveness across stable democracies. Then I consider explanations based on various types of cultural differences (national culture, regional culture, maternalism, and so on). Culture might also determine violence against women by determining rates of violence in general. In the second part of the chapter, I turn to explanations focusing on socioeconomic modernity, such as level of development, labor mobilization and left parties, and industrialization.

A BRIEF OVERVIEW OF GOVERNMENT RESPONSE TO VIOLENCE AGAINST WOMEN

In 1974, most democratic governments had not taken any action to address violence against women (see table 2-1); only the national government of Canada had undertaken any reforms. In 1984, after more than a decade of women's movement organizing around the world, most (twenty-one) of the world's democracies were still doing nothing to address violence against women. Only fifteen of the continuously democratic governments had taken some action.

By 1994, nearly all the national governments (thirty-one of thirty-six) had undertaken some action to address violence against women. The most typical response was to adopt policy initiatives covering two or three of the seven possible areas of policy action discussed in the previous chapter. Only eight countries had addressed five or more areas, making them the most responsive national governments. Australia and Canada had adopted the most comprehensive policies, dealing with all seven areas. The United States had addressed six areas, and Costa Rica, France, Ireland, Israel, and New Zealand had developed fairly comprehensive policies, covering five areas each.

Canada and Australia were also among the earliest to address violence against women, having adopted numerous policy measures in the mid-1980s, while many other governments, such as those in Ireland and Austria, began to deal with these issues only in the 1990s. The government of France was particularly active until the mid-eighties; it had adopted four policy measures by 1984. Sweden and the United Kingdom were also early in enacting reforms, although government response in both countries stalled

Table 2-1: Scope of National Policies on Violence Against Women

1974		1984		1994	
Country	No. of Policy Areas Addessed	Country	No. of Policy Areas Addressed	Country	No. of Policy Areas Addressed
Canada	1	France	4	Australia	7
Australia	0	Sweden	3	Canada	7
Austria	0	U.K.	3	U.S.	6
Bahamas	0	Australia	2	Costa Rica	5
Barbados	0	Canada	2	France	5
Belgium	0	Denmark	2	Ireland	5
Botswana	0	India	2	Israel	5
Colombia	0	Israel	2	New Zealand	5
Costa Rica	0	Netherlands	2	Belgium	4
Denmark	0	New Zealand	2	India	4
Finland	0	U.S.	2	Norway	4
France	0	Costa Rica	1	Sweden	4
Germany	0	Iceland	1	U.K.	4
Greece	0	Luxembourg	1	Austria	3
Iceland	0	Spain	1	Bahamas	3
India	0	Austria	0	Barbados	3
Ireland	0	Bahamas	0	Colombia	3
Israel	0	Barbados	0	Luxembourg	3
Italy	0	Belgium	0	Netherlands	3
Jamaica	0	Botswana	0	Spain	3
Japan	0	Colombia	0	Denmark	2
Luxembourg	0	Finland	0	Finland	2
Mauritius	0	Germany	0	Germany	2
Nauru	0	Greece	0	Iceland	2
Netherlands	0	Ireland	0	Portugal	2
New Zealand	0	Italy	0	Switzerland	2
Norway	0	Jamaica	0	Trinidad & Tobago	2
Papua New Guinea	0	Japan	0	Greece	1
Portugal	0	Mauritius	0	Jamaica	1
Spain	0	Nauru	0	Japan	1
Sweden	0	Norway	0	Mauritius	1
Switzerland	0	Papua New Guinea	0	Papua New Guinea	1
Trinidad & Tobago	0	Portugal	0	Botswana	0
U.K.	0	Switzerland	0	Italy	0
U.S.	0	Trinidad & Tobago	0	Nauru	0
Venezuela	0	Venezuela	0	Venezuela	0

after the early 1980s. Although the United States was one of the first national governments to respond to this problem, addressing two areas in 1978, no further policy development took place at a national level until 1994, when the government adopted measures in four additional areas.

At the other end of the spectrum, four countries (Botswana, Italy, Nauru, and Venezuela) still had not adopted even a single policy measure by 1994. Five other countries (Greece, Jamaica, Japan, Mauritius, and Papua New Guinea) failed to adopt initiatives in more than one policy area to address violence against women. Although Austria, the Bahamas, Barbados, and Colombia had addressed three areas by 1994, they were notable in lacking innovativeness, having had no policy response a decade earlier. In contrast, the other "middling" countries in 1994 (Luxembourg, the Netherlands, and Spain) had begun implementing at least one initiative by 1984.

COMPARATIVE SOCIAL POLICY EXPLANATIONS

Policies on violence against women are social policies: they are important in providing the rights of citizenship to half the population—women. Responding to violence against women requires altering power relationships among social groups (men and women). It also involves a degree of redistribution. As noted earlier, in the United States, federal government spending alone on programs to combat violence against women was nearly a billion dollars in 1998 (Erickson 1998).

The pattern of government response described above presents a challenge to most comparative approaches to social policy because the cross-national patterns on this issue are so unlike those observed in other areas of social policy, such as poverty or motherhood. In most of these other areas, Sweden stands as the model of the most generous or most developed welfare state, while Canada and the United States are viewed as "underdeveloped" or "residual" welfare states (Esping-Andersen 1990; Duncan 1995). Measures of responsiveness to violence against women, though, suggest that Canada, Australia, and the United States have had the most developed social policies, while policy development in Sweden and Finland has remained stunted. The government of Ireland, which is often seen as a traditional society, still "in transition from private patriarchy" (Duncan 1995), is more responsive to violence against women than Sweden, Norway, Finland, or Denmark. Thus, policy development on violence against women appears to follow quite different patterns from more conventional social policy indicators, and it thus requires different explanations. This difference ought to be of interest to scholars of comparative social policy.

STUDIES OF GOVERNMENT POLICY ON VIOLENCE AGAINST WOMEN

Although many governments have been responding to violence against women in one way or another over the past ten or fifteen years, there has been little scholarly attention to cross-national variation in this area of policy. The empirical and theoretical literature on differences in national policies to address the issue is scanty compared to work in other issue areas of concern to women, such as income assistance policies, policies affecting mothers, and policies on reproductive freedom.[3] Sheer novelty (in the sense that violence against women is a newly recognized problem) cannot be considered an explanation when one looks at the exponential growth of the literature on, say, environmental policy (a few examples are Boardman 1992; MacDonald, Nielson, and Stern 1997; and Jamison et al. 1990).

Whatever the reason, there are only three comparative studies of national violence-against-women policy that seek to investigate and explain variation in government response (Elman 1996a; Busch 1992; Heise, Raikes, Watts, and Zwi 1994).[4] All three studies identify the mobilization of a women's movement, and especially a women's movement with some organizational independence from government, as a key catalyst to policy change in this area. In addition, these studies identify the number of women in political office as a possible determinant of government response. But there is no agreement on how or to what extent either of these factors matters (Elman 1996a; Heise, Pitanguy, and Germain 1994). Elman (1996a) finds that federal, pluralist institutional structures create more points of access for women's movements than do corporatist, unitary structures.

Before we turn to the effect of women's movements and women in office (chapters 3 and 4), let us first examine the importance of two factors that have not yet been explicitly considered in the literature on policies to address violence against women: culture and level of development. In taking a global approach to comparing government response to violence against women, I define a set of national policies as comparable across regions and level of development. This will lead many to suspect that culture and level of development are confounding the explanations I present. Because left-wing parties have played an important role in increasing the number of women in politics (Norris 1987), one might expect that the election of left parties to power will spur the development of policies on violence. Let us therefore turn to a consideration of culture, level of development, and political parties.

CULTURE

From the work of feminists and comparativists, we know that certain social norms and attitudes affecting the status of women vary cross-nationally. We know that certain cultural attitudes toward women—for example, "macho" attitudes—are associated with higher levels of violence (Levinson 1989; Heise, Pitanguy, and Germain 1994). Such attitudes might also be associated with resistance to policies that address violence against women.

In the study of comparative public policy, some scholars emphasize the role of "deeply embedded cultural ideas arising from the distinctive historical experiences of nations" (Heidenheimer, Heclo, and Adams 1990) as determinants of policy outcomes. This approach, which is sometimes called the cultural values or the national values approach (Heidenheimer, Heclo, and Adams 1990; Skocpol 1992), may seem particularly well suited to the study of women and public policy. Conway, Ahern, and Steuernagel (1999, 8) note that understanding cultural change is critical to understanding changes in public policies affecting women. Pfau-Effinger (1998) argues that explanations for cross-national variation in women's part-time work have not sufficiently attended to cultural aspects of gender politics. "Gender culture," she writes, importantly influences cross-national variation. She defines gender culture as "common assumptions about the desirable, 'normal' form of gender relations and the division of labor between women and men." These assumptions are "institutionalized as norms" (178). These norms are not shared equally by all social groups in a given society, varying across regions, ethnicities, and social strata. (See also Norris 1987.)

The precise meaning of *culture* can be difficult to pin down. Conway, Ahern, and Steuernagel (1999, 2) define it as "a core of traditional ideas, practices, and technology shared by a people." This broad definition encompasses any number of indicators, including social institutions, the role of women in the family, and the economic conditions of women. Policy itself is one aspect of culture, in this view, but it is also affected by culture.

Although it seems true that culture and policy are interrelated, we need to know the specific aspects of culture that matter, and the mechanisms by which they exert their effect. The aspects of culture that have been found to affect policymaking are numerous, including social practices such as child-rearing norms and the sexual division of labor, public opinion, policymakers' attitudes, and institutional structures (Pfau-Effinger 1998). For example, Mazur (1996) argues that French culture impeded the formulation and implementation of effective sexual harassment legislation. Policymakers "perceived the regulation of sexual harassment as a potential threat to personal freedoms and French culture" (45). These attitudes helped ensure that sexual harassment legislation in France had only symbolic impact. Culture, as Mazur uses the concept, affects policymaking through the attitudes of policymakers. Other scholars have found that culture, or national identity, is also expressed in the structure of institutions. For example, Pauly and Reich (1997) show how national identities are reflected in the activities of political institutions and multinational corporations. In this way, culture indirectly affects policy by determining the structure of institutions.

Almond and Verba (1963) conducted a five-nation study of political culture. They define political culture as "specifically political orientations—attitudes toward the political system and its various parts, and attitudes toward the role of the self in the system. . . . a set of orientations toward a special set of social objects and processes" (13). They measured patterns of political orientation through surveys that asked questions about respondents' feelings about national institutions, about being nationals of their respective countries, and the like. Although Almond and Verba do not undertake to connect political culture to policy, they note that this is one possible way of studying the impact of political culture (28–29). Such a study would "relate systematically types of public policy orientations to types of social structure and cultural values, as well as to the socialization processes with which they are related" (29).

Few would deny that social practices, cultural attitudes, and institutions have some effect on policymaking. But saying that cultural differences explain cross-national variation in policy outcomes does not tell us which practices, institutions, and attitudes matter, and how they matter. As we have seen, the possibilities are numerous. Greater specification is required.

One way of proceeding might be to look, as do Almond and Verba, for indicators of national attitudes toward the policies in question—in our case, policies on violence against women. Conceptually, one would expect policy orientations to bear some relationship to existing policies. Mazur and Stetson (1995), for example, find that political-cultural attitudes toward state intervention are related to equal opportunity policy outcome.

Of course, the relationship between policy and attitudes is complicated. For example, citizens might report greater pride in or support for social policies when they benefit from them, or when policies really help people. Esping-Andersen (1990) argues that universalistic social policies, when they attain certain levels of quality, are the basis for their own support. This may explain why, for example, Canadians in the 1980s expressed a great deal of support for the universalistic social programs (such as health care) while supporting means-tested programs (such as social assistance) less enthusiastically. Similarly, in the United States, it seems that there is broader support for universal programs such as Social Security than for "welfare," or Temporary Assistance for Needy Families (TANF). Esping-Andersen argues that the reason there is more support for universalistic policies in the Scandinavian social democratic welfare states than in the "liberal" welfare states (Canada, the United States, and Australia) is that universalistic policies already exist in the Scandinavian welfare states, and the bulk of people in those countries perceive themselves as benefiting from that state of affairs.

If policies produce attitudes supportive of those policies after the fact, then it is even harder to determine how political attitudes toward policy affect policy outputs. This is especially true in the case of violence against women, where many policies, such as those on public education and training, are aimed specifically at changing awareness. In addition, legal reforms and new legislation can provide legitimacy for claims about violence that were previously unrecognized. So, even if one found a statistical association between positive attitudes and policy outputs, it might be difficult to tell the direction in which a causal relationship ran.

These national values explanations tend to be less useful in explaining big changes in policy. For example, in the United States, domestic violence has gone from being viewed as a private matter to being the subject of wide-ranging federal legislation. In a time of fiscal restraint (the 1990s), large amounts of money were dedicated to fighting domestic violence.[5] How can a single policy orientation explain this change in policy? If policy orientation itself changed, then isn't it possible that the change in policy and the shift in policy orientation are the result of a common cause, say, the long-term effect of a strong women's movement in the United States? Thus, when we are trying to explain major changes in policy orientation, as in this study, such general political culture explanations provide little leverage.

Another problematic aspect of employing the notion of cultural value differences is the tendency to see current policy preferences as the result of a culture that prefers those policies, thereby ending up with a tautological explanation. Cultural preferences, in this view, circumscribe policy processes to such a degree that certain policies are simply not possible, or at least very unlikely. While this may be true in some cases, this argument tends to be misapplied, because the obvious truth that existing policies must not have been selected out by the cultural framework is mistakenly taken to imply that only existing policies were permitted by the cultural context. In this way, existing policies are taken to define the universe of possible policies, implying that the policy process could not have had a different outcome in that the existing policy arrangement is the only possible outcome from that particular cultural context.

This is not to say that cultural predispositions, or attitudes, are not important for understanding policy. But the mechanism by which these attitudes affect policy must be specified. For example, are attitudes expressed in elections? in institutional structure? in opinion polls? If so, how do these particular means of expression affect policy?

Electoral outcomes, attitudes, institutional structures, and other practices often vary within countries and regions (Duncan 1996). This means that it is not always clear *which* attitudes are relevant. As Narayan (1997) argues, "culture," understood as a complex package of attitudes and practices, does not vary according to national boundaries. Social practices and norms vary within countries, and some specific practices and norms are shared by national contexts that are otherwise quite different (Duncan 1995). So assuming a type of uniformity within countries and differences between them involves a sort of cultural essentialism: it falsely posits an essence or nature that undergirds "national culture" (Narayan 1997). Thus, culture varies across regions, classes, and ethnicity. It is also contested within these categories, as feminists and other groups struggle over which attitudes and norms will prevail. Whose norms or attitudes matter, and how?

Of course, once we start to specify whose attitudes make a difference (those of voters, policymakers, feminists?) and how they matter (do they influence voting behavior, the language of legislation, choice of lobbying strategies?), we are no longer giving an explanation based on broadly defined cultural or value differences. We are giving explanations that identify voters or policymakers or feminist activists as the relevant actors, and the media or the legislature or a movement's organization as the relevant arena. Although it would be wrong to say that culture does not influence these activities and arenas, it is much more useful to know which actors and arenas matter, and how. Without such specification, explanations based on attitudes or culture in general are unsatisfying. Unless these elements of the explanation are provided, invoking cultural differences in explaining cross-national policy variation amounts to a "fill-in-the-blanks" strategy: you fill in the category of culture with whatever actors or arenas seem to matter in the case under study. This does not do much to further our understanding of policy change or continuity across countries.[6]

Regional Culture

It may be objected that the above discussion understands culture too narrowly, and that culture does not vary along national lines. Rather, the argument would go, countries in certain areas of the world can be said to share a common history and to interact more with each other than with other parts of the world. In such cases, roughly regional cultures develop, and these are reflected in approximate policy uniformity across countries. For example, one scholar Kaplan (1992, 63) observes that "women . . . are better off in Scandinavian countries than women in other western European nations and the western world." Similarly, Inglehart and Carballo (1997) argue that distinct cultural zones can be identified—Latin America, for example—on the basis of the values that the people of that region hold. The anthology *Women and Politics Worldwide* employs the regional divisions defined by the Overseas Development Council, since these divisions "combine geographic proximity and historical similarity to create a proxy for cultural characteristics" (Chowdhury, Johnson, Nelson, and O'Loughlin 1994, 28). This operationalization is also employed here.

Regional culture, however, does not seem to help much in explaining cross-national policy variation. Table 2-2 groups the democracies in this study according to region. Let us focus on the two regions best represented here, Latin America (seven countries) and Europe (eighteen countries). If regional culture determines national policy outcomes, then surely we would expect to see a difference between the responsiveness of European governments and that of Latin American governments.

In fact, the pattern of national government response in Europe and Latin America appears to be roughly similar. The range of variation is identical: in both regions, there is one country whose national government has adopted not even one of the policy measures specified here, and at least one government that has adopted five initiatives. The modal response in both regions is also the same: the largest number of national governments in both regions address only two or three policy areas. Thus, it seems that region will generally tell us little about the responsiveness of a particular national government.

In the case of Oceania, variation in government response is as great within the region as it is across regions (ranging from o to 7), so knowing that a national government belongs to this region tells us literally nothing about its expected response. In Asia, the variation is somewhat smaller, ranging from 1 to 5—roughly similar to the range in Europe or Latin America.

One way to think about how much information a variable or feature provides is to ask whether knowing the value of that variable—in this case, what region a country is in—will allow you to make a better prediction about the responsiveness of government than just guessing the mean or av-

Table 2-2: Scope of Government Response by Region, 1994 (Number of policy areas addressed)

Africa	Asia	Latin America	North America	Oceania	Europe
Mauritius (1)	Israel (5)	Costa Rica (5)	Canada (7)	Australia (7)	France (5)
Botswana (0)	India (4)	Bahamas (3)	U.S. (6)	New	Ireland (5)
	Japan (1)	Barbados (3)		Zealand (5)	Belgium (4)
		Colombia (3)		Papua New	Norway (4)
		Trinidad &		Guinea (1)	Sweden (4)
		Tobago (2)		Nauru (0)	U.K. (4)
		Jamaica (1)			Austria (3)
		Venezuela (0)			Luxembourg (3)
					Netherlands (3)
					Spain (3)
					Denmark (2)
					Finland (2)
					Germany (2)
					Iceland (2)
					Portugal (2)
					Switzerland (2)
					Greece (1)
					Italy (0)

Note: This table follows the classification defined in Overseas Development Council (OCD), *US Foreign Policy and the Third World: Agenda, 1983* (New York: Praeger, 1983); and Population Reference Bureau, *1984 World Population Datasheet* (Washington, D.C., 1984) and employed in Nelson and Chowdhury 1994. The countries grouped under regional categories are so designated by regional location, rather than language or similar cultural characteristics (e.g., the Bahamas is not a "Latin" country in the latter respect).

erage. For the whole set of countries considered here, the mean, or average, level of government action is to address three policy areas. For each of the regions discussed above (Oceania, Asia, Latin America, and Europe), the mean is also about three. Thus, knowing that a country is in one of these regions tells us little about what we should expect to see in terms of government responsiveness.

Two of the regions, Africa and North America, are represented by only two countries each, which makes it difficult to separate region from shared national-level characteristics (such as federal forms of government or a strong women's movement). In these regions there is also less variation than in the others, suggesting that the statistical principle that variation increases with sample size holds true. It is possible that national governments in Canada and the United States are more responsive because they share a North American political culture, and that national governments in Botswana and Mauritius are less responsive because they share an African political culture. But the small number of countries involved makes it just as likely that other shared features, such as national poverty in the case of Africa or federal governmental structures in the case of North America, make the difference. I return to these points below.

A regression analysis of the impact of region confirms the finding that region tells us little about government responsiveness to violence against women. Recall that scope is a variable that measures how many policy areas a government addresses; it ranges from o (no areas) to 7 (seven areas). A coefficient of 1.00 means that a one-unit change in the independent variable is associated with one additional area of policy action.

In this case, the coefficients should be interpreted as estimating the difference in scope of government response associated with being in that particular region rather than Europe (table 2-3, model 1). In the analysis, region is coded as a dummy variable, that is, each regional category is coded as applying (1) or not applying (0) for all the countries. This makes sense because even though we are interested in the impact of regional culture, we want to know how it affects *national* policy outcomes. So the question can be restated as: How does the region to which a country belongs affect government responsiveness? A positive coefficient means that governments in that region are more responsive than European governments, and a negative coefficient means that they are less responsive.[7]

Even controlling for level of development, the regression analysis does not support standard hypotheses about the importance of regional culture. It appears that Latin American governments may be slightly more responsive than European governments, addressing one additional policy area. This runs counter to the relationship usually predicted in the literature, where the machismo of Latin American cultures is expected to produce less government responsiveness.

In the analysis, North America is associated with an additional three or four areas of policy action. This fits with our initial impression that North American countries seem more responsive than European ones. However, it seems unlikely that the variable North America taps a similar orientation toward social policy in the two countries of the region. Mazur and Stetson (1995), for example, note that Canada is characterized by a "pro-state" culture. In contrast, citizens of the United States are usually described as opposed to government intervention in the area of social policy: "In the United States, strong antigovernment sentiments and the tendency toward pluralist interest group action contributes to the idea of statelessness" in American political culture (Mazur and Stetson 1995, 289).

Moreover, the statistical analysis confirms that (except for the difference

Table 2-3: Coefficients, Dependent Variable = Scope of Government Response,
36 Countries, 1994

Model/ Independent Variables	B	Std. Error	Beta	t	Sig.	R-squared
1/ Level of development	1.90	1.37	0.46	1.38	0.18	0.35
Region-latinam	1.15	1.58	0.23	0.73	0.47	
Region-africa	−0.49	1.90	−0.06	−0.26	0.80	
Region-asia	1.71	1.43	0.24	1.19	0.24	
Region-northam	3.61	1.32	0.42	2.73	0.01	
Region-oceania	1.31	1.20	0.21	1.10	0.28	
2/ Protestant	0.25	0.75	0.06	0.33	0.74	0.13
Other religions	-0.44	1.04	-0.08	-0.42	0.68	
Level of development	1.26	0.70	0.31	1.78	0.08	
3/ Level of development	1.41	0.68	0.34	2.08	0.05	0.12
Maternity-leave index	0.00	0.00	-0.03	-0.21	0.84	
4/ Strong, autonomous women's movement	1.88	0.61	0.48	3.09	0.00	0.28
GNP per capita	0.00	0.00	0.32	2.07	0.05	
5/ Strong, autonomous women's movement	1.81	0.57	0.46	3.19	0.00	0.32
Level of development	1.44	0.59	0.35	2.45	0.02	
6/ Gender Development Index (GDI)	4.33	2.81	0.28	1.54	0.13	0.08
7/ Gender Empowerment Measure (GEM)	4.46	2.47	0.32	1.80	0.08	0.10

between North America and Europe) region is not a good predictor of government responsiveness to violence against women. For example, knowing whether a country is in Latin America or in Europe is a poor basis for predicting government response, since such predictions have large error ranges. This is also true for Africa, Asia, and Oceania, and holds even when controlling for level of development.

As noted, the lack of a compelling interpretation for government responsiveness in the North American region suggests that that coding may be tapping some other, unrecognized feature shared by Canada and the United States, such as a strong, autonomous women's movement, the number of women in cabinet, or a common institutional structure (such as federalism). I discuss these possibilities in chapters 3, 4, and 5, respectively. In addition, level of development is a stronger predictor of government response than any regional difference: the standardized Betas for level of development, North America, and Latin America are .46, .42, and .23 respectively (table 2-3, model 1). I discuss level of development later in this chapter.

Religion

Some will object that the discussion of culture misses one obvious way that culture affects politics: through religious institutions and practices. Religion is thought to be an important aspect of culture (Narayan 1997) and thus might be expected to affect government policy on violence against women. Inglehart and Carballo (1997, 43) note that "in global perspective the historically Catholic societies have relatively similar cultural values—as do the historically Protestant societies." (See also Esping-Andersen 1990.) Weber (1992) speculated that the Protestant work ethic resulted in more rapid industrialization. Looking at cross-national patterns in government responsiveness, we can see that the two most responsive governments, Australia and Canada, are predominantly Protestant countries (see table 2-4). Of the three governments identified as taking no action on violence in 1994, two (Italy and Venezuela) are largely Roman Catholic. Perhaps, as some have suggested, predominantly Catholic countries are less progressive than mainly Protestant ones (see the debates cited in Randall 1987 and Kaplan 1992).

Kaplan (1992) criticizes this common hypothesis as simplistic. She argues that Western Europe is predominantly Catholic and that the few Protestant countries that there are (she identifies Finland, Iceland, Norway, and Sweden as Protestant) are not the most progressive countries in Europe.

The dominant religion is the one to which the largest proportion of people in a country belong. In no country did the dominant religion change over the study period (1974–94). There are six main religions included in the study—Catholicism, Protestantism, Judaism, Hinduism, Buddhism, and Greek Orthodoxy—but for the purposes of analysis, countries were coded as Catholic, Protestant, or other. This was done because the small number of countries in each of the "other" religion categories made it difficult to interpret results meaningfully. There were no predominantly Islamic nations in the group of thirty-six countries in the study. Religion was measured using a dummy variable with Catholicism as the omitted category, since it is the only religion about which there are specific hypotheses.

Using regression analysis, we can test whether there is an association be-

**Table 2-4: Scope of Government Response by Dominant Religion, 1994
(Number of policy areas addressed)**

Roman Catholic	Protestant	Hindu	Greek Orthodox	Jewish	Shinto-Buddhist
France (5)	Australia (7)	India (4)	Greece (1)	Israel (5)	Japan (1)
Ireland (5)	Canada (7)	Mauritius (1)			
Belgium (4)	U.S. (6)				
Austria (3)	New Zealand				
Colombia (3)	(5)				
Costa Rica (5)	Norway (4)				
Luxembourg (3)	Sweden (4)				
Netherlands (3)	U.K. (4)				
Spain (3)	Bahamas (3)				
Portugal (2)	Barbados (3)				
Trinidad	Denmark (2)				
&Tobago (2)	Finland (2)				
Italy (0)	Germany (2)				
Venezuela (0)	Iceland (2)				
	Switzerland (2)				
	Jamaica (1)				
	Papua New				
	Guinea (1)				
	Nauru (0)				

Source: Data on dominant religion are from U.S. Central Intelligence Agency 1993.
Note: Botswana is not included here, as data indicate only that it is Christian and animist, not whether the Christians are Protestant or Catholic.

tween being predominantly Catholic or Protestant and scope of government response. A positive association between the variable Protestant and scope means that being predominantly Protestant is associated with greater responsiveness. A coefficient of 1 means that governments in Protestant countries are likely to address one additional policy area (plus or minus the standard error) in comparison to governments in Catholic countries. When the errors are large in relation to the coefficients, this suggests that the variable in question is a poor predictor of scope.

Kaplan's analysis of Western Europe appears to hold in this study of stable democracies, in which there is a larger number of Protestant countries. Whether a country is predominantly Catholic, Protestant, or of another religion is a poor guide to the probable scope of national government policy on violence against women (see table 2-3, model 2). For 1994, if a country is Protestant rather than Catholic, it is associated with one-quarter of an additional policy area. The standard error is so large (±0.75) that even this small association cannot be predicted with any certainty. Similarly, whether a country is predominantly Catholic or "other" is not a good predictor of scope of government response. This is true even controlling for level of development (table 2-3, model 2).

Thus, it appears that religion as measured here gives us no significant power to predict variation in government response to violence against women. But it may be that the degree, rather than type, of religion is what matters. As Kaplan (1992, 55) writes, "any religion, as long as it has a stronghold on the state and can wield real power, will be a great stumbling block for substantial change in secular matters." For example, Randal (1987) posits that the Catholic Church has been stronger in Ireland than in Italy. Considering the struggle over abortion policy in these two countries, she notes that "the real difference . . . is that in Ireland the Catholic Church has faced no significant challenge to its moral hegemony from an alternative secular or socialist tradition" (282). In Italy, by contrast, the strength of the left-wing tradition and the women's liberation movement meant that the Church could not ultimately prevent abortion-law reform. But in the area of violence-against-women policy, Ireland has adopted more provisions than Italy, and it did so sooner. So the greater entrenchment of the Church in Ireland did not inhibit a more progressive government response to violence against women. Thus, there is little evidence in the data on government response to suggest that religion is an area worth pursuing as an explanation of variation in national policy on violence against women.

Maternalism

Several recent works argue that states in which women are highly valued as mothers enact social policies that are more favorable to women (Skocpol 1992; Koven and Michel 1993).[8] Motherhood, the argument goes, provides access to the rights of citizenship for women, and women's movements have been able to "hijack" maternalism to provoke a state response to women's issues. As Koven and Michel (1993, 31) point out, the maternalist movements of the late nineteenth and early twentieth century "remain important expressions of the subversive potential of claims based on the social and economic value of motherhood joined to women's freedom to define for themselves their relationship to family and work force." Other scholars, however, worry that when concessions are made to women as mothers, traditional values are reinforced. These concessions actually make it harder for women to make progress in other areas—that is, as women, not as mothers (Brush 1996). Do policies designed to benefit mothers have positive or negative spillover consequences for women in areas not related to motherhood? One way of exploring this issue empirically would be to see whether countries with generous maternity benefits also have better policies to address violence against women.

Maternity leave is considered more generous if more total weeks of leave are provided to working women, if the leave is paid, and if a larger proportion of wages is paid out. Overall, the generosity of maternity-leave provisions is calculated as

$$weeks + (weeks * proportion\ of\ wages\ paid).$$

Thus, a government that provided 100 percent of wages during the leave would receive a score of two times the number of weeks. For example, in Austria in 1994, workers were entitled to sixteen weeks at 100 percent of their usual wages, so Austria's score on this variable would be 32. In Belgium, women were entitled to fifteen weeks of leave but were paid only 80 percent of their usual wages, so Belgium's maternity-leave provisions are judged to be less generous than Austria's, receiving a score of 27. Cross-national data on maternity-leave provisions are available only for 1994; they are taken from the International Labour Organization's *Conditions of Work Digest* (1994).

At first sight, the data might seem to suggest that maternalism has a negative relationship to government responsiveness (see table 2-5). For example, Australia and the United States, which are very responsive to violence against women, are the least generous of all developed countries in terms of their provision for maternity leave. The relatively meager provision for working mothers in these countries is widely recognized. Although Canada has somewhat more generous provisions for maternity leave than Australia and the United States, it is not particularly maternalist. On the other hand, Costa Rica and France, which are among the more maternalist countries, are also among the most responsive to violence against women. Thus, there is no obvious relationship between maternalism and government responsiveness to violence against women.

A statistical analysis reinforces this conclusion. If maternity leave were linearly related to scope of government response, one would expect larger or smaller values in the maternity-leave indicator to be associated with differing levels of government response. If maternalism resulted in positive spillovers, then we would expect to be able to predict a positive association; if maternalism created obstacles to addressing women's issues as women, rather than as mothers, then we would expect a negative association.

Analysis of cross-national data for 1994 reveals that there is no rela-

Table 2-5: Maternity Leave and Scope of Government Policy Response to Violence Against Women, 1994

Country	Weeks of Leave	Percentage of Earnings Paid	Maternity-Leave Index	No. of Policy Areas Addressed
Italy	20	80	36	0
Norway	18	100	36	4
Venezuela	18	100	36	0
Denmark	18	90	34	2
Austria	16	Avg. earnings	32	3
Costa Rica	16	100	32	5
Netherlands	16	100	32	3
Greece	15	100	30	1
France	16	84	29	5
Germany	14	100	28	2
Luxembourg	14	100	28	3
Spain	16	75	28	3
Belgium	15	82	27	4
Finland	15	70 to 80	27	2
Canada	17	57	27	7
U.K.	14	90	27	4
Portugal	12.8	100	26	2
Barbados	12	100	24	3
Colombia	12	100	24	3
India	12	100	24	4
Jamaica	12	100	24	1
Mauritius	12	100	24	1
Ireland	14	70	24	5
Sweden	12	90% or flat rate	23	4
Japan	14	60	22	1
Israel	12	75	21	5
Trinidad & Tobago	13	60	21	2
Bahamas	8	100	16	3
Iceland	8	Fixed allowance	16	2
Switzerland	8	100	16	2
Botswana	12	25	15	0
New Zealand	14	Unpaid	14	5
Australia	12	Unpaid	12	7
U.S.	12	Unpaid	12	6
Papua New Guinea	6	Unpaid	6	1
Nauru	—	—	0	0

Source: International Labour Organization 1994.

tionship between the generosity of maternity provisions and the scope of government response to violence against women, even when level of development is taken into account (table 2-3, model 3). The coefficients (both standardized and unstandardized) are roughly zero, suggesting neither a positive nor a negative association.

Status of Women

It may be that attitudes toward women or sexual equality are the relevant cultural variable, and that all this discussion of region, religion, and political culture misses the point. Perhaps the general position of women in society is the best predictor of government responsiveness to violence against women. If women are generally better off in some countries than in others, then we would expect this overall advantage to be reflected in greater government responsiveness to violence against women.

One important problem with this argument concerns interpreting an association between women's status and the scope of government response. If countries that are more responsive to violence against women are more responsive to women's concerns in general, then looking for an association begs the question of what makes governments more responsive to women's concerns. To say that some governments are more responsive to violence against women because they are more responsive to women's concerns, without specifying what makes them so, is not very satisfying.

In any case, it seems unlikely that the relationship between women's status and policy outcomes is so simple. Responsiveness varies across policy areas within countries. The national governments that are the most progressive on violence against women are not the ones that do best in addressing women's poverty. It seems likely that there are different dynamics behind the various policy outcomes that affect women's status.

Indeed, the evidence does not support a simple association between the status of women and government response to violence against women. The Gender Development Index (GDI), developed by the United Nations, is the Human Development Index (HDI) adjusted for gender inequality. The HDI measures the average achievement of a country in basic human well-being. "The HDI indicates whether people lead a long and healthy life, are educated and knowledgeable and enjoy a decent standard of living"; the GDI measures achievement in the same basic categories "but takes note of inequality in achievement between men and women, and imposes a penalty for sex inequality" (UN Development Programme 1995, 73). For the countries in this study, the GDI ranges between 0.401 and 0.919 (see table 2-6).

The UN Development Programme (1995) also developed the Gender

Table 2-6: Gender Development, Gender Empowerment, and Scope of Government Policy Response to Violence Against Women, 1994

GDI Rank	Country	GDI (1990–92)	GEM (1990–92)	No. of Policy Areas Addressed
1	Sweden	0.919	0.757	4
2	Finland	0.918	0.722	2
3	Norway	0.911	0.752	4
4	Denmark	0.904	0.683	2
5	U.S.	0.901	0.623	6
6	Australia	0.901	0.568	7
7	France	0.898	0.433	5
8	Japan	0.896	0.422	1
9	Canada	0.891	0.655	7
10	Austria	0.882	0.610	3
11	Barbados	0.878	0.545	3
12	New Zealand	0.868	0.637	5
13	U.K.	0.862	0.483	4
14	Italy	0.861	0.545	0
15	Belgium	0.852	0.479	4
16	Switzerland	0.852	0.479	2
17	Netherlands	0.851	0.625	3
18	Portugal	0.832	0.435	2
19	Bahamas	0.828	0.533	3
20	Greece	0.825	0.343	1
21	Ireland	0.813	0.469	5
22	Spain	0.795	0.452	3
23	Luxembourg	0.790	0.542	3
24	Trinidad & Tobago	0.786	0.533	2
25	Venezuela	0.765	0.391	0
26	Costa Rica	0.763	0.474	5
27	Mauritius	0.722	0.350	1
28	Colombia	0.720	0.435	3
29	Jamaica	0.710	—	1
30	Botswana	0.696	0.407	0
31	Papua New Guinea	0.487	0.228	1
32	India	0.401	0.226	4
Unranked	Iceland*	—	—	2
Unranked	Germany*	—	—	2
Unranked	Israel*	—	—	5
Unranked	Nauru*	—	—	0

Source: UN Development Programme 1995.

Note: GDI = Gender Development Index; GEM = Gender Empowerment Measure.

* Data not available.

Empowerment Measure (GEM). The GEM examines whether women and men are able to actively participate in economic and political life and take part in decision-making. The GEM is an index composed of the proportion of seats held by women in parliament, the proportion of administrators and managers that are women, the proportion of professional and technical workers that are women, and women's share of earned income. For the countries in this study, the GEM ranges between 0.22 and 0.75 (see table 2-6).

The very ranking on the GDI is likely to provoke questions. How did Finland come to be ranked second in the world in terms of women's status? Experts on women's status in the Nordic countries suggest that Finland has lagged behind the other four in many important areas (Bergqvist 1999). Japan is also characterized by very regressive attitudes toward women's work and sexuality, and it seems strange to see that country ranked so highly.[9] Nevertheless, the GDI and the GEM are the best cross-national indicators of women's overall status that are currently available. Country scores on the GDI and GEM are taken from the United Nations' *Human Development Report* (UN Development Programme 1995).

Neither of these gender equality indicators explain much of the variation in scope of government response, reducing errors by less than 10 percent (with R-squared equal to .08 or .10) (table 2-3, models 6 and 7). A score of .30 higher on the GEM index (the difference between Finland's score and that of Japan, for example) is associated with a little more than one additional area of government action, plus or minus three-quarters of an area. This is a small effect when one considers that the biggest differences in ranking on both the GEM and the GDI indices are about .500. Even these largest differences would not allow us to predict big changes in government response with confidence. Regression analysis suggests that we can predict with 95 percent confidence that a GDI or GEM score that is .500 higher will be associated with somewhere between one and four additional areas of policy action. Such a wide range of possible association suggests that predicting the scope of government response from rank on gender equality indices could result in big errors, even when the differences on the indicator are stark. Thus, the general position of women vis-à-vis men, as measured by the GDI and GEM, is a poor guide to scope of government response to violence against women.

Policy Styles

Another possible explanation of cross-national variation is differing policy styles. A policy style is a "characteristic approach to problem-solving" and "a characteristic relationship between government and other actors in the policy process" (Richardson 1982, 197). National policy style vary across sectors and types of issues. For example, one theoretical ap proach sees different policy styles as being associated with compensatory distributive, regulatory, redistributive, self-regulatory, and constitutional is sues (Richardson, Gustafson, and Jordon 1982).

Few would deny that relationships between government and other im portant actors affect policy outcomes. The strength of the policy styles ap proach is that it emphasizes the relationship between different types o determinants of policy outcomes. As Hoberg (1998) notes, instead of talk ing about ideas, interests, and institutions, we ought to be talking about th relationships between these three categories. He calls these constellations o factors "policy styles."

The weakness of the policy styles approach is that it is not clear whicl actors and relationships ought to be relevant for a particular policy issue The question is, which aspects of the relationships between which actors de termine policy outcomes regarding violence against women? In the case o violence against women, a policy issue that involves redistributive, compen satory, and regulatory policies, the policy styles framework suggests that i range of actors and policy arenas should be relevant (Richardson Gustafson, and Jordon 1982). But which of these actors is most important Which arena matters the most? And which aspect of the relationship be tween government and other actors is relevant here? Is it the power differ ences between actors? Is it the frequency of interaction? The policy style approach raises more questions than it answers. For that reason, I focus o the specific actors and aspects of relationships that appear to be importan for violence-against-women policy and eschew more general discussion o policy styles.

Bigger Problems Provoke Better Policies

Cultural differences may also affect policy outcomes by determinin rates of violence to begin with. Kingdon (1984) suggests that problems are more likely to make it onto the government agenda when their sheer mag nitude forces action or when a noticeable change in the problem occurs This means that there might be greater government attention to violenc against women where such violence is more of a problem. If this argumen held, we would expect to see higher levels of violence associated with broader, earlier government response and lower levels of violence associatec with a weaker, later response.

While it is difficult to produce any fine measure of the prevalence of vi olence against women, the evidence we do have suggests that it is not re ated to government response in this way. As I have noted, it is not easy to obtain cross-nationally comparable data on levels of violence. However, a 1992 survey allows us to make some comparisons (United Nations, 1996). For example, the rates of sexual assault and victimization in sexual incidents were at least twice as high in Papua New Guinea as in Costa Rica. But the government of Costa Rica has done much to address the problem of violence against women; Papua New Guinea has done almost nothing. The higher rates of violence reported there cannot be attributed to greater awareness of the problem; in Costa Rica, there have been extensive public education campaigns regarding violence against women, while in Papua New Guinea these efforts have been much more limited. Similarly, recent studies suggest that Japan has a very high rate of domestic violence (see appendix A), yet there is virtually no government response to this problem.

Some countries with very high rates of violence also have a very highly developed government response to violence against women. In both Canada and Belgium, for example, about 50 percent of women have been victims of violence against women, and these countries are among the more responsive. In such cases, however, it is more likely that the high rates of violence reported are products of the fact that (1) in these countries, the governments undertook national surveys to assess the level of violence in order to better address the problem, whereas other countries are only now developing the information required for an effective response; and (2) the more aggressive government response has resulted in increased awareness and a better criminal justice response, leading to higher rates of reporting to authorities and survey researchers.

LEVEL OF DEVELOPMENT

In most studies of policy on violence against women, the level of a country's development is implicitly assumed to have an effect, so that we see studies of either developed countries (Elman 1996a) or developing ones Heise, Pitanguy, and Germain 1994). But the one study that compares countries across levels of development (Busch 1992) appears to demonstrate that starkly different levels of development do not preclude strikingly similar policy processes in the area of domestic violence.

In general, one might expect socioeconomic factors to affect government response to violence against women. After all, Call, Nice, and Talarico 1991) find that socioeconomic factors (specifically, racial composition, urbanization, and educational level) explain policy variation across the United States in rape law reform. In 1975, Wilensky argued that "economic growth makes countries with contrasting cultural and political traditions more alike in their strategy for constructing the floor beneath which no one sinks" (27). This "policy convergence" perspective has enjoyed a renaissance in recent comparative scholarship on policy.[10] In this view, economic and social policy is becoming more similar around the world as nations grapple with similar problems. Overbye (1994), for example, argues that "social security arrangements in European as well as Anglo American countries may gradually become more similar" because there are "similar social and political mechanisms at work in different countries, pushing towards convergence in policy outcomes, despite persistent variation in institutional arrangements" (147). Similar arguments have been made in regard to developing countries, where integration into the globalizing economy is said to require particular kinds of policy responses, although for these countries the argument has mostly been applied to economic policy (Sachs 1989; Krugman 1993; Cook and Kirkpatrick 1997).

At first glance, a kind of modernization perspective might seem to explain cross-national variation in the development of violence-against-women policy. In 1974 there was only one country that had undertaken any legal reform in this area; by 1984 fifteen countries had addressed between one and four policy areas; and by 1994 all but four of the thirty-six stable democratic countries had undertaken some kind of policy initiative to address violence against women (see table 2-1). If these countries were indeed crossing some threshold of development or abundance that allowed them to respond to violence against women, this pattern would explain a good deal of the variation in the timing and comprehensiveness of policy action.

However, on closer examination, this explanation has less plausibility. First, as individual countries have "modernized," the trajectory of violence-against-women policy has not been linear. For example, in Canada, the rape shield provision was struck down in 1991 and then replaced a year later. The national governments of both Belgium and Jamaica provided some funding for shelters in the late 1980s, but this has since ceased. The United States had a federal government office to address domestic violence in the early 1980s, but few people even know about that office now (Elman 1996a; Gelb 1998).

Second, level of socioeconomic development does not appear to explain why some national governments are more responsive than others. The national governments of Costa Rica and Israel, for example, address a large number of policy areas (five) but cannot be said to be among the most economically developed of the stable democracies. In addition, some advanced industrialized countries, such as Japan, Italy, and Greece, rank among the least responsive governments (see table 2-7).

In order to test this hypothesis statistically, I employ two different measures of economic development: gross national product (GNP) per capita and the United Nations' (1995c) classification of countries as developed or developing. GNP per capita is the total material wealth of a society, public and private, divided by the population. Since GNP is an average, it is a poor measure of distribution; grossly unequal societies may have the same GNP per capita as those in which wealth is relatively equitably distributed.

GNP per capita is one reasonable measure of the concept of economic development in modernization theories. Aggregate national wealth as mea-

Table 2-7: Scope of Government Policy Response by Level of Development, 1994

Developed Countries		Developing Countries	
Country	No. of Policy Areas Addressed	Country	No. of Policy Areas Addressed
Australia	7	Costa Rica	5
Canada	7	Israel	5
U.S.	6	India	4
France	5	Bahamas	3
Ireland	5	Barbados	3
New Zealand	5	Colombia	3
Belgium	4	Trinidad & Tobago	2
Norway	4	Jamaica	1
Sweden	4	Mauritius	1
U.K.	4	Papua New Guinea	1
Austria	3	Botswana	0
Luxembourg	3	Nauru	0
Netherlands	3	Venezuela	0
Spain	3		
Denmark	2		
Finland	2		
Germany	2		
Iceland	2		
Portugal	2		
Switzerland	2		
Greece	1		
Japan	1		
Italy	0		

Source: Classification of countries as developed or developing is from UN 1995c.

sured by GNP is conventionally used as a key indicator of economi growth. GNP per capita is usually used to distinguish among lesser devel oped countries (LLDCs), less developed countries (LDCs), and advanced in dustrialized countries. Some of the wealthiest countries have declining level of industrialization as they shift from manufacturing to service-base economies. This means that GNP per capita may be a better measure of eco nomic development than proportion of gross domestic product (GDP) de rived from manufacturing (a standard measure of industrialization) o proportion of labor force employed in manufacturing. GNP per capita fo the years 1974 to 1994 is taken from World Development Indicators (for merly World Tables), an electronic database provided by the World Ban (International Bank for Reconstruction and Development 1998).

For 1994, there is a very weak linear relationship between GNP pe capita and scope of government response (table 2-3, model 4). A differenc in GNP per capita of $20,000 is associated with a difference of a little les than one additional policy area. The average GNP per capita among thes stable democratic countries for 1994 is $10,333, and the standard deviatio is $6,726. Since the differences in GNP per capita are too small to be asso ciated with much of a difference, it is unlikely that GNP per capita, or na tional wealth, is a major determinant of variation in policies on violenc against women.

The fact that it takes such big differences to see an effect suggests tha there may be a threshold effect of national wealth that is not being ade quately tested by using GNP as a measure. A threshold effect on policy de velopment would not be linear and therefore might not show up in a multiple regression analysis of GNP. It may be that once countries attain a certain level of national wealth, they are more likely to devote resources t social policy than when resources are scarce.

In order to test for a threshold effect, I categorized the thirty-six stabl democracies as developed or developing for the years 1974–94 according t the UN classification. If there is a threshold effect, we should expect a valu of 1 (developed) to be positively associated with scope of government pol icy on violence against women.

There does appear to be a small but significant association between leve of development and scope of government response. Development is associ ated with one or two additional areas of policy action, and the errors ar not too big in relation to the predicted effects. Note, however, that stron and autonomous women's movements are better predictors (standardize Beta of .46) than level of development (.35). These two factors together ex plain a small proportion (about 32 percent) of the total variance in policie on violence against women (R-squared = .32).

One possible interpretation of the weak, nonlinear relationship between national wealth and scope of government response to violence against women is that greater national wealth can improve institutional effectiveness. Putnam (1993, 86) argues that economic development is clearly associated with high performance of public institutions. Richer countries are more likely to have the resources to design and implement policies, although they may not do so. This suggests that economic development is a weak enabling factor, rather than a fundamental determinant of government responsiveness to violence against women. This hypothesis seems more plausible than the modernization arguments outlined above, especially given the powerful effect of institutional structure on policymaking that I demonstrate later in this study (chapter 5).

Left Parties, Right Parties, and Labor Mobilization

There are some suggestions in the literature that when labor parties are in power, governments appear to be more responsive to women's concerns. For example, Mazur and Stetson (1995) find that the most effective women's policy agencies were created under the initiatives of social democratic governments. Norris (1987, 126) notes that left parties provide more opportunities for women in politics (see also Christensen 1999, 83). A study of abortion policy in the United States found that women state legislators in the Democratic party had a greater effect on policy than women in the legislature in general (Berkman and O'Connor 1993). Perhaps the strength of left or labor parties is associated with greater responsiveness to violence against women?

The categorization of "left" or "labor" parties must be used with care in a comparative study in order to avoid the superficiality that results from taking party labels such as "labor" or "social democratic" at face value. These labels cannot be assumed to have similar meanings across different political systems or even over time in one country. The "new" Labour Party in Britain, for example, has been criticized as having abandoned the traditional agenda of the left. Premier John Buchanan, a Progressive Conservative leader in Nova Scotia, Canada, was a proponent of set-aside seats for women in the national Senate, while this position was rejected by members of the Liberal party. In addition, since the political spectrum is so different across countries, the most left-wing party in one country might be the most right-wing party in another. The Democrats, for example, are often considered the left party in the United States, but by Canadian or Scandinavian standards, the Democratic platform of welfare reform, tax credits, and family values looks like a right-wing, or at best a centrist, agenda.

In addition, there are important political divisions within parties. Nor are all party systems divided along a left-right continuum defined by the participation of organized labor. Where would religious parties fall on the continuum? Where would the Icelandic women's party fall? Where would environmental parties fall, when they put conservation above jobs? Where would the Canadian Bloc Québécois, whose main demand is the independence of Quebec, fall? These ambiguities suggest that "left parties" may not be as meaningful a category for cross-national analysis as it first appears to be.

Still, there must be some way of getting at the seeming impact of left parties cross-nationally. One possible conceptualization of this finding is that political mobilization of labor affects government responsiveness to violence against women. Esping-Andersen (1993) uses the proportion of legislative seats held by labor parties as a measure of labor mobilization. Another possible measure might be membership in trade unions.

Comparable data of sufficient quality on labor mobilization are difficult to obtain for these thirty-six countries, but the data we do have provide little evidence to support this hypothesis (table 2-8). The most responsive countries are those in which labor is less extensively organized: Australia, Canada, and the United States have weaker labor organizations than Norway, Sweden, Germany, Finland, or Austria (see table 2-8). Gelb (1989, 211) argues that in Sweden, unions and political parties "preempted" feminist demands to such a degree through their gender-neutral equality policies that "issues of power sharing and male dominance have largely been left untouched." Elman (1996a, 1995) finds that in Sweden, important advances in government response to violence against women occurred under the conservative party, and that the labor party acted as an obstacle to such action. In Canada, the most significant improvement in national policies to address violence against women came during the Progressive Conservative administration of Prime Minister Brian Mulroney. Among the most responsive governments, important policy recommendations have often been articulated by bipartisan commissions or committees—for example, in Ireland, the United States, and Canada. In addition, periods of reform have often spanned more than one administration, thus involving both left and right parties (see table 2-9). There is no clear relationship between left parties and greater responsiveness to violence against women.

Thus, there appears to be little evidence to support the idea that labor mobilization is associated with greater government responsiveness to violence against women. Indeed, the broader relationship between labor mobilization, political parties, and women's issues is complex. Gelb (1989, 80) notes that although trade unions have sometimes been important allies for

Table 2-8: Labor Mobilization and Scope of Government Policy Response, 1994

Country	Organized Labor as Percentage of Labor Force (1993–94)	No. of Policy Areas Addressed
Finland	80	2
Sweden	80	4
Belgium	70	4
Norway	66	4
Denmark	65	2
Austria	60	3
Iceland	60	2
Ireland	58	5
Luxembourg	55	3
Portugal	55	2
Germany	47	2
Italy	43	0
New Zealand	43	5
Australia	40	7
U.K.	40	4
Mauritius	35	1
Barbados	32	3
Canada	30	7
Japan	29	1
Netherlands	29	3
Bahamas	25	3
Jamaica	24	1
Trinidad & Tobago	22	2
France	20	5
Switzerland	20	2
U.S.	16	6
Costa Rica	15	5
Greece	13	1
Spain	10	3
Colombia	8	3
India	5	4
Botswana	—	0
Israel	—	5
Nauru	—	0
Papua New Guinea	—	1

Source: Figures on organized labor are from U.S. Central Intelligence Agency 1993.

Table 2-9: Political Parties in Power during Main Periods of Policy Innovation, Eight Most Responsive Governments (to 1994)

Country	Years of Main Policy Innovation	Political Parties in Power
Australia	1986–93	Liberal and National Party coalition; Labor
Canada	1981–87; 1990–94	Liberal (center-left); Progressive Conservative (center-right)
U.S.	1993–94	Democratic (center-left) president and Republican (right) Congress
Costa Rica	1986–94	Partido Nacional Liberacion (socialist); Partido Unitad Social Cristiana (conservative)
France	1983–90	Socialist
Ireland	1990–94	Fianna Fáil and Progressive Democrat (right-wing liberal) coalition
Israel	1982–94	Labor-Likud coalition (1986–92); coalition of Labor, Meretz, and Shas (1992–94)
New Zealand	1992–94	National Party (right)

Source: LeDuc, Niemi, and Norris 1996; Nelson and Chowdhury 1994; Stetson and Mazur 1995.

feminist activists, "an aversion to the creation of special interests within unions, as well as the persistence of a 'male culture,' has prevented women from gaining access to substantial internal power in unions." Great progress has been made in incorporating feminist organizing into contemporary unions and left-wing parties, but historically, the debate over whether gender or class was more fundamental obstructed solidarity between feminists and socialists (Brownmiller 1999; Elman 1996a; Gelb 1989; Young 1990a).

Some have suggested that the reverse relationship between political parties and violence-against-women policy would be likely to hold. Policies on violence against women, the argument goes, are mainly symbolic measures that involve little redistribution. For this reason, they present an opportunity for right-wing or neoliberal governments to mollify women's organizations without spending any money. This line of thinking might seem to explain why the Anglo-American governments were so responsive to violence against women. In the 1980s, elections in Canada, the United States, and Britain brought the neoliberal governments of Brian Mulroney, Ronald Reagan, and Margaret Thatcher, respectively, to power (Bashevkin 1998).

The trend towards adoption of neoliberal policies might also seem to explain the increasing government responsiveness to violence across all democratic governments from 1974 to 1994.

But the history of policy development in the most responsive countries fails to support this argument. As noted above, important advances have involved both right- and left-wing governments. In France, for example, the development of policy on violence against women ended abruptly when the Socialists were voted out of government in 1990. The most important piece of national legislation in the United States, the Violence Against Women Act of 1994, was proposed by the Clinton administration. Before 1994, such legislation was strenuously resisted by Presidents Reagan and Bush and by other Republicans. Although we probably want to call Clinton a neoliberal of some variety, it is hardly the case that his election in 1992 represented greater neoliberalism than the Reagan-Bush era.

Government attention to violence against women in Canada, the United States, and Australia preceded neoliberalism. Moreover, some neoliberal administrations of the past (such as that of Reagan in the United States) have refused to act on the issue, viewing it as a political hot potato or a private issue of conscience and therefore not political. More recently, however, the neoliberal governments of these countries began spending hundreds of millions of dollars on programs to address violence against women. In an era of budget cutting, funding for these programs has expanded; in the United States, a Republican Congress authorized almost a billion dollars for violence-against-women programs in 1998 (Erickson 1998). Thus, the rise of neoliberalism does not help explain the expansion of government response to violence against women, either over time or cross-nationally.

More generally, although left political parties have been important conduits for women's presence in government (Norris 1987), political parties of both the right and the left have been poor mechanisms for the articulation of women's issues. Bashevkin (1993) notes that the political mobilization of women has often raised issues not on the agendas of traditional political parties and has often challenged existing party systems. Party discipline has been exerted (with varying degrees of success) to keep women "in line" within both labor and conservative parties (Elman 1996a, chap. 4). A cross-national study of the correlation between attitudes on particular issues and left-right attitudes found that views on abortion were only weakly correlated with left-right orientation (Dalton 1996). This may indicate that neither established parties of the right nor of the left have strongly associated themselves with this or other "women's issues." As Gelb (1989, 53) notes in regard to parties and unions, "existing political structures give little priority to feminists' interests; rather than seeking to solidify feminist strength and advancing women's interests, they have aided in their dissipation and fragmentation."

CONCLUSION

In this chapter I have examined the theoretical and empirical basis for claims that cultural differences, level of development, or the political power of left parties fundamentally determine government responsiveness to violence against women. I argue that explanations relying on broadly defined, national cultural differences are theoretically problematic. Empirically, I find that other proxy measures for "general" cultural differences, such as region and religion, offer little insight into government responsiveness to violence against women. This does not amount to arguing that culture does not matter in explaining policy. Rather, it suggests that more specific hypotheses about the mechanism by which culture affects policy need to be developed, and that such hypotheses are likely to focus on proximate variables, such as institutional structure or electoral processes, rather than on a direct effect of culture itself.

While level of development appears to have some relationship to government responsiveness, it is a weak, nonlinear relationship that is far from determinative of government response. Nor does labor mobilization, in terms of levels of unionization or the prevalence of left or right parties, seem to explain changes in violence-against-women policy. I conclude that the concepts of cultural difference, level of development, and power of left political parties leave unexplained the bulk of the variation in government response. The standard comparative social policy explanations appear to offer very little insight indeed. In the following chapters, I develop an explanation of government responsiveness to violence against women in terms of the interaction between the women's movement and the institutional structure of the state.

3

Social Movements and Policies to Address Violence Against Women

> Defying police degradation
> Tossing aside tradition
> We have come!
> Dalit, battered women, worker, farmer
> In an army together
> We have come!
> To end dowry, rape, misused authority
> To stop wife-beating and cruelty
> We have come!
> To wipe women's suppression
> To remove police oppression
> To free this humanity
> In a rally we have come!
>
> PROTEST MARCH SONG, INDIAN WOMEN'S GROUP

> The government has succeeded in avoiding the political strength
> of a united national women's movement on this Panel [to address
> violence against women]. But fifteen months is a long time and
> we can raise a lot of hell.
>
> LEE LAKEMAN, CANADIAN ASSOCIATION OF
> SEXUAL ASSAULT CENTRES, 1991

■ Social movements, such as the women's movement, the environmental movement, and the civil rights movement, have important, long-term effects on democratic political systems. In addition to provoking or stopping particular government actions, such movements have been credited with changing social values and transforming government institutions (Rochon and Mazmanian 1993; Bystydzienski and Sekhon 1999; Costain and McFarland 1998; Dryzek 1990; Piven and Cloward 1993). Do social movements affect government responsiveness to violence against women? If so, how?

In this chapter, I find that strong, independently organized women's movements improve government responsiveness to violence against women. In fact, women's movements are a necessary condition for the articulation of this issue. It is always women's movement activists and organizations that work to get violence against women recognized as a public problem rather than a private affair and thus put it on the public agenda. Women's movements are most effective in this when they are organized independently of political institutions and parties.

These important effects of women's movements are inadequately accounted for in the policy literature. In fact, the current conceptualizations of women's movements in the policy literature—as interest groups, policy networks, or policy entrepreneurs—actually obscure the most important effects of these movements. I offer an alternative account of how social movements influence policy processes.

WOMEN'S MOVEMENTS AND SOCIAL MOVEMENTS

A women's movement is a form of social movement. A social movement is a form of political mobilization in which membership and action are based on claims of justice: "Social movements have in common individual mobilization through a sense of morality and (in)justice, and social power through social mobilization against deprivation and for survival and identity" (Fuentes and Gunder Frank 1989, 179).[1] Women's movements are social movements aimed at improving the condition of women. They include all forms of voluntary collective action—where this connotes "solidarity in pursuit of common goals" (Molyneux 1998, 70)—that aim to promote the well-being or status of women (Tilly 1978).[2]

Women's *movement* suggests a broad social movement and not the isolated activity of a few people (Molyneux 1998). The existence of a few small-scale organizations is not in itself a movement. However, a large number of small associations (even when they are not consciously coordinated) or a single broadly based association (even when it is rife with conflict) can have a cumulative effect on political life that we would refer to as a movement. We must also be careful about defining a women's movement as encompassing a broad proportion of the population, as this may prejudge the issue of the strength of the women's movement. A weak women's movement may have little effect on the broader population but still be a movement. Thus, an assessment of the potential political mobilization a movement is capable of is relevant to the assessment of the strength of a movement, but not to its existence (Kingdon 1984, 155).

The term *women's movement* may seem to suggest a singular, unified movement. In reality, of course, it always involves a variety of groups, usually with goals that conflict on some level (Bystydzienski and Sekhon 1999). Often, subgroups of women are organizationally separate and isolated from each other. For example, women of color and lesbians have often estabished organizational bases separate from white and/or straight women's organizations, even when pursuing similar goals (Matthews 1993). Thus, women's movements (plural) may be a more accurate way to refer to this phenomenon.

Are all these women's movements *feminist* movements? The meaning of feminism is contested within and across national contexts. One of the central disputes among women's movements in most countries is the meaning of feminism, and in this sense there are many feminisms within most national contexts. Feminism, like democracy, can be conceived of as a continuum, with organizations and institutions being more or less feminist on several (sometimes conflicting) dimensions. Many feminists argue that as an ideal, feminism requires a commitment to combat the interlocking oppressions of sexism, racism, classism, and compulsory heterosexuality. It requires a commitment to egalitarian, participatory decision-making processes (see, for example, Naples 1998; hooks 2000; Mansbridge 1995; and Vargas 1997).

Few, if any, feminist organizations or activists meet this standard in practice, just as few democracies approximate the ideal democracy (Ferree and Martin 1995). Still, we can distinguish between organizations or institutions that are at least minimally feminist and those that are not. At a minimum, feminism requires "an explicit consciousness of gender as a distinct category affecting women's position—in conjunction with other social, economic, and political factors—and action to change gender inequality" (Bystydzienski and Sekhon 1999, 387). This may include activists or organizations that do not consider themselves to be feminists, or who have conflicting understandings of feminism.[3] It would exclude those conservative women's groups who claim that women's status does not require improvement. It would not exclude conservative or traditional women's groups who focus on women's differences or distinctive contributions as mothers or caregivers, as long as these groups aimed to improve women's status or shared similar goals. In this minimal definition of feminism, the women's movements discussed in this book are feminist movements.

WOMEN'S MOVEMENTS AND VIOLENCE AGAINST WOMEN

In every country for which detailed accounts are available, it is women's movements that first articulate the issue of violence against women and press for recognition of it as a public problem, one that requires state action. Although in most places it is recognized that rape and wife beating do occur, it takes women's movements to publicize the extent of these problems and to make the case for public responsibility for protecting women's human rights. As a result, policies on violence against women are always traced to pressure from an organized women's group. For example, in her discussion of government response to domestic violence in India and the United States, Busch (1992, 599) notes:

> Public recognition of domestic violence against women as a social problem in both countries paved the way for further movement demands. Initially, the BWM [battered women's movement] and ADVM [anti-dowry violence movement] attempted to challenge the hegemonic ideology that the family was a private sphere, not subject to state interests or action, and that the state had no interest in the family. These movements also challenged the notion that women's interests were identical with "family interests." In both countries, SMOs [social movement organizations] began to focus on changing police practices as a concrete way to help women survivors and prevent further violence. Both sets of movements were able to get reform enacted that criminalized domestic violence against women.

In a comparative study of violence-against-women policy in Sweden and the United States, Elman (1996a) finds that government response to violence against women depends on the articulation of the issue by a strong, autonomous women's movement. Morken and Selle (1995) observe that the women's shelter movement in Norway "emerged primarily out of the feminist women's movement." They describe the movement as playing "an important role in bringing the abuse of women to the public's attention and subsequently in lending legitimacy to the idea that abuse of women is a serious social problem which requires comprehensive government action" (177; see also Bergman 1999, 114). Gillian Walker (1990) traces the process by which the women's movement first articulated the issue of male violence against women in Canada and how the state responded to this articulation with policy.

In a study of violence prevention in the Andean region, Marin (1997, 88) notes that "women's organizations in all of the Andean countries have struggled for over ten years to get laws passed or revised in order to permit intervention in the home, which is where, under the veil of privacy, the greatest number of crimes occur, and typically go unpunished." Babb (1997) outlines how the Rape Crisis Society in Trinidad and Tobago came to organize around the issue of violence against women and agitate for government action. Writing about the Caribbean region, Clarke (1997, 60) notes that "women's organizations have been in the forefront of action to eliminate violence as well as to provide services to victims of violence against women." She observes that violence against women is generally seen as a problem internal to the family in most countries across the region, and that this makes it difficult for women to get help (53).[4] In India, the antirape movement began in the late 1970s when women's organizations and democratic-rights organizations took up cases of gang rape by the police (Patel 1991). Women's groups in Bombay and Delhi raised the issue of domestic violence around the same time (ibid.).

In virtually every case where I could find out details about the development of government response, women's groups were identified as the catalysts for government action. Not surprisingly, women's groups were always the ones responsible for first articulating the issue. This is clear for all eight of the most responsive national governments: Australia, Canada, the United States, Costa Rica, France, Ireland, Israel, and New Zealand. It is also clear for some moderately responsive states, such as India, Norway, Sweden, and the United Kingdom. In some "laggard" states, such as Italy, Denmark, and Spain, it is clear that the women's movement was responsible for articulation of the issue, although it was less successful in getting the issue on the government agenda.

WOMEN'S MOVEMENTS AND POLICY PROCESSES

There is little disagreement in the studies of policy on violence against women that it is women's movements that are the catalysts for change: their actions and demands set the wheels of government response in motion. The literature suggests that the presence of a women's movement influences variation in policy outcomes on violence against women in some way. Indeed, many studies of women and public policy in general identify women's movements as important influences on policy outcomes (Bergqvist 1999; Bystydzienski and Sekhon 1999; Randall 1987; Freeman 1975; Gelb 1989; Gelb and Palley 1982; Katzenstein and Mueller 1987; Koven and Michel 1993; Stetson and Mazur 1995). Feminist activists are responsible for developing the very concept of violence against women, and it is hard to imagine the issue framed as a public one before the women's movement transformed public discussion of what had previously been seen as a private matter.

Activists as Lobbyists

How exactly are women's movements influencing policy outcomes? The dominant model for thinking about the influence of women's movements on policy conceptualizes women's movements as lobbying groups seeking to influence policymakers. Gelb and Palley (1982) describe feminist groups as successful in influencing policy when they work within the system for incremental change. Their main tools are the provision of information and the mobilization of allied groups. Women's movements are successful when they form policy networks. Women's groups are "like other interest groups" in that they struggle over the framing of issues, over symbolic issues (7–8). Although many other tactics are employed from time to time, lobbying, according to Gelb and Palley, is the main tool of the women's movement. Elman (1996a) argues that feminist groups in the United States are able to present themselves as autonomous experts, as specialized providers of information, and that this explains their policy influence. The lack of such access to the Swedish state on the part of organized groups partially explains why the women's movement was locked out of the policy process in Sweden.[5]

In this model, whether or not the women's movement affects policy depends on the lobbying capacity of women's organizations (the information and expertise they can provide). "Group resources including staff, funding and membership constrain political influence" (Gelb and Palley 1982, 35). In fact, Gelb and Palley argue that the more disruptive, protest-oriented techniques of the women's movement have been ineffective in influencing policy in the United States. Being insiders, or good lobbyists, rather than being autonomous or independent of institutional rules, is what determines policy influence.

Women's Groups as Part of a Social Movement

Other scholars have questioned this model of the women's movement as overly narrow (Costain 1998; Ferree and Martin 1995). Costain (1998, 178) notes that the influence of organized women's groups in the United States depends on the broader context of the women's movement: "The history of organized women applying political pressure is one of periodic success. Congress is most likely to respond favorably during times of mobilized women's movements." Gelb (1989, 1995) argues that independent women's organizing contributes to the vitality of the women's movement.

These viewpoints suggest that women's groups are a special type of organized group, one that is best understood as embedded in a larger social movement. Such groups may use lobbying techniques and "play within the rules," as Gelb and Palley suggest. But the success of these measures depends in large part on other types of activities, such as meetings, protests, publications, and the like, which may not be directly aimed at influencing the government agenda. These activities focus more on articulating a women's agenda or issue.

Jack Walker's study (1991) of interest groups in the United States provides some support for this way of conceptualizing the women's movement. According to Walker, social movement organizations such as women's groups play the role of representing the broader social movement in the nation's capital. These "citizen" groups tend to adopt what Walker calls an "outside" strategy to influence policy. Citizen groups mainly use "outside" strategies based on appeals to the public through the mass media and try to mobilize citizens on a broad scale at the grass roots (9). In contrast, occupation or industry groups that pursue an "inside" strategy rely mainly on their financial resources, substantive expertise, and concentration within certain congressional constituencies as a basis for influence.

Elman (1996a) argues that women's groups in the United States are able to participate in policymaking processes as autonomous experts. But Walker finds that citizen groups in the United States reported that they had little access to policymakers because they were viewed as too political. He observes, "Rather than being consulted as experts, citizen groups were more likely to be consulted as part of an effort to hear all sides of an issue, especially when there is a perceived conflict on the part of policymakers" (1991, 133).

Recent analyses of women's organizations have stressed the importance of examining them as part of the broader movement. Women's organizations are only one aspect of the women's movement (Ferree and Martin 1995), and only one way by which women's movements can affect policy. Social movement organizations depend on the activities of the broader movement for their very creation and subsequent effectiveness. Thus, citizen groups such as women's organizations influence policy outcomes "when public support for the cause they represent swells to such a great extent that policymakers must address their claims or risk losing their political legitimacy" (Walker 1991, 133).

Women's Movements and the Policy Agenda

In order for policy to be enacted, it must appear on the government agenda (Kingdon 1984). The government agenda is "the list of subjects or problems to which governmental officials, and people outside of government closely associated with those officials, are paying some serious attention at any given time" (3). Women's movements are important in getting violence against women on the governmental agenda because they are the first to articulate and draw public attention to the issue. They put it on the public agenda, where it can be taken up and made part of the governmental agenda by government bureaucrats, legislators, and other policymakers. Even in Finland, where the women's movement is relatively weak and where shelters and other programs tend to be run by the state, it is clear that the women's movement was the first to articulate the issue of violence against women (Bergman 1999, 114).

According to Kingdon (1984), social movements, or social movement advocates, work to get certain events interpreted in a specific way or to get particular ideas recognized as problems. They latch onto high-profile events to draw attention to their interpretation of social problems and conditions. Getting an existing condition to be perceived as a public problem, as women's groups did with domestic violence and sexual assault, is important for eliciting a policy response.

In addition, social movements work to change the "national mood" or "civil society" in less issue-oriented ways. For example, a national mood can be broadly antiregulatory, without reference to a particular issue. Civil society involves, in the words of Maria Markus, "the whole network of the voluntary and particular (that is, not all-encompassing) associations and organizations, together with the autonomous instruments of opinion formation, articulation and oppression which are distinct both from the state and from the proper institutions of the economy" (cited in Young 1990a, 82). Social movements affect public discussion and interpretation of events. So, in addition to drawing attention to particular problems, social movements can have more diffuse effects on the way people interpret the world. As Rochon and Mazmanian (1993, 77) note: "By changing social values, movements expand the range of ideas about what is possible. This ultimately has an effect on politics because it changes perceptions of what the most important political problems are. In so doing, movements redefine the political agenda." Both the struggle over the interpretation of specific events and this broader diffusion of a particular perspective throughout society are ways that social movements can influence public policy agendas.

Women's movements employ at least three distinct modes of intervention in civil society. The first mode of affecting public discourse is "everyday politics," that is, the range of everyday activities aimed at changing attitudes, including challenging assumptions in discourse and changing behavior and language (Molyneux 1998; Mansbridge 1995; Katzenstein 1995). In the article "Redefining Politics: Patterns of Women's Political Engagement from a Global Perspective," the authors note, "The richest, most varied, and most typical arena of women's political engagement is found in the politics of everyday life" (Chowdhury, Nelson et al. 1994, 18). Mansbridge (1995) explains how feminist activists develop "street theory," that is, explanations for gender domination in their daily lives. They develop this theory through discussion with one another. In addition, when feminists say "the personal is the political," part of what they mean is that in their daily lives they try to create more just norms for gender relations by adhering to those norms themselves. For example, feminists' efforts to redefine marriage from a model of legal and economic dependency (of women on men) to a shared equal partnership included both their attempts to obtain legal reforms and working to create such relationships for themselves (Stetson 1998). These latter efforts (insisting, for example, on equal responsibility for housework, cooking, and child care) are what I am trying to get at with the notion of "everyday politics." The idea is that such incremental change on an individual level will eventually result in changing norms at an organizational or societal level.

The second way the women's movement affects public discourse is through women's cultural productions, such as books, movies, magazines, theater, and the like. These arenas for discussion are critical to the development of street theory that can make its way into a more general public discussion in workplaces, daily newspapers, and television shows. Finally, the third way the women's movement influences public discourse is through regular social movement organizing and activities, such as forming networks to exchange information and conduct discussions, letter writing, street protests, petitions, lobbying. Note that all three forms of political activity involve what Katzenstein (1995) calls "discursive politics," or the struggle over meaning (cf. Fraser 1989). Most social movements make struggle over the meaning of key political concepts (justice, basic needs, equality) central to their activities, and the women's movement is no exception (Fuentes and Gunder Frank 1989; Fraser 1989).

One way that women's movements intervene in public discussion about violence against women is through their attempts to influence the interpretation of key events. On December 6, 1991, for example, in what has become internationally known as the Montreal Massacre, Marc Lepine burst into an engineering class at the École Polytechnique in Montreal, separated the women from the men, shot fourteen of the women, and then killed himself. He left a note blaming feminists for his inability to gain entrance to an engineering program. Canadian feminists interpreted this event as an act of violence against women, as an example of how violence is used to prevent women from breaking out of their gender roles (by, for example, entering a nontraditional career). As a result, December 6 has been designated as a national day of awareness of violence against women, and people wear ribbons and attend vigils for women victims of male violence on that day each year.

Women's groups also employ the traditional protest politics associated with the social movements of the 1960s to raise awareness about violence against women. In Canada and the United States, activists have used similar methods of creating awareness of violence against women. These include "speak-outs," where women are encouraged to stand up and tell the story of their victimization in a public forum, and "take back the night" marches, where women symbolically march at night to signify that they wish to walk at night free from sexual violence.

Women's cultural productions also raise awareness of violence against women. In India, women activists drew public attention to high-profile cases of rape and abuse. Feminists there have written songs of solidarity and produced skits and plays, street theater festivals, slide shows, and other audiovisual material about violence against women. These materials, which are more effective than "distribution of pamphlets, leaflets or delivering speeches," are judged to have "empowered an increasing number of women to challenge the situation" (Patel 1991, 161). Women's movements in India have also produced booklets, poster exhibitions, journals, and training manuals on violence against women, which "have been used to sensitize the government officials, lawyers and judges, police staff and community workers" (161). Some activists also prepared materials explaining the criminal justice system to women.

Women's movements influence public discussion by advancing moral and political arguments to create public support for their claims and to exert pressure on policymakers. Women's movements also work to diffuse a women's perspective or agenda throughout society. For example, in places where there is a strong women's movement, most people have a sense that there are some issues that are "women's issues," and they can even identify some of them. When women's movements are extremely effective, they can affect the legitimacy of a democratic government by creating a broad groundswell of support for their policy issue that politicians ignore at their peril (Walker 1991).

Thus, although women's groups can achieve an effect on policy through lobbying, the main way that women's movements influence public policy is through the more diffuse strategy of transforming the public agenda by political argument. Awareness and interpretations of events are advanced in cultural productions, protest politics, and everyday politics as well as through formal channels of "professional politics," such as the production of policy briefs. It is through these mechanisms that the women's agenda or perspective, articulated by autonomous women's groups, enters the public policy arena. The diffusion of this perspective raises new issues for public discussion and sometimes changes public priorities. Thus, women's movements affect the public agenda in both direct and indirect ways.

A WOMEN'S AGENDA

I am arguing that in all the nations considered here, the diverse and often divided women's movements collectively infuse a women's agenda or perspective into the policymaking process. But the idea that women share something like an agenda is likely to be controversial. In fact, the central question for feminist theory over the past decade has been how the group "women" can be seen as politically relevant in itself, when class, race, ethnic, and other differences significantly divide women. Even within one national context, the argument goes, women are too different from each other to be characterized as having a common identity or interest.[6]

Women of different classes may, for example, have conflicting interests regarding the regulation of domestic workers: many bourgeois women benefit from the cheap domestic labor of working-class women and women of color who clean their houses and look after their children. In fact, the labor of working-class women or women of color may make possible the participation of bourgeois women in the labor market on a more equal footing with men of their class. This is just one example of a possible conflict of interest between women.

Another is the historical conflict between African American women and white women during the battle for women's suffrage in the United States. Some white women exploited racist arguments that would have excluded black women from the vote in order to support arguments for suffrage for white women (hooks 1981). Sometimes, while interests between different women have not conflicted, they have nevertheless not provided an adequate basis for political solidarity. For example, black women and white women in the United States have had serious struggles over how to define reproductive freedom. White women were denied access to birth control and abortion while African American, Hispanic, and Native American women were forcibly sterilized, giving them very different perspectives on what "choice" required (Davis 1990, 15–26). These and other examples of differences or conflicts of interests between women make it very difficult to assert a single "women's interest."

The assertion of a common identity is perhaps even more questionable. As we all know, many women deny that their identity as women is the most important, or even an important, aspect of their identity. Women of different races and sexual orientations may have dramatically different experiences and identities, even when it comes to issues as seemingly fundamental as motherhood.[7] As Fraser (1992) points out, this lack of a common identity applies not only to women but to all social groups. Social identities are too complex, shifting over time and across groups and subgroups, to say of any group that its members share an identity.

Growing awareness of the differences between women lends credibility to the postmodern critique that talking about women as a political group essentializes the group "women"—that is, attributes a fundamental essence or nature to the group that is not, in actuality, there (Spelman 1988; Butler 1990). Lugones (1994), for example, has argued that the idea of political representation for oppressed groups such as women involves a "logic of purity" that does violence to the complexity of social groups.[8]

Women as a Social Group

I find these arguments about the lack of a shared interest or identity convincing. Yet, at least sometimes, women appear to act on the basis of nothing more than solidarity with other women, and this can have important political effects. At the 1995 United Nations' Fourth World Conference on Women in Beijing, for example, women's groups from all over the world were able to establish a set of issues for discussion that they agreed constituted women's issues. What is the basis for the political solidarity so often observed among very different women?

Young (1996) has suggested one way of solving this problem. She argues that women are not a group with a shared experience or identity, but rather are a group defined by social norms and institutions—what she calls a structural social group. Each structural social group has a unique perspective on political life (Young 2000). It is this perspective that I am saying produces a women's agenda.

The concepts of perspective and agenda recognize both the divisions among women and the relationship among the issues they share. But before I explain exactly how, let me first explain the idea of a structural social group. Structural social groups are defined by their relations to other groups, not by an essential identity or characteristic. Thus, they are defined by objective relations, rather than by subjective identities or experiences. In a caste system, for example, some classes are privileged in relation to others: the existence of a privileged class depends on there being a disadvantaged class (Young 2000). Social norms and institutions create relations of advantage and disadvantage among groups. For example, social norms privileging heterosexual relationships result in social privileges (heterosexual relationships are more widely supported), economic privileges (such as spousal benefits through employment), and even legal privileges for heterosexual couples.

Similarly, social norms disadvantage women as a group. By custom, women assume primary responsibility for child and elder care, housework, and other unpaid activities. Since most workplaces assume that workers have few such responsibilities, women workers are disadvantaged compared to men, who often have someone else taking care of these family matters. In addition, women's association with the private sphere still disadvantages them in politics: even in the United States, where there has been a strong women's movement, many people still think that women ought not to be involved in public life. These are just two examples of social practices or norms that disadvantage women in relation to men.

Women are defined as such by society, marked out as women by others, even when they themselves feel that their identity or interest as women is not important. When asked whether she was running "as a woman," Pat Schroeder, a representative in the U.S. Congress, replied, "Do I have a choice?" Women still have little choice about whether their gender becomes salient for others. In April 1999, a headline in the *New York Times* read "Woman Sets Out to Lead Kohl's Party out of Its Crisis" (Cohen 1999). The headline did not specify the name or other features of the new party leader, but merely that she was a woman. The category "woman" is made salient by social conditions in a way that "red-headed" is not.

The notion that social structures shape women's lives does not mean that they affect all women in the same way. For example, in societies where race and class structure social relations, relations between women and men are expressed in class-specific and racially specific terms. Black feminists in the United States, for example, have argued that African American women have been marked out as black women, vis-à-vis black men and white women (hooks 1981; Collins 1994). But recognizing the important differences in women's experiences should not obscure the fact that these different conditions are related, often even structurally interdependent.

For example, white women in the United States have traditionally agitated for access to abortion, while African American women protested forced sterilization. These are different issues, but they both relate to women's control of their reproductive capacities, or reproductive freedom. This is not just a coincidence: women's reproductive capacities have been placed in the service of maintaining race relations. Racist concerns about growing numbers of people of color resulted in forced sterilization of women of color. Similarly, concern for the "survival of the race" resulted in restrictions on access to abortion for white middle-class women. Indeed, many of the privileges associated with maternalism were motivated by concerns for the continuation of the race (Koven and Michel 1993). These same concerns resulted in practices discouraging poor women and women of color from having children. Thus, the valuation of motherhood for white women (to the exclusion of other important aspects of life) was structurally related to the devaluation of motherhood for women of color.

Similarly, in the conflict between bourgeois and working-class women over rates of pay for child care, women on both sides are struggling to deal with the obligation for the primary care of children and with the lack of remuneration or recognition for this work. In both cases, it is women who are divided over what to do about child care because it is women who have responsibility for children. What bourgeois and working-class women have in common, in this example, is that they must both figure out the value of child care, while their male partners do not have this conflict. Thus, the value of caring for dependents and the unequal distribution of this burden between men and women is an issue that confronts both groups of women, although they have conflicting interests.

When people interact with other members of their social group to discuss the status of their group, they can identify the norms and practices that set them apart from others, that advantage and disadvantage them in their everyday lives. The set of issues identified by the group constitutes its social perspective: what does the world look like from the perspective of members of that group? What issues are salient for them? A social perspective is more like an agenda than a position, more like a list of problem areas than a list of possible solutions or policy options (Young 1996, 2000).

If we organize the set of issues and complaints articulated by women's organizations, we notice some common themes across very different groups of women; these constitute issues that affect all women, albeit in different ways. If we take the total list of issues raised by women's activism, we have a picture of social structures that create the group called "women." The greater the diversity of women involved, the more information we have about the social structures that create the series. In the United States, Latina women, African American women, Jewish women, lesbian women, business and professional women, union women, poor women, homemakers, mothers, and countless others have created their own organizations. The organization of these subgroups of women has facilitated the articulation of their perspective as women. As a result, we have a better understanding of how the social practices and institutions that constitute race, class, and sexual orientation structure womanhood for all women.

In Beijing, this diversity was multiplied greatly by the inclusion of women from all over the world. The result was a list of issues of concern to women everywhere: poverty, violence, racism, ethnic differences, religion and custom, health, education, and so on. These issues, of course, matter in different ways and degrees for women in different subgroups and countries. Nevertheless, the issues identified name major categories of social practices and norms that affect all women's lives. We learn a lot about gender as a social practice by examining the different ways and degrees to which social practices privilege men over women, the masculine over the feminine, for women of different classes and countries. For example, social practices limit women's choices about and control over their own sexuality and reproductive capacities, although such limits are most severe for women of color and poor women. Women's work, both paid and unpaid, is devalued across class, race, sexual orientation, and national contexts.

The notion of a shared agenda, then, acknowledges that women may be divided among themselves by the conditions they face. Although groups of women probably never share anything as specific as a policy position, or a specific interest, they do share a set of issues that structure their lives as women. The identification of the set of issues is accomplished by women's group discussions of their experiences in confronting the social institutions that inhibit them. The cumulative product of these discussions constitutes a women's agenda. This alternate picture of the world, or perspective, is what women's movements communicate to the mass public and to policymakers.

Women's Movements as Powerless to Affect Policy Outcomes

A competing literature sees policy outcomes as relatively isolated from women's movements or their characteristics and primarily determined by socioeconomic structures, such as capitalism and/or patriarchy.[9] This position may find support in a recent study of the U.S. states. Murphy (1997) examines state-by-state variation in policy on police reforms with respect to domestic violence. She finds that the strength of the women's movement (which she operationalizes as the number of women belonging to the National Organization for Women in each state) has no impact on policy outcomes.[10]

Although such studies are not concerned with national policies, they nevertheless may have implications for how we interpret the findings in studies of national policy. It could be that women's movement mobilization really does not matter to this policy area, as Murphy's state-level study suggests, and that further analysis will reveal that the finding of the importance of women's movements is the product of generalizing from knowledge of a few cases. On the other hand, we may not see the importance of the women's

movement in the state-level studies because mobilization does not vary sufficiently across states to produce an important effect. In particular, these
studies could miss the fact that the mobilization of the women's movement
is actually a necessary condition for state action because it is relatively constant across states within the United States (that is, relative to variation in
the women's movement across countries). If this is the case, it should come
out in a cross-national study, where there is a greater degree of variation in
the mobilization of women across units of observation.

CROSS-NATIONAL PATTERNS OF INFLUENCE OF
WOMEN'S MOVEMENTS

The existence of women's movements can be studied cross-nationally
based on a coding of historical and other narrative accounts of the women's
movement in each country. Where accounts distinguish between the
women's movement and the feminist movement, or second-wave feminism,
starting in the last half of the twentieth century, the latter is coded as the beginning of the feminist movement. In most cases, a number of historical accounts were used to date the beginning of the women's liberation movement
and to assess its strength comparatively. There are few disputes among
country experts about whether there is a women's movement and when it
began, making coding relatively easy. Sources of data by country are listed
in appendix C. A country that does not have a women's movement is coded
0, while those that do receive a 1. The vast majority of nations in this study
had active women's movements by 1994 (see table 3-1).

If women's movements had a big, direct impact on the scope of policies
on violence against women, we would expect the presence of a women's
movement to be strongly associated with increased government action. Recall that government response is coded from 0 to 7, depending on the number of policy areas that are addressed. For each one-unit increase in the
independent variable—that is, for each women's movement starting up—we
would expect to see a number of new areas of policy action, so we would
expect the presence of a women's movement (an increase of one unit) to be
associated with action in several additional areas of policy.

In fact, the existence of a women's movement is only weakly associated
with scope of government response, explaining only 6 percent of the variance in policies on violence against women (see table 3-2). This variable was
a poor predictor of scope of government response, because the standard errors are almost as big as the effect itself. The presence of a women's movement could be associated with anywhere between one and five additional

Table 3-1: Characteristics of Women's Movements in Stable Democratic Countries and Scope of Government Policy Response to Violence Against Women

Country	Movement?	Year Movement Began	Strong?	Autonomous?	No. of Policy Areas Addressed, 1994
Sweden	Yes	1975	No	No	4
Norway	Yes	1968	Yes	Yes	4
Finland	Yes	1965	Yes	No	2
Denmark	Yes	1970	Yes (until 1983)	Yes (until 1983)	2
Netherlands	Yes	1967	Yes	Yes	3
Germany	Yes	1968	No	Yes	2
Iceland	Yes	1968	Yes	?	2
Austria	Yes	1972	No	No	3
New Zealand	Yes	1969	Yes	Yes	5
Luxembourg	Yes	1975	No	No	3
Trinidad & Tobago	Yes	1978	Yes (since 1989)	Yes (since 1989)	2
Canada	Yes	1966	Yes	Yes	7
Switzerland	Yes	1975	No	No	2
Spain	Yes	1975	No	Yes	3
Italy	Yes	1970	Yes	No (until 1990s)	0
Costa Rica	Yes	1973	Yes	Yes	5
Ireland	Yes	1973	Yes	Yes	5
Belgium	Yes	1972	Yes	Yes	4
U.S.	Yes	1966	Yes	Yes	6
Jamaica	Yes	1977	Yes (in 1994)	Yes (since 1992)	1
Colombia	Yes	1973	Yes (since 1985)	Yes (since 1979)	3
Barbados	Yes	1974	Yes (since 1990)	Yes (since 1981)	3
Botswana	Yes	1984	No	No	0
Australia	Yes	1969	Yes	Yes	7
U.K.	Yes	1968	Yes	Yes	4
Israel	Yes	1973	Yes	Yes	5
Portugal	Yes	1975	No	No	2
Bahamas	Yes	1974	No	Yes (since 1983)	3
India	Yes	1970	Yes	Yes	4
France	Yes	1968	Yes (until 1985)	Yes	5
Venezuela	Yes	1974	No	No	0
Greece	Yes	1975	No	No	1
Mauritius	Yes	1978	No	No	1
Japan	Yes	1975	No	Yes	1
Papua New Guinea	Yes	1972	No	No	1
Nauru	No	—	—	—	0

areas of government action. This wide range suggests that the mere existence of a women's movement is not sufficient to influence policy outcomes.

However, it is possible that women's movements are necessary but not sufficient for government response. If so, the impact of the women's movement would be observed only when additional conditions obtained—conditions that, together with the presence of the women's movement itself, would create sufficiency. Such a relationship could be tested by examining the interactions of the women's movement with other conditions, or by observing additional features of the women's movement that resulted in an effect on policy.

Thus, despite the lack of a linear association between women's movements and scope of government response to violence against women, extensive case evidence suggests that women's movements are indeed necessary but not sufficient for the development of a government response: in all stable democracies over the period 1974 to 1994, there was not one single government initiative adopted in the absence of a women's movement.

This evidence is important, but it leaves many questions unanswered. Almost all of the countries in this study now have women's movements of some kind, but there is great variation in policy outcomes. This is not surprising, since even those scholars who give women's movements a central explanatory role see the impact of movements on policy as being mediated

Table 3-2: Coefficients, Dependent Variable = Scope of Government Response, 36 Countries, 1994

Model/ Independent Variables	B	Std. Error	Beta	t	Sig.	R-squared
1/ Does a women's movement exist?	2.97	1.99	0.25	1.49	0.14	0.06
2/ Does a women's movement exist?	2.17	1.98	0.18	1.10	0.28	0.15
Level of development	1.22	0.68	0.30	1.81	0.08	
3/ Level of development	1.44	0.59	0.35	2.45	0.02	0.32
Strong, autonomous women's movement	1.81	0.57	0.46	3.19	0.00	
4/ Strong, autonomous women's movement	1.76	0.64	0.45	2.73	0.01	0.27
GNP per capita	0.00	0.00	0.23	1.19	0.24	
Log10 of number of reps	0.29	0.35	0.16	0.84	0.41	

by the characteristics of women's movements, political parties, institutional structure, political culture, and the like (Elman 1996a; Stetson and Mazur 1995; Randall 1987; Gelb 1989; Katzenstein and Mueller 1987; Koven and Michel 1993). I turn now to investigate some of these possibilities.

AUTONOMY AND THE ARTICULATION OF A WOMEN'S PERSPECTIVE

Many scholars identify the autonomy of women's groups as important for their success in influencing policy (Elman 1996a; Busch 1992). An autonomous women's movement is a form of women's mobilization that is devoted to promoting women's status and well-being independently of political parties and other associations that do not have the status of women as their main concern.[11] For example, if the only women's organizations are women's wings or caucuses within existing political parties, the women's movement is not autonomous. "Autonomous organizations . . . are characterized by *independent* actions, where women organize on the basis of self-activity, set their own goals, and decide their own forms of organization and struggle" (Molyneux 1998). These organizations must be self-governing and must recognize no superior authority, nor be subject to the governance of other political agencies. Bashevkin (1994, 144) notes, for example, that major Canadian women's organizations have attempted "to remain formally independent of the parties, believing that independence could guarantee autonomy, control and a degree of distance from established party organizations."

The cross-national evidence suggests that the autonomy of the women's movement is important. It is difficult for women's movements to get violence against women on the government agenda when they are organized *only* inside political parties. For example, for two decades, the Italian women's movement, organized mainly within political parties, was unsuccessful at persuading the parties to accept recommendations for legal reform on the issue of sexual assault. However, in the 1990s, the movement decided to adopt the strategy of organizing outside the state, collecting signatures on petitions and so on. As a result, legislation on violence was finally passed in 1996.

It also appears that it is difficult for women to simultaneously maintain strong intraparty organizations and autonomous organizations. In Denmark in the 1960s, a strong, autonomous women's movement began outside the state in small consciousness-raising groups and other decentralized structures. With the creation of women's branches inside the political parties, the women's organizations outside the state, which had been responsible for the beginning and growth of the feminist movement, all but disappeared. But the intraparty organizations were not as successful as the autonomous ones had been in drawing attention to women's concerns. By the early 1970s, the political parties had decided to close their women's branches in the name of gender equality (Christensen 1999; Borchorst 1995). With this dissolution, women's organizing outside the state was revitalized, and flourished throughout the remainder of the 1970s and into the early 1980s (Kaplan 1992, 79).

Women's movements can be coded as *autonomous* if they have an organizational base outside political parties, unions, and other political institutions. They must also be independent of organizations that do not make the condition of women their primary concern. Autonomous women's organizations are not subsidiaries, auxiliaries, or wings of larger, mixed-sex organizations. Data on organizations were taken from narrative accounts (see appendix C) and encyclopedias of women's organizations (for example, Barrett 1993).

Women's movements also vary in terms of how strong or influential they are. Movements might be autonomous or independent but have little impact on the attitudes or awareness of those outside the active group or groups. Strong women's movements can command public support and attention, while weaker ones have trouble convincing the media and others that their positions and opinions are important for public discussion. Given what we know about democratic policymaking, it seems likely that strong women's movements will influence policy outcomes more than weak ones. But note that strong movements do not always influence policy outcomes. McAdam (1999) notes that although the women's movement in the United States is generally agreed to be strong, it has not had much success in changing policy outcomes.[12]

Movements can be coded as strong if they are described in narrative accounts as strong, influential, powerful, mobilizing widespread public support, or the like. Narrative accounts of women's movements often explicitly assess their strength over time and/or relative to women's movements in other countries.[13] Strength can also be assessed through an examination of the number of women's organizations, the number of members they have, and the degree of support for them. The existence of a large number of organizations or a few well-supported and highly visible ones usually indicates a strong women's movement. The numerical data on organizations generally supported the assessments of strength in the narrative accounts. Where the women's movement is both strong and autonomous according to these criteria, the country is coded 1; where either strength or autonomy is absent, the country is coded 0. For a summary of codings, see table 3-1. All eight of the most progressive countries (scores of 5 to 7) have strong, autonomous women's movements, or at least did at the time of policy development.

With this coding, multivariate regression analysis can be used to test whether the presence of a strong and autonomous women's movement appears to be associated with more government action on violence against women (table 3-2). Again, government response is coded from 0 to 7, depending on the number of areas of policy action that a national government undertakes. If strong and autonomous women's movements produced better policy outcomes, we would expect a one-unit increase—that is, the presence of such a movement—to be associated with some marked change in government response, such as addressing a number of additional areas.

In the multivariate analysis, the presence of a strong and autonomous women's movement is indeed associated with one or two additional areas of government action, and this association is statistically significant (that is, it is unlikely to be due to chance). Moreover, a strong and autonomous women's movement appears to be more important (with a standardized Beta of .45) than GNP or the number of women representatives in the lower house (with standardized Betas of .23 and .16 respectively).

Why is autonomous organization so important to the impact of the women's movement on violence-against-women policy? The literature appears to identify two main reasons that autonomy from the state is important for women's movements: avoiding bureaucratic forms of organization and avoiding contact with male-dominated organizations. However, as I show below, these explanations do not adequately account for the effect of women's movement autonomy.

The Women's Movement and the Bureaucratic State

Some studies of government responsiveness to violence against women emphasize that the bureaucratic nature of states prevents an effective response (Walker 1990; Busch 1992). Indeed, some early feminist theorists of bureaucracy argued that bureaucratic forms in themselves suppress feminist activities (Ferguson 1984). Perhaps autonomous movements are more successful in influencing policies because they are better able to maintain their focus on feminist issues.

The bureaucratic nature of the state, however, does not seem to account for the importance of the autonomy of women's movements in explaining policy responsiveness to violence. In Britain, the women's movement was

more autonomous and committed to avoiding cooperation with bureaucracy than was the U.S. women's movement, but the latter has been much
more successful in influencing government policy (Gelb 1989, table 1).

In addition, it is no longer possible to maintain a strict distinction be-
tween bureaucracies on one hand and feminist organizations on the other.
This distinction has been undermined by the development of what seem to
many observers to be feminist bureaucracies, such as the National Action
Committee (NAC) in Canada or the National Organization of Women
(NOW) or the National Coalition Against Domestic Violence in the United
States (Gelb 1995). As Molyneux (1998, 70) notes, "the varied history of
women's activism reveals a considerable diversity of institutional arrangements, within which . . . genuinely non-hierarchical organizations have been
the exception rather than the rule." Moreover, as Katzenstein (1998) observes, there is a long tradition of feminist protest within male-dominated,
hierarchical organizations such as the Catholic Church and the U. S. Army.
Feminist activists and many other bureaucratic reformers have experi-
mented with a variety of organizational forms, attempting to lessen degrees
of hierarchy, improve communication, and the like (Gelb 1995; Ferree and
Martin 1995). Thus, current scholarship has begun to ask which bureaucratic forms most effectively promote feminist values and which do not
(Stetson and Mazur 1995; Staudt 1998; Duerst-Lahti and Kelly 1995).

Thus, it is not the bureaucratic nature of the state that necessitates the
autonomy of women's organizations. The women's organizations that press
for government action on violence are frequently themselves bureaucracies.
If independent organization is indeed important in order for women's
movements to succeed in putting violence against women on the public
agenda, it must be for some other reason.

The Women's Movement and the Male-Dominated State
Another possible reason for arguing that the autonomy of women's organizations is important is that mainstream state organizations are dominated by men. Elman (1996a, 24) argues that autonomy from male-
dominated organizations was an important ingredient of the relative success
of the U.S. women's movement in influencing policy.[14] Within federal systems, Elman observes, policies are the result of bargaining among specialized but autonomous interest groups; women's organizations in the United
States are able to participate in the policy process without being co-opted by
the state. In Sweden, in contrast, women's organizing was limited to caucuses within the male-dominated political parties and unions. In male-dominated organizations, it is difficult for women to articulate and defend their

interests. Indeed, Cockburn (1991) documents male resistance to the implementation of equality policies inside organizations.

Perhaps surprisingly, however, the disproportionate number of men in state institutions does not appear to account for the importance of women's movement autonomy. The extant research shows that the ratio of men to women in an organizational setting influences the likelihood that women will voice a dissenting position.[15] Currently, the proportion of women in Scandinavian political parties exceeds the level at which women supposedly voice their distinctive concerns. But the large proportion of women in Scandinavian political parties has not translated into greater responsiveness to violence against women in those countries. In fact, the Scandinavian states may be less responsive than some states where there are very small numbers of women in the legislature, such as the United States, France, and Australia. If autonomy is important because state institutions are dominated by men, then autonomy should be less important where women are more numerous inside state institutions. But, as Elman shows, the lack of autonomy on the part of the Swedish women's movement prevents the effective articulation of the issue of violence against women as a public issue, despite the large number of women in the legislature.

Cross-National Evidence on Women's Movement Autonomy

What, then, can explain the apparent importance of the autonomy of women's movements? As noted, the important women's organizations that press for government action are themselves bureaucracies, so it cannot be that autonomy from the state is important because the state is a bureaucracy. Nor is it satisfactory to say that autonomy is important because men dominate the institutions of the state.

This finding seems to hold for both federal and corporatist states. At a national level, the United States was one of the last countries to implement many reforms relating to violence against women, despite having one of the strongest, most autonomous, and earliest-organized women's movements.[16] The Canadian and Australian governments had both addressed six or seven areas by 1990; France, five; and Costa Rica, India, Israel, and Norway, four. All of these governments were quicker to respond to the demands of the women's movement than the government of the United States. When the latter did finally respond, with the 1994 Violence Against Women Act, many areas were addressed at once, but this reform was late in coming. The women's movement of the United States has been organized nationally and pressing for national reforms in this area since the early 1970s, but in countries such as Costa Rica, women's movement organizing began later and received concessions much more quickly. This suggests that strong, autonomous women's movements need more than a federal structure to access the institutions of the state.

To sum up, the evidence reviewed thus far suggests that women's movements are necessary but not sufficient to provoke a government response to violence against women, and that the autonomy of the women's movement likely influences the comprehensiveness of government policies. But existing accounts of why autonomy matters seem unsatisfactory as explanations for this finding. Below, I develop an alternative account of why autonomy of the women's movement matters for violence-against-women policy.

Why Women's Movement Autonomy Matters

The autonomy of women's groups from established political institutions such as political parties is necessary for the articulation of the issue of violence against women and for placing it on the public agenda. The strength and autonomy of the women's movement is key to the development of government policy to address violence against women for two reasons. First, women must be independently organized *as women* in order to articulate women's perspective. It is not just the proportions of women and men in an organization or group that matter. Recall that social perspectives or agendas are developed through interaction among the members of a social group or subgroup. Thus, no individual member on her own has special access to knowledge about the group. Social perspectives are not immediately obvious to individual members of the group. Only where women have formed groups in which they mutually identify as women can they articulate their perspective interactively. Individual women, for example, do not necessarily know which issues are important to them as women and which are important to them as, say, students at a public university until they talk to other women about it.

In order for women to develop their distinct perspective, they must have the room to focus on their priorities as women. When women's groups are subgroups of a broader chapter, such as a trade union or political party, their own priorities are always implicitly second to those of the organization as a whole. This is why, as Molyneux (1998, 70) notes, "From the earliest moments of women's political mobilization, women activists in political parties, trade unions, and social movements have argued that they needed a place within which to elaborate their own programmes of action, debate their own goals, tactics and strategy free from outside influence." Thus, the presence of men, and the male-dominated nature of the political process does not account for the difficulty of articulating and pursuing feminist goals within political parties and other established institutions. Whether the organizational structure facilitates women's organization *as women* is also important.

The second reason independent organization is important relates to the effective translation of the women's agenda into the organizational agenda. Agencies that are not mainly focused on women's concerns are more likely to adopt as priorities only those "women's issues" that fit easily into the existing organizational agenda. Women's issues that are more difficult to absorb into existing priorities will tend to be passed over. This makes it difficult to get certain issues, such as violence against women, adopted as part of overall organizational agendas. Thus, women's wings or suborganizations will have a harder time using organizational resources to articulate a women's agenda than independent women's organizations, which can directly translate women's priorities into organizational priorities.

When women's organizations are independent, they can devote their resources to drawing public attention to women's issues. When they are only subsidiaries or wings of larger organizations, it can be difficult for them to make the case that considerable amounts of organizational resources should be spent on a women's issue. Violence against women is an issue that is of concern mainly to women. Political parties, trade unions, and other political organizations may have more difficulty adopting such an issue as a priority than they would other women's issues that can be adopted under a universal category, such as old-age pensions, minimum wage, or family and medical leave.

Some autonomous women's movements articulate the issue of violence against women but remain weak and ineffective. Women's organizations or activists must be sufficiently influential to convey these priorities to the rest of the public. Thus, the strength of the women's movement is also important.

A corollary to the argument about the necessity of autonomy is that autonomous organizations for women of color should improve their ability to voice their concerns within the organized women's movement and within civil society more generally. As we shall see in chapter 6, an examination of policy development in Canada and Australia appears to bear out this hypothesis.

CONCLUSION

The women's movement affects the policy process mainly through what has been called discursive politics. These effects are not well captured by conceptualizations of social movements that focus on lobbying and insider bargaining tactics. I return to this theme later in the book, arguing that a structural understanding of social movements offers a better conceptualization of their policy impact (see chapter 7).

Autonomy, I contend, makes social movements much more effective in changing policy. In fact, a strong, autonomous women's movement is *necessary* for the initial articulation of the issue of violence against women as a public issue, because (1) women must be independently organized in order to articulate women's issues; and (2) a strong, independent organization is better able to use organizational resources to draw public attention to women's issues.

Women's movements, then, are critical for identifying the issue of violence against women. Yet recognition of an issue is only necessary, and not sufficient for, an impact on policy. Strong, autonomous women's movements and level of development together explain only 32 percent of the variance in scope of government response to violence against women. Under what conditions are these articulations translated into policy influence? I take up this question in the following chapters.

The Effect of Women in Government on Policies on Violence Against Women

In policymaking structures, the absence of women is obviously significant; the presence of women, however, does not necessarily imply change. Institutions and processes are much more than 'conglomerations of individual biological men' and much more has to change than the bodies in control.

CATHERINE HOSKYNS, 1996

■As social movements, women's movements are the first to identify the issue of violence against women and put it on the public agenda. But issues on the public agenda do not always make it onto the government agenda (Kingdon 1984). Sometimes governments ignore these public articulations, or take them up halfheartedly. What determines whether these public articulations are translated into policy action?

Many recent studies of the impact of women legislators on public policy conclude that the existence of a greater proportion of women in elected office makes governments more responsive to women's concerns. Although much of this research focuses on the United States, (for example, Thomas 1994; Murphy 1997) similar findings have been generated for Canada (for example, Gigendil 1996; Gigendil and Vengroff 1997; and Tremblay 1998) and some European countries, such as Sweden, Norway, and the United Kingdom (Bystydzienski 1992a; Gelb 1989; Lovenduski and Norris 1993; Matland 1993). There have been fewer systematic studies on women legislators in the developing world, but there is some research suggesting that women legislators in those countries have been important in developing policies on violence against women and other women's issues (Gonzalez-Suarez 1994; Valenzuela 1998). Kingdon (1984) argues that government officials are the most important influences on government agendas. Are governments that include more women more likely to respond to violence against women? Perhaps the presence of women in government is the missing piece of the puzzle.

Before examining this question empirically, I first discuss some common conceptual weaknesses in studies of how women policymakers affect policy outcomes. First, many studies look at the impact of women in public policy by investigating whether individual female legislators are different from male legislators. This assumes that one can infer an impact on policy merely by adding up the preferences of individual legislators. But the preferences of legislators may combine in nonadditive ways to produce policy, so deducing an impact on policy from differences in the behavior of individual legislators constitutes a fallacy of aggregation. Second, a focus on sheer proportion or number of legislators ignores the importance of the institutional structure in which they are embedded (Davis 1997; Duerst-Lahti and Kelly 1995; Kathlene 1995; Tamerius 1995). Some positions to which women may be elected or appointed are likely to be more influential than others and thus to have a greater impact on policy. Third, most studies of the impact of gender on policymaking implicitly or explicitly assume that simply because they are women, individual women share a feminist analysis of public policy problems and wish to promote feminist goals (Lugones 1994; Varikas 1995). Fourth, there is little analysis of the impact of the women's movement in these studies of gender differences (Dobrowolsky 1998),[1] and there is no attention to a possible interactive relationship between women in government and the presence of a women's movement. Thus, a better conceptualization of the impact of women legislators on public policy, and of gender on policymaking more generally, is needed.

This cross-national study of the impact of women legislators on policies to address violence against women finds no relationship between proportion of women in the legislature and policy outcomes on violence against women. I find only a very weak, nonlinear relationship between number of women and more responsive policy outcomes. This does not imply that individual women or groups of women are unimportant as political actors in the development of violence-against-women policy; indeed, the case evidence I review in this chapter suggests the opposite. However, it is unlikely that women's impact can be understood in terms of the number or percentage of women in the legislature, or without reference to the institutional and organizational context in which these women find themselves.

WOMEN IN GOVERNMENT AND POLICIES

THEORETICAL WEAKNESSES IN THE CURRENT LITERATURE

There is now an extensive literature examining the consequences and determinants of better representation for women and minorities in bureaucracies and legislatures, especially in the United States (Darcy, Welch, and Clark 1987; Darden 1984; Grofman, Handley, and Niemi 1992; Hill 1981; Jones 1996; Matland 1993; Matland and Studlar 1996; Meier, Wrinkle, and Polinard 1999; Nixon and Darcy 1996; Rule and Zimmerman 1994; Sapiro 1981; Shugart 1994; Singh 1998; Welch 1990; Welch and Studlar 1990; Zimmerman 1994). Issues of representation for women are also becoming increasingly important in European and Latin American scholarship. In part, this increased interest reflects current policy debates in these regions: in France, the "movement for parity" has pressed for laws guaranteeing equal representation for women (Le Doeuff 1995; Varikas 1995), while in Latin America, the large number of countries adopting gender quotas has stimulated discussion of women and representation (Archenti and Gómez 2000; Jones 1996; Schmitter 1998).

This literature has produced many fascinating findings about the different backgrounds, roles, and performance of men and women as policymakers (Davis 1997). In this chapter, I focus specifically on arguments that women policymakers make *governments* more responsive *in terms of policy outputs* in the area of violence against women. A close examination of the research reveals that the link between women's preferences as a group, women policymakers, and actual policy outputs is not well conceptualized or established.

The Fallacy of Aggregation

In a study of U.S. states, Murphy (1997) argues that women in government focus on different issues than do their male colleagues and that we ought to expect them to be more responsive to concerns about police reform on domestic violence because this is a women's rights issue. In explaining why the election of more women to state legislatures would lead to more reform in this area, Murphy relies mainly on the many studies charting the differences in behavior of individual women and men in government. Plenty of research finds differences between women and men in legislatures in general: women tend to emphasize social policy, while men tend to focus more on business.[2] In addition, women are generally more successful in introducing and promoting legislation in regard to women, children, and family. It is clear from this research that, inside and outside the legislature, women face different constraints and opportunities than do men, and this affects their behavior as legislators.[3]

However, using this research to argue that the proportion of women in the legislature is likely to have an impact on policy involves a fallacy of aggregation. Such a fallacy occurs when one assumes that something about a whole unit can be understood merely by aggregating the characteristics of the parts. But the whole may be more than the sum of its parts. The fact that individual women in legislatures behave differently from individual men tells us little about how the legislature as a group acts. It is possible that one may merely aggregate the actions of the individual legislators in order to predict correctly the behavior of the legislature as a whole, but it is also possible that this is incorrect. For example, Thomas (1994, 151) reasons that since women, on average, introduce and pass .35 more initiatives reflecting "women's distinctive concerns" than do men, an increase of ten women legislators will result in the "introduction of three or four more children's bills per session." But this is true only if additional women introduce new bills as opposed to working on the bills that other women propose. It is also possible that as the number of women increases, the number of women's bills per additional woman decreases, as women team up to work on issues of importance to them.

Most of the research on the impact of women legislators examines individual-level variables, such as policy preferences, legislative or leadership style, and party or other political affiliations. But these differences do not necessarily aggregate in ways that make the activities of legislatures reflect these different characteristics. For example, women legislators may feel that social policy is more important than defense policy, but they may not be successful in convincing others in the legislature of this view. They may also speak more tentatively about their representation of women in a public setting than in a private interview with a female researcher. Thus, many questions remain as to how the differences that have been documented aggregate in the legislature to affect policy outcomes.

Some studies examine the impact of the number or proportion of women in legislatures. First, some evidence from the United States and Norway suggests that when there are large numbers of women in public office, women in legislatures behave differently than do men—for example, introducing more bills on women, children, and the family (Thomas 1994; Bystydzienski 1992). These studies build on research on gender dynamics in classrooms and other deliberative settings that has identified the phenomenon of a "critical mass," that is, a proportion at which minority groups feel comfortable expressing themselves in the context of a mixed group (Kanter 1977; Etzkowitz et al. 1994). Once the number of women officeholders reaches a "tipping point," typically hypothesized to be between 10 and 20 percent, differences between men and women emerge. For example, a comparative analysis of twelve U.S. states finds that in legislatures composed of less than 10 percent women (in this study, Pennsylvania and Mississippi), women members did not exhibit "women's distinctive concern" by introducing more legislation regarding women, children, and the family (Thomas 1994; Welch and Thomas 1991).[4] However, it is important to note that the latter findings only support the idea that the proportion of women in the legislature affects the behavior of women, not that it affects policy outcomes. Thus, these data do not establish a link between a large proportion of women and more women-friendly policy *outcomes*.

Moreover, another analysis of the U.S. state legislature data found that "the number of women who served in a chamber in the legislature had little effect on the extent to which women *or* men gave priority to women's distinctive concerns" (Dodson and Carroll 1991, 68; emphasis in original). Women were just as likely to mention support for "women's distinctive concerns" when there were fewer than 15 percent women in the legislature as when there were more. In addition, although Thomas (1994) finds that 10 percent is necessary for women's distinctive concerns to emerge, she observes that 25 to 30 percent is not enough for women to have an impact on policy outcomes and thus does not constitute a critical mass. This leads her to hypothesize that the impact of women on policymaking would only become evident where a greater proportion of women occupy political office.

Inadequate Conceptualization of the Women's Movement

Some studies of the U.S. states avoid the fallacy of aggregation and more straightforwardly find that the number or proportion of women in political office matters to policy outcomes. Statistical analyses of fifty-one state legislatures (the fifty states and the District of Columbia) have revealed that the number of women in the legislature has an impact on policies on abortion and domestic violence. Hansen (1993) and Berkman and O'Connor (1993) find that a large enough proportion of women in the legislature prevents the adoption of restrictive parental notification measures in regard to abortion. According to Murphy (1997), the proportion of women in the legislature influences policy outcomes on domestic violence.[5]

More detailed studies of smaller numbers of states, or of individual states, have resulted in similar findings. Again, in their study of twelve U.S. states, Welch and Thomas (1991) find that in state legislatures with more than 10 percent women, a larger proportion of bills on women, children, and the family are successfully passed. In a study of Arizona, Saint-Germain (1989) notes that as women increase their numbers in the state legislature, they are more effective in altering legislative content.

None of these state-level analyses adequately controls for the impact of the women's movement.[6] Berkman and O'Connor (1993) do not even consider variation in the organization or strength of the women's movement to be a relevant factor. Saint-Germain notes the changes in policy outcome over time in Arizona, but these changes could have been the result of growing mobilization of the women's movement as much as the result of more women in government. Murphy (1997) considers the women's movement impact on police-reform policies, but she uses membership in the National Organization for Women (NOW) as a measure of women's mobilization across states. Employing this measure, she finds women's mobilization to have no significant impact on policy outcomes. But, as we have noted, counting the membership of formal organizations does not adequately capture the strength of the women's movement. Many important feminist activists are not formally members of any organization.

Moreover, membership in NOW is an inappropriate operationalization of the women's movement for comparing women's mobilization across states. NOW is a national organization that focuses on national policy. It has been very active in lobbying for improvements to the national Violence Against Women Act (VAWA) and VAWA II. But its activities are likely to have less impact at a state or local level, since the coordinated activities of the organization concern national policy. In Pennsylvania, for example, the main women's organization that works on state-level policy on wife battering is the Pennsylvania Coalition Against Domestic Violence. In order to assess the strength of the women's movement within a state, in a way that is meaningful for state politics, one would want to assess whether women are organized at a state level. It could well be that in states with strong state and local movements, women are *less* likely to join national organizations. If one is going to use women's organizations as a measure of feminist activity at all, it would make more sense to look at the number of state or local organizations or their membership, using a directory of women's organizations to identify them.[7]

Murphy herself points out another aspect of her findings that may suggest caution in generalizing from her results. There is a negative correlation between the police reforms she is using as an example of a women's rights policy and other areas of women's legal status, including rape-law reform. Murphy suggests that this may be because police reform as she has identified it may not be a women's rights issue. In spite of this concession, she states that "the most significant contribution of this research is the finding that the more women there are in state legislatures, the more likely there is to be legislation designed to help battered women. Women politicians do make a difference" (1997, 47). This strong conclusion is not well supported by the evidence.

Thus, none of the state-level studies investigating the impact of women legislators on policy outcomes has adequately addressed the influence of the women's movement as a possible rival explanation. This is important because, as we saw in chapter 3, many scholars have shown women's movements to have a significant impact on the policy process. The strength of the movement may have a kind of threshold effect, such that all of the U.S. states are past the threshold at which the women's movement makes a difference, so its effect is not visible from state to state in the way that it is cross-nationally. In any event, this seems an important area to explore further, because cross-national evidence (discussed in chapter 3) suggests that women's movements do make a difference to policy outcomes, at least in the area of violence against women.

Position Power of Women Legislators

Focusing on the impact of a greater number or percentage of women in the legislature ignores the importance of positional power in institutions (Mazur 1995b; Duerst-Lahti and Kelly 1995). It is a mistake to conceptualize the impact of women in the legislatures solely in terms of numbers, even in terms of percentages. This oversimplifies the way legislators interact with each other.

The structure of the institution and the positions within which women act are likely to affect the impact women have (Davis 1997; Kathlene 1995). Individual women in positions of power may have a greater impact than large numbers of female legislators, especially when a strong women's movement supports them. For example, although the United States still lags behind other nations in terms of the proportion of women elected to legislatures, women were much better represented in President Bill Clinton's cabinet than in past cabinets. A similar situation prevailed in Canada in the late 1980s. In Norway, Prime Minister Gro Harlem Brundtland appointed women to her cabinet at a greater rate than they were elected, which resulted in her cabinet's being dubbed "the women's cabinet."

Women in such positions may wield greater influence than their numbers would suggest. Such influence can be called position power, that is, power that stems not from the individual herself but from her position in an institutional structure (Kathlene 1995; Duerst-Lahti and Kelly 1995).[8] Such position power is likely to be especially effective when women have been appointed to positions of prestige in response to a strong feminist movement. Defying powerful women legislators or members of the executive who have the support of the women's movement may seriously undermine the challenger's legitimacy.

The Problematic Notion of the Transparency of Women's Interests

Studies of the impact of policymakers' gender on violence-against-women policy, and the literature on gender and policymaking more generally, share a common theoretical problem (Thomas 1994; Dodson and Carroll 1991; Berkman and O'Connor 1993; but cf. Mezey 1994). They implicitly or explicitly assume that simply because they are women, individual women have (the same) feminist analysis of public policy problems and wish to promote feminist goals. The assumption of a common interest or concern that is obvious to politically active women by virtue of their being women is extremely problematic, but very common in the literature on gender and public policy.

For example, in her study of twelve American states, Thomas (1994) assumes that all women share "distinctive concerns." Larger proportions of women in the legislature, according to Thomas, allow women legislators to "cast aside inhibitions related to minority status and support issues central to their lives" (1994, 98). Similarly, Sapiro (1981) argues that the presence of women themselves in political bodies promotes women's interests for many reasons, including that women representatives are more responsive to women's interests. Note that the argument that individual women are more receptive to women's interests can hold only if women have identifiable interests as women and if the women in government know what these interests are and are more responsive to them.

Although she takes the opposite position on the impact of the gender of policymakers, Elman (1996a) makes a similar assumption about the transparency of women's common interest in her study of policymaking in Sweden. She assumes that women in the legislature are prevented from pursuing feminist goals by male-dominated parties and trade unions. A "higher proportion of women in the Riksdag [legislature] has not translated into greater commitment to policies that would radically alter male dominance" because "party discipline has been so acute that (male-dominated) parties control candidate nominations and determine which policies to promote and which to ignore. Women's interests have, thus, been subsumed by gender-neutral approaches to sex-equity" (29). Elman argues that women are a sort of sisterhood with shared interests based on their sex. Thus, she implies that women's common interests would emerge directly from the greater number of women if party discipline were not so strong that it prevented them from articulating those interests.

The assumption of a common interest or concern that is transparent to politically active women by virtue of their being women is extremely problematic (Lugones 1994; Varikas 1995). First, women have many "distinctive concerns" that cannot be characterized as promoting feminist concerns. For example, women buy more bridal magazines and have more plastic surgery than men, but these practices, and the interest in them, hardly reflects a feminist consciousness. Much of the discovery of differences between male and female legislators in the 1980s can no doubt be traced to the influence of the feminist movement, but much of this discovery results from an expanded definition of what counts as women's concerns to include not only specifically feminist issues, but also those areas traditionally thought of as female: that is, children, the family, moral turpitude, and social reform (Mezey 1994). This broader operationalization of "women's concerns" could include many policies that one would hesitate to classify as promoting women's interests. For example, a policy to prevent increased welfare payments to women who have additional children while on welfare would have to be called a policy concerning women and the family, but it would hardly be considered an example of a policy promoting women's interests.

The point is that we must not assume that if women legislators behave differently from their male counterparts, women or their interests are necessarily better represented by those female legislators. As I argued in the previous chapter, it is unlikely that all women share anything so concrete as a common interest that can be translated into a policy option. The level at which all women have something in common is so general that even if we could identify what they had in common—for example, "motherhood" or "female body experience"—it is unlikely to be obvious how to translate such an interest, experience, or concern into specific policy positions. All that these studies can really claim to have discovered is that women legislators tend to introduce or support certain kinds of policies, not that women better represent other women or their interests. Thus, these problems undermine arguments that greater numbers of women in government result in better policies for women.

WHEN WOMEN POLICYMAKERS AFFECT POLICY

Despite these weaknesses in the theoretical and empirical literature, women policymakers appear to play a prominent role in getting specific pieces of legislation on violence against women passed. How are we to interpret the apparent importance of women policymakers in these cases, given the concerns raised above?

In the many cases in which individual women have seemed to play an important role in policymaking at a key moment, those women often saw themselves as having an obligation to other women, as representing women. In a recent study in the United States, Coleman, Brudney, and Kellough (1998) investigate the likelihood that minority bureaucrats create policies that are more reflective of the interests of the minority groups they seem to represent. They find that such bureaucrats make little substantive difference to policy outcomes unless the individual bureaucrats identify themselves as representatives of their group.

It seems plausible that a similar phenomenon is at work with women legislators. Women legislators may be more motivated to represent what they take to be "women's concerns" when they self-identify as responsible for women in some sense. But, as I have noted, many women do not see themselves as representing women. What determines whether a women is likely to self-identify as a representative of women?

Women policymakers are more likely to feel a responsibility to represent women when there are fewer of them. Dodson and Carroll (1991) find that after a certain point, as the proportion of women increases, women are less likely to report that they feel that they represent women. In addition, women who are involved in women's organizations, such as women's caucuses, networks, and the like, are likely to anticipate explaining their actions to other women and may thus be more motivated to take their group concerns into account.

Women who are part of women's organizations or who participate in feminist activities (going to lectures, reading feminist newspapers, and so forth) are likely to be best acquainted with women's issues, since such sites of interaction are where women's perspective is mainly developed (see chapter 3). Thus, they are likely to have both the motivation and the knowledge to make a difference. Indeed, according to Haussman (1992), women who are not members of any women's organization are barely distinguishable from men as a group on many important women's policy issues.

In Australia, for example, feminists involved with the Women's Electoral Lobby (WEL) consciously strove to enter the government bureaucracy to promote feminist aims. It was in this context that the term *femocrat* was coined. As one observer writes, "So many WEL members took up these positions that the phenomenon became known collectively as 'WEL entering government'" (Sawer 1994, 25). In fact, a 1985 survey of state and federal women M.P.s (members of Parliament) found that 28 percent were, or had been, WEL members. In state governments, WEL members had penetrated the bureaucracy at high levels: for example, three of five cabinet ministers in Western Australia were former WEL activists (ibid., 78). Stetson and Mazur 1995) judge the feminists working in the women's policy machinery in Australia as being highly accessible to women's movements and also as having a high level of policy impact. The large number of feminists in government bureaucracies may have contributed to the broad, multifaceted government response to violence against women in Australia. Of course, these women entered government as part of a conscious strategy of the women's movement, and they remained connected to women's organizations and activities even after taking office.

Women policymakers not only need motivation and knowledge to promote women's issues, they also need power. Although in some cases a single woman or a handful of women can effectively oppose an initiative, the coordination needed to introduce new policies usually requires some positional or organizational power. Women cabinet members with the motivation and the knowledge are more likely to be able to effect change than women legislators in less powerful positions. A legislative women's caucus can also supply the needed influence by providing organizational resources and presenting a united front (cf. Thomas 1994).

In general, women in government (whether elected or appointed) are unlikely to be able to make policy more reflective of women's perspective in the absence of a strong, autonomous women's movement. Such a movement greatly magnifies the influence of a women's caucus or a women's cabinet, and it provides an external base of support and legitimacy to counterbalance internal government resistance to the enactment and implementation of feminist policies.

Individual women can play an important role in promoting policies to address violence against women.[9] Whether they are likely to play such a role depends on whether there is a strong, autonomous women's movement and whether the individual women are influential enough to affect policy. These two factors are much more important than the number or percentage of women in the legislature.

Thus, in the case of policies on violence against women, we would expect an interactive relationship between the presence of a strong, autonomous women's movement and feminists in influential decision-making positions in government. This would not necessarily be reflected in a relationship between the number or proportion of women in the legislature and policy outcomes. Small numbers of women can also be effective partners for autonomous women's movements.

CROSS-NATIONAL PATTERNS OF POLICY DEVELOPMENT

The argument I have made here better fits the case evidence of how poli cies on violence against women come to be passed than does an accoun based on number or proportion of women legislators. Indeed, in the eigh most responsive countries, a large number or proportion of women legisla tors is conspicuously absent at the time of the main phase of policy devel opment on violence against women. Most of these countries lack a critica mass during that period even by the most minimal definition (10 percent) and in two countries policy innovation occurred when there were as few a four or eight women in the legislature (see table 4-1). Two of the most re sponsive countries (Australia and France) have been singled out as bein among the worst globally for low numbers of women in the legislature (In terparliamentary Union 1995).

The top ten countries in terms of percentage of women in the legislatur in 1994 all have 20 percent or more (see table 4-2), a large enough propor tion to constitute a critical mass by most accounts. The absolute number o women ranges from 12 to 141. Yet in this group, the predominant govern ment response to violence against women is to address only two or thre policy areas. Even if we take the more stringent standard of 30 percent fo a critical mass, three of the five countries that meet this standard addres only two or three areas, and none addresses more than four. This group o countries is thus no more responsive—and may be somewhat less respon sive—than the set of all stable democratic governments taken as a group.

Table 4-1: Women in Lower House during Main Period of Policy Innovation, Eight Most Responsive National Governments

Country	Main Years of Policy Innovation	Percentage and Number of Women in Lower House
Australia	1986–93	5.4 to 8.8% (8 to 13)
Canada	1981–87	5.0% to 9.6% (14 to 27)
U.S.	1993–94	11% (48)
Costa Rica	1986–94	10.5 to 14% (4 to 8)
France	1983–90	7.1 to 6.9% (35 to 40)
Ireland	1990–94	7.8 to 12.7% (13 to 21)
Israel	1982–94	7.5 to 9.2% (9 to 11)
New Zealand	1992–94	8.7 to 21.2% (12 to 21)

Source: Interparliamentary Union 1995.

Table 4-2: Proportion of Women in Legislature and Scope of Government Policy Response, 1994

Country	Election Date	Total Seats	Women (#)	Women (%)	No. of Policy Areas Addressed
Sweden	9-94	349	141	40.4	4
Norway	9-93	165	65	39.4	4
Finland	3-91	200	78	39.0	2
Denmark	9-94	179	59	33.0	2
Netherlands	5-94	150	47	31.3	3
Germany	10-94	672	176	26.2	2
Iceland	4-94	63	16	25.4	2
Austria	11-94	183	43	23.5	3
New Zealand	11-93	99	21	21.2	5
Luxembourg	6-94	60	12	20.0	3
Trinidad & Tobago	12-91	37	7	18.9	2
Canada	10-93	295	53	18.0	7
Switzerland	10-91	200	36	18.0	2
Spain	6-93	350	56	16.0	3
Italy	3-94	630	95	15.1	0
Costa Rica	2-94	57	8	14.0	5
Ireland	11-92	166	21	12.7	5
U.S.	11-94	440	48	10.9	6
Jamaica	3-93	60	7	11.7	1
Colombia	3-94	166	18	10.8	3
Barbados	9-94	28	3	10.7	3
Botswana	10-94	40	4	10.0	0
Australia	3-93	147	14	9.5	7
U. K.	4-92	651	62	9.5	4
Belgium	11-91	212	20	9.4	4
Israel	6-92	120	11	9.2	5
Portugal	10-91	230	20	8.7	2
Bahamas	8-92	49	4	8.2	3
India	6-91	528	42	8.0	4
France	3-93	577	37	6.4	5
Venezuela	12-93	203	12	5.9	0
Greece	10-93	300	186	6.0	1
Mauritius	9-91	70	2	2.9	1
Japan	3-93	511	14	2.7	1
Papua New Guinea	6-92	109	0	0	1
Nauru	11-92	18	?	?	0

Source: Interparliamentary Union 1995.

Notice, though, that there are some women in the legislature of ever country where there is some response to violence against women.[10] It ap pears that it is usually women (although men are also involved in som cases) who are the prime movers behind this type of legislation. For exam ple, Monique Begin and Kim Campbell, important female cabinet member in Canada, played an important role in the development of the country' policy on violence against women (Sproule 1998; Vickers, Rankin, and Ap pelle 1993). Similarly, although two male names (Orrin Hatch and Josep Biden) are generally associated with the 1994 Violence Against Women Ac in the United States, Gelb (1998) points out that an influential feminist aid to Biden was key in ensuring that the feminist content of the bill was no gutted during bargaining. The women's caucus also played a significant rol (Gelb 1998). Individual women legislators and bureaucrats also played a important role in the development of legislation in Ireland and France. Thi suggests that women legislators and legislative aides and other women bu reaucrats may have an impact on violence-against-women policy but tha that impact is not a direct result of the quantity (number or percentage) o women.

Number and Percent of Women in the Legislature

The regression analysis (table 4-3) supports the argument that the per centage of women in the legislature is a poor predictor of policy outcome in the area of violence against women. Nor is the absolute number o women in the legislature a good predictor of greater responsiveness: in multivariate regression analysis, the standard errors are as large as the pre dicted effect (see model 8). It is clear that there is no linear relationship be tween number or percentage of women in the legislature and policy outcomes.

Some scholars have used the log of the number of women to capture the threshold effect associated with a critical mass (Berkman and O'Conno 1993; cf. Hansen 1993). It appears that there may be a weak, nonlinear re lationship between the number of women and more responsive policy out comes (model 2). This type of relationship suggests there may be a point o diminishing returns after which additional women have less of an effect or policy.[11] Specifically, an additional ten women legislators may be associatec with a fraction (.25 to .75) of one additional area of policy action. An ad ditional one hundred women would be associated with about one addi tional area of policy action. This is not much of an effect out of a range o 0 to 7 possible areas of policy action addressing violence against women.

Although the effect is very small, it may have practical importance in

Table 4-3: Coefficients, Dependent Variable = Scope of Government Response, 6 Countries, 1994

Model/ Independent Variables	B	Std. Error	Beta	t	Sig.	R-squared
1/ Strong, autonomous women's movement	1.76	0.64	0.45	2.73	0.01	0.27
Log number of reps	0.29	0.35	0.16	0.84	0.41	
GNP per capita	0.00	0.00	0.23	1.20	0.24	
2/ Strong, autonomous women's movement	1.66	0.60	0.42	2.80	0.01	0.28
Log number of reps	0.49	0.25	0.30	1.97	0.06	
3/ Strong, autonomous women's movement	1.69	0.62	0.43	2.73	0.01	0.19
Proportion of women cabinet members	0.02	0.03	0.09	0.58	0.57	
4/ Strong, autonomous women's movement	1.32	0.66	0.34	2.01	0.05	0.23
Proportion of women subministers	0.04	0.03	0.23	1.35	0.19	
5/ Strong, autonomous women's movement	1.88	0.61	0.48	3.09	0.00	0.28
GNP per capita	0.00	0.00	0.32	2.07	0.05	
6/ Strong, autonomous women's movement	1.35	0.59	0.34	2.29	0.03	0.33
Effective women's policy machinery	2.13	0.85	0.37	2.51	0.02	
7/ Strong, autonomous women's movement	1.41	0.61	0.36	2.32	0.03	0.34
Effective women's policy machinery	2.01	0.88	0.35	2.28	0.03	
Number of women in legislature	0.00	0.01	0.08	0.54	0.60	
8/ Strong, autonomous women's movement	1.84	0.61	0.47	3.02	0.01	0.23
Number of women in legislature	0.01	0.01	0.16	1.06	0.30	
9/ Strong, autonomous women's movement	2.56	1.14	0.65	2.24	0.03	.23
Percent of women in legislature	0.37	0.35	0.20	1.06	0.30	
Strong, autonomous women's movement * percent of women in legislature	−0.05	−0.06	−0.25	−0.80	−0.43	

certain cases. Where there had previously been no women in the legislature a few additional women could make the difference between no policy and some official action on the problem of violence against women. However after the election of more than a handful of women, the effect of additional women in the legislature is even smaller. Since most national legislatures in stable democracies now have more than a handful of women (see table 4-2) this finding is of limited use for the purposes of this study.

The presence of a strong, autonomous women's movement is a better predictor of policy outcomes than the logged number of women in the legislature, with standardized Betas of .45 and .16 respectively (table 4-3, model 1). Such a movement is associated with a larger increase than that associated with one hundred additional women legislators. Controlling for level of development (measured by GNP per capita), the presence of a strong, autonomous women's movement produces about two additional areas of policy action on violence against women ($1.76 \pm .64$). In contrast, still controlling for level of development, large numbers of additional women in the legislature would likely yield little or no change in policy—somewhere between no additional action and half of one additional area (B = $.29 \pm .35$).

One possible modification of the hypothesis that the presence of more women legislators results in better policies is to posit an interactive relationship between women's mobilization and women in government. This effect would be muted in a state-level comparison if women's movement mobilization did not vary as much intranationally as it does cross-nationally.

Even taking such an interaction into account, the most responsive countries are not those with the largest number of women in the legislature. Recall that France and Australia, although they had strong, autonomous women's movements at the time of policy innovation, are notorious among advanced industrialized countries for electing a very small number and proportion of women. In fact, throughout the study period (1974–94), France never had more than about 6 percent women in the legislature, suggesting that a critical mass of women is not a necessary condition for being responsive to the problem of violence against women.[12] Thus, it is also unlikely that a greater number of women in the legislature interacts with women's movements to produce better policy outcomes. Regression analysis reveals similar results: a variable aimed at capturing the interaction between women's movements and the number of women in the lower house also proved to be a poor predictor of policy outcome, with standard errors larger than the coefficient (table 4-3, model 9).

Women in Cabinet and Women Subministers

As noted, it may be that women must be in positions of power, such as in the cabinet, to make a difference in policy (Davis 1997). However, even when we focus on women with position power—whether we use the proportion of women in cabinet or the proportion of subministers (high-level administrators) who are women—there is little evidence of any association with the scope of government response to violence against women. Data on the number of women in decision-making positions are only available for two years, 1987 and 1994, and are taken from the UN (1995c) publication *The World's Women*.

The proportion of women in ministerial positions and subministerial positions were included (in different models) in the regression equation. Multivariate analysis shows that the proportion of women cabinet ministers is a poor predictor of scope of government response, with a standard error (.03) larger than the coefficient (.02) (table 4-3, model 3). The proportion of subministers is also a poor predictor, with a large standard error (.03) relative to the coefficient (.04) (model 4). A strong, autonomous women's movement is much more strongly associated with scope of government response than either proportion of women in cabinet or proportion of subministers: standardized Betas for these three variables are .43, .09, and .23 respectively (models 3 and 4). Thus, there is little evidence to suggest that the number or proportion of women in either ministerial or subministerial positions is associated with the scope of government response to violence against women.[13] In addition, it appears that institutional variables (such as an effective women's policy machinery) are more strongly associated with responsiveness to violence against women (models 6 and 7). These variables are discussed further in the next chapter.

CONCLUSION

The received wisdom in the study of women and public policy is that a greater proportion of women in the legislature leads to more women-friendly outcomes. My review of the empirical literature, however, suggests that this finding rests on shaky conceptual and empirical grounds. Moreover, this cross-national study of the impact of women legislators on policies to address violence against women finds only a very weak, nonlinear relationship between number of women and policy outcomes. This pattern would be consistent with the pattern of a "point of diminishing returns" only if the threshold point is a very small number of women. It may be that individual feminist women are important in getting policies passed as policy entrepreneurs. Indeed, it may be that the presence of at least one woman is a necessary condition for policy development in this area. But there is no linear relationship between the overall number of women in government and government responsiveness to violence against women. In general, it is possible that focusing on numbers or percentage of women may misoperationalize the way in which women legislators influence public policy.

More importantly, however, the study of gender power and policymaking must move beyond the study of women as policymakers. The presence of a strong, autonomous women's movement explained more of the variation in scope of government response than any of the variables relating to women in the legislature. In the next chapter, I consider how the structure of political institutions affects government responsiveness to violence against women. I show that these variables are more important than the individual-level variables on which much of the literature on gender and public policy tends to focus.

5

Sexing the State

The Impact of
Political Institutions on Policies
on Violence Against Women

■Many activists believe that institutional reforms will improve government responsiveness to violence against women and women's issues in general. In India, one report on women and violence calls for "the setting up of a Women's Commission as a watch-dog agency with . . . powers and autonomy" (Krishnaraj 1991). Activists in Latin America call for specialized family courts and police stations (Brasiliero 1997). Feminists in Canada, Norway, and the United States have agitated for commissions on women, equal status offices, and other institutional changes aimed at improving conditions for women (Geller-Schwartz 1995; Bystydzienski 1992a; Stetson 1995).

Does the structure of government agencies affect government responsiveness to violence against women? If so, how? The turn to the "new institutionalism" in political science has spawned numerous studies exploring the connections between institutional structure and public policy (Weaver and Rockman 1993; March and Olsen 1989; Hall 1986; Skocpol 1992; Immergut 1992; Knight 1992; Sproule-Jones 1993; Steinmo, Thelen, and

Longstreth 1992; Weir, Orloff, and Skocpol 1988; Heclo 1974; Atkinson 1993; Tuohy 1992). Feminist studies of social policy and public administration have examined the interaction of the women's movement and the state in policy processes (Stetson and Mazur 1995; Staudt 1997; Busch 1992; Walker 1990; Stivers 1993; Cockburn 1991). Below, I explore the contributions and limits of these approaches for explaining cross-national differences in policies on violence against women. As we shall see, the structure of political institutions is critical for understanding responsiveness to violence against women, but this effect cannot be fully accounted for by the extant literature.

DEFINING INSTITUTIONS

With the rise of the new institutionalism in policy studies and in political science more generally, many people now agree that institutions are important determinants of policy outcomes. But few agree on how or why institutions might matter to policy outcomes, or even what institutions are.

For rational choice scholars, institutions are defined as the "rules of the game" (Knight 1992; Immergut 1992; Sproule-Jones 1993). Institutions provide a complex structure within which actors must pursue their ends. Institutions, in this definition, include particular rules and socially shared prescriptions (Knight 1992), constitutional structure (Immergut 1992), and the nested configuration of rules that constitute a federal system (Sproule-Jones 1993). This definition of institutions includes both social conventions and formal structures such as legal codes. It also includes both state and private bureaucratic or administrative structures. Although it may be useful in some contexts, this category seems to me to be too broad for the purposes of explaining the impact of institutions on policy, because it would include local social norms, the rules of English grammar, the rules of Monopoly, and the tradition of having bridal showers. While some of these things may have an impact on policy outcomes, some conceptual distinctions are required in order to construct an account of how these "rules of the game" influence policy.

The institutions that constitute the state may have a different impact on the authoritative decisions and actions of the state (that is, on policy) than do private rules and practices. Collapsing state and private institutions into a single category obscures any such difference, and little conceptual leverage is gained.

Atkinson (1993) distinguishes between state and nonstate institutions. He defines the state as "those political institutions that together comprise a

ystem of order that claims a monopoly on the exercise of coercive power
ind the authority to issue determinations that are binding on all of those liv-
ng within a prescribed territory" (7). Weaver and Rockman (1993, 8) de-
ine political institutions to mean governmental structures, including
ederalism, bureaucratic structures, electoral rules, number of legislative
:hambers, and so on. Although, as Hall (1986) points out, state and non-
.tate institutions are often closely related, they are conceptually distinguish-
ible.

I follow Atkinson in distinguishing between political or state institu-
ions and nonstate institutions. Politics is the means by which "relatively
arge and permanent groups of people determine what they will collectively
lo, settle how they will live together, and decide their future, to whatever
:xtent this is within their power" (Hannah Pitkin, cited in Young 1990a). In
)ther words, politics is the means by which a political community governs
tself, or makes decisions about its collective life. Political institutions, then,
ire those institutions concerned with determining the conditions of collec-
ive life, what we owe one another, and when we are free from mutual obli-
;ation. Political institutions are distinguished from nonstate institutions by
rirtue of the legitimacy and authority they claim over all citizens or mem-
)ers of the political community. In this chapter, I focus on the policy impact
)f political institutions defined as the rules and administrative structures of
;overnment for a given community or country.

As I noted earlier, political institutions are conceptually distinguishable
rom government, that is, the agencies of highest public authority for a par-
icular territorial unit. Governments act through but are not identical to po-
itical institutions or administrative structures. Political institutions can also
)e distinguished from the concept of the state. The term *state* is often used
o refer to the totality of government, political institutions, laws, policies,
ind the like. Since I am examining subcategories of the concept of the state
policy, governments, institutions) and the relationship between them, I will
nostly use these more specific terms, except when I am discussing broader
:heories of state.

NEOINSTITUTIONALISM AND PUBLIC POLICY

How do political institutions affect policymaking? With the resurgence
)f interest in the state and political institutions, two distinct types of ac-
:ounts of how institutions affect public policy have emerged (Ostrom 1995;
Atkinson 1993).[1] The first variant of institutionalism assumes that policy
)utcomes are best understood as the aggregation of the actions of self-

interested individuals (Immergut 1992; Sproule-Jones 1993). Actors make rational decisions based on their preferences and the choices that confront them. These decisions drive their behavior. The policy process can be understood as a cumulation of such decisions. The second variant of the institutionalist approach to policymaking, the structural, or historical, approach, focuses on institutions as organizers of political actors and policy. Political institutions enable some actors and exclude or disempower others through their structure (Weaver and Rockman 1993; Weir, Orloff, and Skocpol 1988; Skocpol 1992; Hall 1986; Atkinson 1993; Offe 1984).

Both of these approaches offer insight into how institutions affect policymaking. Although the method of analysis often differs, I see the central tenets of structural institutionalism as compatible with, and even complemented by, the main conclusions of rational choice analysis. These central tenets direct the analyst's attention to four key characteristics of political systems: (1) the organization of actors outside the state; (2) the organization and historical roots of the administrative structure; (3) processes of institutional feedback; and (4) variation in institutional structure.

The organization of actors outside the state: Neoinstitutional approaches emphasize the impact of institutions on the organization of political actors, that is, on the groups, agencies, individuals, and networks whose behavior affects collective life. Institutional structures can affect whether certain group interests are ever articulated, and how strongly they are articulated (Hall 1986; Skocpol 1992). For rational choice theorists, the organization is important because it affects how individual preferences are aggregated (Immergut 1992), while for structural theorists institutional structure can be transformative, changing the values or identities of actors (Atkinson 1993; Skocpol 1992). But both approaches hold that institutional structures can either empower or disable actors, give them voice in the policy process or deny them access to it. For example, labor laws can make it much easier for unions to organize and thus express their members' collective interests. When interests are more effectively articulated, they are better represented in the policy process. This is one key way in which institutions shape policy outcomes.

The organization of the administrative structure: Rational choice theorists and structural theorists argue that the structure of the administrative system affects policy outputs because it constrains actors inside political institutions (Immergut 1992; Weir, Orloff, and Skocpol 1988). Rational choice theorists focus on how the rules of the institution (such as voting procedures) affect policy outcomes at a microlevel—at the level of each decision or action. Structural theorists emphasize the importance of the structure of the administrative system in determining whether and how governments will produce policies. Federalism, or the division of power between central and regional governments, is one example of a type of administrative structure. Administrative systems may also vary as to whether they include, say, a centralized statistical agency or an education department. Different structures not only afford different capacities for policymaking and innovation, they also result in different proclivities: administrations are likely to formulate policies in ways that "fit" into the existing administrative structure and language (Weaver and Rockman 1993; Tuohy 1993; Weir, Orloff, and Skocpol 1988; Hall 1986). For example, a government with a department of the environment might be more likely to address environmental problems.

The organization of political institutions reflects past political struggles between groups (Skocpol 1992; Weir, Orloff, and Skocpol 1988; Hall 1986; Atkinson 1993; March and Olsen 1989). The Canadian provinces and the U.S. states were important actors in shaping the federal systems that constrain or enable them today (Atkinson 1993; Morrison, Commager, and Leuchtenberg 1980). Thus, "the institutions that organize group relations act as a kind of social memory, imprinting the conflicts of the present with the institutional legacy of the past" (Hall 1986, 233). Of course, this does not mean that institutions simply mirror social conflicts: "Organization does more than transmit the preferences of particular groups; it combines and ultimately alters them. Accordingly, economic policy may not faithfully reflect a struggle among competing interests precisely because organization refracts that struggle" (ibid.).

Processes of institutional feedback: We often hear of "backlash" against particular policy initiatives. In Canada, Prime Minister Mulroney's popularity was said to have plummeted partially in response to his government's introduction of the Goods and Services Tax in 1990; pro-life groups in the United States are said to have mobilized in reaction to the Supreme Court's 1973 decision in *Roe v. Wade;* the Supreme Court of India's 1985 decision in favor of a Muslim divorcée named Shah Bano met with rioting and protests. Such reactions to policies can be thought of as a kind of feedback that government gets about policy.

Policy feedback occurs continuously as policy alternatives are debated and implemented. Lobbying, protests, and shifts in public opinion may all be considered types of feedback. The amount and type of feedback depend partly on the degree of access that affected groups have, both to the policymaking process and to the administrative structure in general. As Atkinson (1993, 36) puts it: "The institutional design of political systems is understood to be a key variable in the degree to which citizens are able to participate in the policy process." This means that the organization and formal structure of the institution, in addition to affecting the structure and strength of political actors and the structure of policy, can affect how groups or individuals interact with administrative systems and how much input they actually have in policymaking that affects them.

Variation in institutional structure: Finally, both structuralists and rational choice theorists conceive of institutional structure as varying across institutional units (such as departments or offices), as well as over time and space. They also acknowledge that institutional capacity can vary from policy issue to policy issue, even within an institutional unit. These variations in institutional structure, may thus be of differing degrees of importance for different policy issues.

NEOINSTITUTIONALISM AND GENDER

How, then, is institutional structure likely to affect policies on violence against women? One relevant group of actors outside the state is the women's movement. How does the organization of the state affect the ability of women to organize and articulate their interests? The neoinstitutionalist literature has, for the most part, not considered this question.[2] March and Olsen (1989) note that historic struggles among social groups, such as gender groups, affect the structure of political institutions. Although this observation is suggestive, theorists of political institutions have not taken it much further. How, if at all, do historic struggles over gender affect contemporary policymaking? The neoinstitutionalists have provided little insight into this question. Nor have they considered how the structure of political institutions might constrain those within the institutions who are attempting to address violence or other women's issues. Thus, there are few answers to be found in neoinstitutionalist political science as to how the structure of political institutions affects and is affected by gender structures, that is, relations between men and women as groups.

This is partly because of the intellectual history of these approaches: they aimed to distinguish the independent effects of institutions, to show that they could not be collapsed into social structures and processes. In addition, because of their interest in organizational factors, neoinstitutionalists have studied social groups mostly in terms of their formal organizations, such as labor unions or women's clubs, rather than as social cleavages or forces more broadly understood (Weir, Orloff, and Skocpol 1988; Skocpol 1992). This work has contributed many significant insights about the importance of such organizations for the policy influence of groups. However, social groups such as women and minorities are much more than official organizations. The effects of social structures such as gender, race, and class groups are broader than those of such officially representative organizations.

Research by feminist political scientists working mostly outside the neoinstitutionalist literature suggests some answers to the question of how social structures of gender affect political institutions and vice versa. In a study of women's commissions in the United States, Duerst-Lahti (1989) finds that women's commissions played an important role in strengthening the women's movement. In a series of case studies of organizations in Britain, Cockburn (1991) argues that equal opportunity policies are more likely to be successful when there is a women's movement inside the institution that seeks to implement the policy. Other scholars contend that bureaucracies such as development organizations and the European Union bear the imprint of the men who created them and thus tend to reflect masculine perspectives and values (Staudt 1997; Hoskyns 1996).

In spite of these and other suggestive studies, we still lack an adequate theoretical account of how political institutions are gendered. Specifically, we need a theory of political institutions that can explain both (1) the respects in which political institutions are gendered, that is, how they affect and are affected by social relations between men and women, the masculine and the feminine; and (2) how the relationship between political institutions and gender relations changes over space and time. Although neoinstitutional approaches suggest many possible ways for thinking about variation in political institutions, they are not much help in understanding whether or how institutions might be gendered.

Conversely, as I will show below, although feminist theorists have provided accounts of how institutions are gendered, they have not accounted for change or variation in political institutions. In the early feminist theories of state and bureaucracy of the 1970s and 1980s, the administrative structure of the state was either ignored or assumed to be uniformly bureaucratic and therefore male-biased. This opposition to bureaucracy has given way to a more nuanced view of the state as sometimes women-friendly and sometimes male-biased. However, even these more nuanced studies tend to collapse the concepts of the state and social policy and thereby overlook variation in the administrative structure as a possible source of policy change. In spite of a developing body of empirical work, then, there is still very little feminist theorizing about variation in the gendered nature of the administrative structure of political institutions.

FEMINIST THEORIES OF THE BUREAUCRATIC STATE

Early feminist theories of the bureaucratic state tended to see all bureaucratic forms as antifeminist by virtue of being bureaucratic. The classic feminist theoretical study of bureaucracy is the work of Kathy Ferguson, who argues that bureaucratic systems can never promote feminist goals because they are systems of domination (1984, 83). Even if feminists were able to secure positions of power in bureaucracies, they would be prevented from using their position to promote feminist goals because of what is required of managers in bureaucratic systems: they must conform to bureaucratic norms in order to procure promotion and other rewards; they must support "goal consensus" (which really means forcing a unified vision of reality on workers) in order to ensure the smooth running of the organization; and they must remain distant from subordinates. Outside such structures, in contrast, feminists can organize in "active and authentic" ways (82).

More recently, Camilla Stivers (1993) has argued that there is a male bias built into the structure of public administration in the United States. She notes, "Like other public sector activities, public administration is structurally male despite its apparent neutrality: it can only go on as long as it does because women bear a lop-sided share of the burden of domestic functions without which life would simply not be possible" (5). She maintains that the norms and practices of administration privilege men and their work over women and their work. Bureaucratic norms of objectivity, expertise, leadership, and virtue may appear to be gender-neutral. But in practice they disadvantage women, because women are not seen as embodying these virtues. For example, our models of leadership require that women violate norms of femininity. This creates tension for women who wish to be leaders in public bureaucracies.

This view of bureaucracy as inherently biased against women and the feminine has had a strong influence on many studies of policies to address violence against women.[3] Busch (1992) develops this argument in a study of policy response to domestic violence in India and the United States. Following Ferguson (1984), she argues that policy processes neutralize women's movement demands because bureaucratic structures are incompatible with feminist goals. Because of this bureaucratic structure, in this view, even where states appear to be acting to address feminist concerns, on closer analysis we find that state action works to disempower women. For example, state policies on violence against women construct women as passive subjects of policy, as victims and clients. Feminist organizations, on the other hand, emphasize empowerment over treatment. Moreover, Busch argues, "the bureaucratic structure of the liberal democratic state means that state response to women's movement demands criminalizes violence against women without recognizing that such violence is rooted in unequal gender relations" (1992, 603).

A similar analysis can be found in Walker's study (1990) of government response to violence against women in Canada: a problem initially framed by the women's movement as a problem of social inequality (violence against women) is translated by expert bureaucratic discourse into a fragmented, apolitical problem (family violence). This makes it subsumable within the helping professions as a "special problem" of dysfunctional families, easily administered by the mental health, social service, and criminal justice systems. Daniels (1997) develops a similar analysis for the United States.[4]

It is easy to understand why scholars who have studied the history of government response to violence against women would be skeptical of the emancipatory potential of state policy. In the United States, for example, until the legal reforms of the past ten or twenty years, the state was involved in legitimizing and supporting patriarchal dominance within the family by, for example, permitting a marital exemption for rape. In judicial decisions and policies, agents of the state have legitimized male violence against women by explicitly considering such violence a private matter, and they have sometimes explicitly named wife beating as a husband's prerogative. Moreover, government involvement in funding shelters and crisis centers has often been held responsible for the professionalization and subsequent depoliticization of rape crisis centers and women's shelters. Activists complain that government funding brings too many strings, requiring formal credentials and training, hierarchical forms of organization, eligibility requirements, and other invasive bureaucratic practices that interfere with the empowerment that crisis centers and shelters originally took as their main goal (Dobash and Dobash 1998; Walker 1990; Elman 1996a; Everett 1998; Reinelt 1995; Arnold 1995; Matthews 1995; Patel 1991; Sanchez and Gonzalez 1997).

Nevertheless, there are good theoretical and empirical reasons to look beyond this one-sided view of bureaucracy (Haney 1996). More recent theorizing about organizational structure and bureaucracy has produced a more nuanced view of the possibility for feminist organizing within hierarchical structures. In view of the wide variety of organizational forms that feminists have adopted, it seems unlikely that all bureaucratic forms of organization are equally inimical to feminist goals (Ferree and Martin 1995). Indeed, many large feminist organizations can claim some degree of success in promoting feminist action. Women's groups can take a variety of forms, but most of the big ones (such as NOW in the United States, the National

Action Committee in Canada, and the Women's Electoral Lobby in Australia, to name a few) must these days be described as bureaucracies (Ferree and Martin 1995; Molyneux 1998). Even those that are formally nonhierarchical are not free of domination, as revealed by the proliferating critiques of consciousness-raising groups by African American, lesbian, and other women. There are degrees of hierarchy, and some bureaucracies are more decentralized and less hierarchical than others (Staudt 1997; Yudelman 1997; Gelb 1995).

Both women's groups and bureaucracies in modern society take a variety of forms. The notion of bureaucracy as uniformly male-biased is also difficult to maintain in light of the significant variation in government policy that bureaucracies have produced across space and time. If we think there is a difference between providing shelters, crisis centers, and hotlines and not providing such services, and if we think that having wide-ranging public education programs is better than not having them, then we must concede that the variation in policy does indeed matter to those concerned with violence against women. If we think there is real policy variation despite the male-biased nature of bureaucracy, then we must find out what circumstances permit policymakers to produce better policies and what circumstances prohibit such innovation. This suggests that we ought to investigate the consequences of variation in bureaucratic forms to discover which forms are most likely to produce policies that benefit women, and which are not.

COLLAPSING THE STATE AND SOCIAL POLICY

With the realization that state policies affecting women vary so much over space and time, and even within particular institutions, many scholars of gender and policy began to theorize the relationship between the state and social policy in a more nuanced way. However, much of this feminist scholarship has ignored the administrative structure of the state by collapsing the concepts of state and policy. The most egregious example of such theoretical slippage is MacKinnon (1989), who equates law and state, and sometimes even the courts and the state, making little reference to either the legislative or executive branch.

More subtle examples are evident in feminist scholarship on the welfare state, which equates the state with the structure of social policy. As Leira notes, whether a state is "woman-friendly" or male-biased is usually determined by examining the policies of different welfare states: "Analytically, the concept of the 'woman-friendly state' is difficult, as a range of different criteria may be applied to argue the woman friendly or unfriendly character of the policies of different welfare states" (1993, 50). Sassoon (1987) equates the structure of the welfare state with the structure of social policy, examining the effect on women workers of the organization of state services around a male model of work. Similarly, Saraceno (1994) equates changes in state welfare policy with changes in the state; she examines the effects of Italian social policy on families and women and uses this as evidence to support arguments about the structure of the Italian welfare state. Lewis (1998) investigates changes in the structure of the welfare state by examining changes in social care policies, such as government provision for child care and elder care. In a book entitled *The State and the Family*, Gauthier (1996) does not define the state, and focuses primarily on state support for families—that is, family *policy*.[5]

While valuable in other ways, these studies share the feature that they collapse the concepts of state and social policy. These feminist scholars analyze the state by examining assumptions about women or gender that are built into the pattern of social legislation and by examining the impact of policies on women and families. But states are more than policies: they are administrative, decision-making systems. Treating policy as equivalent to the state turns the administrative structure of the state into a black box.

Collapsing the state and policy makes intranational policy variation very difficult to analyze. When a state enacts contradictory policies, it appears to be in conflict with itself (Dahlerup 1987; Haney 1996). But in some cases, policy conflict can be reconceptualized as policy variation within a state across policy areas. If this is the case, we can ask (for example) whether differing administrative structures of the responsible agencies could account for the differing outcomes. An important area of inquiry is being obscured by the mode of analysis that equates state and social policy.

FEMINIST INSTITUTIONALISTS

Over the last decade, a handful of feminist scholars have begun directly studying the structure of political institutions (Duerst-Lahti and Kelly 1995; Elman 1996a; Gelb 1989; Malloy 1999; Stetson and Mazur 1995; Staudt 1997). These studies suggest that two main types of institutional structure may have an impact on women's policy issues: federal and corporatist institutional structures, and women's policy machineries.

Centralized Corporatist Structures versus Decentralized Federalism
Institutional structures may indirectly affect policy processes by stifling or encouraging the organization of women's movements. In a study of Sweden, the United States, and Britain, Gelb (1989) argues that the degree of

corporatism or political centralization is a crucial variable affecting the emergence and activism of a women's movement. Pluralism or dispersed power "makes the system accessible to a wider range of interest groups" (20). In a comparison of the United States and Sweden, Elman (1996a) similarly argues that centralized, corporatist political structures suppress women's autonomous organizing and that fragmented federal republics encourage it.

Corporatism rests on a tripartite division between government, business, and labor. These sectors are represented through hierarchical organizations whose leaders are taken to be able to make commitments and express positions on behalf of the whole sector or group. As Schmitter puts it, corporatism is

> a system of interest representation in which the constituent units are organized into a limited number of singular, compulsory, non competitive, hierarchically ordered and functionally differentiated categories, recognized or licensed (if not created) by the state and granted a deliberate representational monopoly within their respective categories in exchange for observing certain controls on their selection of leaders and articulation of demands and supports. (Phillippe Schmitter, cited in Peters 1991, 168)

Generally, critics of corporatism focus on the elitism and exclusionary character of the tripartite bargaining system (Peters 1991; Yeatman 1990). In particular, new social movements raise issues that cannot be addressed within the framework of the traditional categories of social democratic thinking, namely, class inequality and employment-related concerns. Peters argues that even in Sweden, where the process is relatively inclusive, certain features of the corporatist processes of decision-making make it difficult to include new social movements. The organizations that speak for these movements can rarely make binding commitments on behalf of their constituents. Furthermore, the purpose of membership in an environmentalist organization, for example, is different in important ways from the purpose of membership in a union. Insofar as these interests are noneconomic, they do not necessarily lend themselves to bargaining between elites (Peters 1991).

Elman (1996a) argues that the problem with corporatism is that it prevents women's autonomous organizing by limiting women to organizing within the tripartite structure of corporatist decision-making. The emphasis on organizing only on the basis of class obstructs gender-based organizing, which is seen as subsidiary or even detrimental to class solidarity. There has been male resistance to feminist demands in unions and other labor organizations in the United States, Sweden, and Britain (Brownmiller 1999; Elman 1996a; Cockburn 1991). The point is that corporatist decision-making procedures privilege these class-based organizations and deny access to independent women's groups.

But in Norway and Denmark, corporatist political processes did not prevent women from organizing outside as well as within the formal institutions of government. Gelb identifies both Sweden and Britain as being closer to the corporatist, centralist end of the pluralist-corporatist continuum. Yet a strong, autonomous women's movement emerged in Britain but not in Sweden (Gelb 1989, 8). So women *can* organize independently in the context of corporatism.

In addition, response to violence against women varies across the Scandinavian countries, where centralized, corporatist decision-making structures are the norm. The Swedish state, for example, has been much more innovative and comprehensive in its response to violence against women than Denmark and Finland have been. Moreover, the Swedish government has recently become even more responsive to violence against women, yet Sweden is still a centralized state with a corporatist decision-making structure. Thus, corporatism alone cannot explain the lack of an autonomous feminist movement (since Britain had one but Sweden did not); and it does not appear, alone, to account for a lack of government response to violence against women.

It is possible that corporatism has a stifling effect on women's movements where they do successfully organize, limiting the concessions that governments can provide to these organizations. This may be due to the elitist character of corporatist decision-making. The male-dominated character of the process has been documented: the main players tend to come from those segments of society (business and trade union leaders) from which women are most completely excluded (Yeatman 1991). But is this elitism so different from the political bargaining processes in federalist states? Women have also been excluded from the leadership of unions, business, and other "nonpartisan" special interest groups in federal systems.

Elman (1996a) argues that corporatist structures are more centralized and that federal systems provide more points of access for organized groups. It is important to note that although Elman compares corporatist systems to federal systems, it is certainly possible to combine a federal structure with corporatist decision-making processes. Federal systems are political conglomerations of regional units in which there is a division of power between the member polities as a collective and the individual member polities. "The essential institutions of federalism are, of course, a government of the federation and a set of governments of the member units, in which both kinds of governments rule over the same territory and people and each kind has the authority to make some decisions independently of the other" (Riker 1964). There is no reason to think that this type of arrangement is incompatible with corporatism. Indeed, Germany is one such federal, corporatist system (Esping-Andersen 1990).

It may indeed be that federal systems, because they involve a division of power between levels of government, offer more points of access for social movement organizations (Elman 1996a; Sabatier 1999). But federal systems vary greatly in the degree to which they are decentralized, and this decentralization often varies across policy issue areas. Moreover, unitary systems are often more decentralized in practice than they are on paper. This makes it exceedingly difficult to use a formal classification of federal versus unitary to predict the actual degree of decentralization in a polity that exists for any given policy issue. At any rate, the eight most responsive countries are equally divided into federal, decentralized states (the United States, Australia, New Zealand, and Canada) and unitary, centralized states (France, Costa Rica, Israel, and Ireland).

The very "specialization" that Elman credits with granting women access to the policymaking process under the federal system in the United States has itself been criticized as exclusionary, admitting only certain types of people who qualify as "experts" while excluding many others (Walker 1990; Fraser 1989; Stivers 1993). In other words, it is not only corporatist policy processes that are male-dominated, and we need to know more about how the exclusion of women from *these* corporatist processes (as compared with other male-dominated processes) prevents women from pressing for reforms from the outside.

Women's Policy Machinery

Most democratic governments in the world, and almost all the national governments considered here, have implemented some kind of institution that ostensibly promotes the status of women. There is even some evidence that the institutionalization of feminism can have an impact on policy outcomes (Stetson and Mazur 1995; MacKinnon 1989; Staudt 1998).

A women's policy machinery is a set of one or more government institutions (an office, department, commission, or ministry) whose main purpose is to promote the status of women. Feminist proponents of women's policy machineries concede that in many respects political institutions have historically been male-biased (Staudt 1998; Stetson and Mazur 1995). They rightly point out the importance of disaggregating the concept of the state into its component parts and considering the theoretical possibility that the impact of political institutions might vary across institutional structures (Stetson and Mazur 1995; Haney 1996; Pringle and Watson 1992; Brown 1992; Alvarez 1997). But this disaggregation of the state is inadequate to explain why a women's policy machinery might have an effect on policy different from that of agencies that are *not* designed to focus on women. Is a women's policy machinery more effective in developing and implementing policies than are feminist bureaucrats working in regular departments? Why or why not?

GENDER BIAS IN INSTITUTIONS

The feminist literature does not answer this question directly, but there is much that is instructive in the extant research. Feminist policy scholars have developed concepts that reveal gender bias in policies that appear, on their face, to be gender-neutral. They have done this by examining the assumptions embedded in the very categories and language the policy employs and by showing that these assumptions often concern the appropriate roles for, and relationships between, men and women.

There may be such a bias in the administrative structure of the state, that is, in the organization of political institutions. The *administrative structure of the state* refers to the substantive categories around which administration is organized (for example, health, education, or defense) and relationships between the agencies responsible for specific categories. As March and Olsen (1989, 26) note, "internal divisions of labor normally result in polities built around the principles of division of labor and specialization, and so a partitioning of citizens and officials into relatively self-contained collections of roles and rules."

Modern administrative structures tend to be bureaucratic in the sense that they involve a fairly stable arrangement of roles and assignment of tasks. But administrative structures vary across bureaucracies: for example, one state bureaucracy might have a department of marine affairs, and another might not; one structure might have a central statistical office, while another is organized so that each department gathers its own information. The question is, which administrative structures facilitate responsiveness to violence against women and which obstruct government response?

We know that all forms of organization privilege some categories and subordinate others, a phenomenon known as the mobilization of bias. As

March and Olsen (1989, 27) point out, "attention is a scarce good in politics; and control over the allocation of attention is important to a political actor. . . . By inhibiting the discovery of an entry into some potential conflicts, a structure of rules organized into relatively discrete responsibilities channels political energies into certain kinds of conflicts and away from others." Bureaucracies are set up to deal with a certain set of problems, and they tend to define these problems in characteristic ways. By doing so, they may exclude particular ways of thinking about problems or solutions.

The structure of administration can affect the ease with which problems are addressed. For example, if one agency has the resources and responsibility to deal with a major problem, the issue can be more easily addressed. If responsibility for a problem is divided among functional areas, this can present difficulties for effective policy design and implementation. "By suppressing links across partitions, the division of labor creates significant barriers between domains of legitimate action. . . . Coordination across boundaries is more difficult than within them. Different sets of rules tend to evolve independently in different domains" (March and Olsen 1989, 26).

In addition, the combination of agencies having responsibility for policy design and implementation can have a substantial impact on the success of a policy or program. If responsibility for a policy issue is not explicitly assigned to a specific agency, agencies will likely give priority to those tasks for which they already have explicit responsibility. "If multiple agencies are assigned responsibility for implementing the program, lack of coordination among them could mean that responsibilities are carried out with different degrees of rigor or that different standards are applied by each agency. This problem has affected several policies of particular importance to women, such as employment, education and credit" (Conway, Ahern, and Steuernagel 1995, 10).

Some assumptions about the policy environment are necessarily built into the way that administrative categories are defined. These assumptions reflect the social and physical world in the context of which the administrative structure was designed. Often, administrative divisions persist even when they are no longer appropriate for the environment in which they are situated. For example, Finnemore (1996) points out that because many African states copied administrative structures wholesale from Western states, some landlocked states in Africa have navies.

The categories of administration often reflect assumptions about social relations that make it difficult to enact feminist policies. For example, in the United States, addressing the double burden of individuals' paid work and their unpaid work in the family should involve policy coordination among agencies from both Health and Human Services (which handles, for example, subsidies for daycare) and the Department of Labor. A similar division into administration of the paid workplace and administration of family affairs is evident in Canada, Norway, Costa Rica, and many other countries. This division reflects an assumption that the problems of paid workers (assumed to be men who are not primary caregivers for children) are separate from family issues, such as the care of children (taken to be mainly the province of women). Policies that aim to recognize the family responsibilities of workers, therefore, usually involve at least two major administrations. The challenge of policy coordination is not insurmountable, of course, but it does add some complexity to addressing the policy issue.

In most countries, policies to address the status of women tend to cut across traditional administrative categories as they are currently constructed; that is, the functional areas of responsibility are usually divided so that women's issues, such as violence against women, child care, and reproductive freedom, are addressed by a number of different agencies. This creates the administrative challenge of coordinating women's policies and programs, which, as a result, often end up as a low priority for all agencies concerned.

Even when women's concerns should fit into a department's area of responsibility, it is often hard to make an issue that is critical for achieving sexual equality seem like a priority for that department. Each department constructs its agenda so that it can take care of the things it has traditionally taken care of (usually not the business of promoting women's issues). The promotion of the status of women is not, senior bureaucrats might argue, a primary responsibility of these departments. So policy priorities that focus on women have to be justified in terms of their relationship to traditional agenda items. This means that even where women's agenda items fit into traditional areas of bureaucratic responsibility, they fall through the cracks, because it is not clear to senior bureaucrats that their mandate includes ensuring that they address men's and women's concerns equally. Leading officials of the European Union, for example, at one point viewed its gender equality directives as marginal to the main work of the EU (Hoskyns 1996, 154). Such attitudes likely affect how issues are ranked in terms of their importance throughout the institution.

Designing, implementing, and evaluating policy to address the status of women sometimes requires developing new ways of collecting and analyzing data. There is often a lack of information for designing and implementing new policies. Women's policy machineries can help provide the resources and expertise to generate this data.

Most feminist and mainstream state theorists agree that one of the functions of an administrative system is the maintenance of a social order (March and Olsen 1989; Fraser 1989). Most modern state administrative structures were at one time responsible for a social order that disadvantaged women and rendered them subordinate to men. The categories of administration often retain assumptions about social relations (for example, that paid work and child welfare are cleanly separable issues) that make it difficult to enact feminist policies. Policies that aim to promote the status of women usually require policy action across administrative categories, or the reordering of traditional priorities within departments. Thus, the institutional remnants of this historical origin create an organizational disadvantage that makes it difficult to employ the administrative structure to change gender relations.

FEMINIST INSTITUTIONALISM

How, then, do political institutions affect actors outside the state in the case of violence-against-women policy? The key relevant social groups that have struggled on this policy issue are women's movements. Providing symbolic, material, and research support to feminist activists is one way that states can strengthen women's movements (Duerst-Lahti 1989). Providing formal opportunities for access to the state is another important way. Examples of such support include the advisory committees set up in both Canada (until 1995) and Australia whereby women's organizations had regular access to government officials. In addition, in Australia (and in Canada until the early 1990s) there were regularized annual meetings between political officials and women's movement representatives to discuss a women's agenda. Thus, one determinant of state responsiveness might be whether states provide formal avenues through which women's movements have access to state decision-making. We would expect increased access and resources for women's groups to result in greater policy responsiveness on the part of the institution.

The neoinstitutionalist approach suggests that the categories of administration—that is, the substantive categories that are the focus of the major departments—and the distribution of resources across these categories construct policy capabilities. Our discussion suggests that the current construction of administrative categories in most of the political institutions in question makes it difficult to address issues of concern to women. We have noted that government response to violence against women requires policy action in areas as diverse as criminal justice, education, and income assistance. But these areas are usually the responsibility of a variety of different agencies, which poses considerable coordination problems. This may be one reason that government response to violence against women has often been so fragmented and partial.

The categories of administrative structure may obstruct an effective response to women's concerns. The way that institutions organize work makes it hard for them to address women's concerns, even when they have the political will to do so. Policy responses to the issues of provision of child care, violence against women, the protection of reproductive freedom, and advancing economic equality between men and women usually require coordination among a number of major government departments. As Malloy (1999, 267) notes, "Movements and groups such as women, indigenous peoples, people with disabilities and others form and frame new policy fields that challenge traditional departmental and functional boundaries. Their specific policy interests and goals—such as domestic violence prevention or same-sex spousal rights—commonly do not fit in existing portfolios but require the coordination of multiple departments and agencies."

It has long been recognized that all forms of organization privilege some categories and ways of seeing the world and ignore or repress others. The current mobilization of bias in political institutions disadvantages women and their concerns, creating a sort of gender bias in the fundamental structure of the institutions. Existing institutional structures are likely the product of past struggles and thus tend to reflect the view of the historically dominant group (Hall 1986; Atkinson 1993). Social groups struggle to get their way of looking at the world formalized in political institutions, or to preserve the existing institutionalization of their perspective, because this greatly privileges that group over competing groups in future struggles. "Dominant groups create environments to which others must respond, without themselves attending to the others. This is a fairly standard characterization of the position of dominant ethnic or gender groups, of persons in authority in totalitarian regimes, or of leading firms in a concentrated industry" (March and Olsen 1989, 47).

Although it happened in different ways in the many countries considered here, the general account of the development of political institutions is that powerful groups of men were successful in having the social perspective of privileged men codified in the functional divisions of the state. As Hoskyns (1996, 10) points out, "Virtually all public policy making on women's issues takes place within structures that are male-dominated, in the sense that they reflect male life-patterns, are largely controlled by men, and support a process that presents different but essentially male views of problems and solutions."

As we have seen, administrative structures are designed to address particular problems in particular contexts. This has meant that they are usually set up to address problems other than women's issues, in contexts that tend not to feature sexual inequality. According to Staudt (1997, 10), "Gender is a social construct that differentiates men and women in ways that become embedded and institutionalized in the political and bureaucratic authority of the state. Women rarely have voice in conceptualizing such institutional forms." Thus, women's general powerlessness at key historical moments of institutional design partially accounts for the survival of an administrative structure that obscures their concerns.

We noted above that neoinstitutionalists emphasize that institutions are organizations, and that the framework in which new problems are approached will likely be determined largely by the usual way of organizing and approaching things. In her discussion of policies on domestic violence, Busch (1992) similarly argues that the form of policy response to domestic violence depends partially on which problems existing institutional structures already address. For example, if a health policy bureaucracy already exists, then the problem will be understood as a health problem. In the United States, where there is a highly developed criminal justice system, violence against women is taken up as a criminal justice problem. We can extend her argument by observing that in European countries, where the social-distributive apparatus is more developed, violence-against-women policy will tend to focus more on provision of services to victims and less on criminal justice response. Busch explains that this feature of bureaucratic response precludes a comprehensive policy to address violence against women because the problem will necessarily be fragmented and the response uncoordinated—and probably partial—as it is taken up by one or another of these administrative structures. Hoskyns (1996) argues that the efforts of the women's bureau of the EU to raise the issue of racism against migrant workers were partially thwarted by the absence of any administrative unit that could take primary responsibility for the problem (an observation to which I will return in later chapters). Thus, it is clear that the current administrative structure of many states lacks the policy capabilities required to address feminist issues effectively.

This suggests that altering the administrative structure of the state will improve policy responsiveness. Introducing new categories, such as administrations that focus on women and permit coordination of policies across existing administrative categories, can facilitate the formulation of policies to promote the status of women. Where women's movements have introduced women's issues as categories of the administrative structure of state ınd policy, we would expect political institutions to be more effective in implementing feminist policy.

Indeed, such a rationale lies behind the creation of many women's policy agencies. Hoskyns (1996, 122) notes that efforts in Ireland and Germany to implement gender equality directives adopted by the EU led to "an increase in the bureaucratic structure around equality policy, and to facilities which at a certain level at least made it easier for women's issues to be articulated." In Germany, the Arbeitsstab Frauenpolitik (working group on women's issues) of the Federal Ministry for Youth, the Family, and Health was increased in size and given both cross-departmental authority and responsibility for funding women's projects and disseminating information. In Ireland, the Employment Equality Agency, an office focusing more narrowly on employment equity, was established in 1977 in response to the EU directives. Similarly, some governments originally created their gender office or women's bureau to help prepare for international women's rights conferences.

Women's policy agencies are one way of creating state institutions that reflect women's perspective, as defined in chapter 3. A women's policy machinery can address issues of concern to women (such as violence) without segmenting such problems into their health, criminal justice, and other aspects. Thus, women's policy machineries introduce the category "women" as a legitimate subject—indeed, a priority—of policy. It follows that violence against women will be more effectively addressed where there is a women's policy machinery.

Virtually all of the countries in this study had created a women's policy machinery of some kind by 1994. There is great variety of form among these institutions: some are women's desks stationed in lowly subdepartments, as in Botswana; other policy machineries, such as those in Canada and Belgium, consist of a complex array of advisory bodies and agencies focused directly on service provision. Some policy machineries, such as that in Australia, include mechanisms through which women's movement activists can be included in national policymaking processes. Only Nauru had no women's policy machinery at all.

Perhaps unsurprisingly, these diverse institutional measures do not appear to have had a uniform effect on policy responsiveness to violence against women. Indeed, the very fact that nearly every country has such a policy machinery should suggest to us that its mere existence will not have much explanatory power. As Malloy (1999) notes, "conventional bureaucratic wisdom dismisses most agencies as peripheral to actual decision-making and irrelevant except as external political symbols" (Malloy 1999, 268).

As we have noted, in order to improve policy responsiveness, the women's policy agency must have sufficient power to coordinate policy across a variety of sectors. The mere presence of a women's policy machinery may not be as important as having an *effective* women's policy machinery. A token advisor at a low level in the department of sports and tourism should not be expected to have the same effect on policy as a women's office that has strong support from and interaction with women's movements, considerable resources, and a mandate to use those resources to comment across departmental divisions on a wide range of government policy issues of concern to women. Indeed, we should not expect minimal, superficial reforms to have any effect at all, but we should expect a major institutional reform to have some effect. But how can we determine which reforms are likely to be effective and which are not?

THE EFFECTIVENESS OF WOMEN'S POLICY AGENCIES

Mazur and Stetson (1995) have developed a typology of women's policy machineries based on their cross-national analysis of women's policy machineries and equal employment opportunity policy in twelve countries (fig. 5-1). For each women's policy machinery, they ask whether the institution has the capacity to influence policy outcomes and whether it provides access to women's advocacy organizations. Having categorized the agencies according to these criteria, Mazur and Stetson ask what determines these two features of women's policy machineries. They examine the impact of organizational forms, political culture, politics of establishing the agency, and the form of the women's movement. Since we have already discussed the last three, let us stay focused here on the first explanatory factor, organizational form. Mazur and Stetson observe that a women's policy machinery is more effective when it has broad, cross-sectoral responsibility than when it has a primarily advisory capacity or is at a subdepartmental level, as is, for example, the Women's Bureau in the U.S. Department of Labor. While this is an interesting finding, Mazur and Stetson do not offer a theoretical account of why this is so.

The women's policy offices that Mazur and Stetson judge to be generally effective in influencing policy appear to have had some positive impact on government response to violence against women. Effective women's policy offices in Australia and France were apparently important in developing a response to violence against women. Indeed, in France, the main policy initiatives in this area seem to have stemmed from the work of the feminist activists who staffed the Ministère des Droits de la Femme (MDF) until 1986.

Level of Policy Influence	High Level of Policy Access	Low Level of Policy Acces
High	Australia, OSW The Netherlands, DCE Norway, NESC Denmark, DESC	Sweden, JÄMO Great Britain, EOC France, MDF
Low	Germany, FB United States, WB Canada, several	Ireland, MSWA, JOCWR Italy, ESC, ESONC

Source: Stetson and Mazur 1995, 277
Note: Spain is included in the original figure but is not shown here because it is considered a contrasting case and thus is not part of the initial development of the typology of state feminist offices.

Fig. 5-1. Stetson and Mazur's Comparative Typology of State Feminist Offices

Mazur (1995b) charts the ministry's influence as declining after 1985. But it was between 1980 and 1985 that the largest number of policy initiatives on violence against women were adopted in France. Similarly, in Australia, the establishment of the Women's Affairs Section in the Department of the Prime Minister and Cabinet in 1974, the expansions of the Section in 1975 and 1977, and, finally, the establishment of the Office of the Status of Women in 1982 preceded, and may have facilitated, the Australian government's response.

Mazur and Stetson develop their assessments of effectiveness based on their measures of the impact of women's policy offices on equal employment policy. This study of violence-against-women policies suggests that the differential outcomes observed by Mazur and Stetson may be an artifact of the policy issue they chose to examine (John and Cole 2000). For example, Elman (1995) notes that the Swedish policy agency Jämställdhetsenheten, or JÄMO (The Equality Affairs Division in the Ministry of Public Administration), was "conspicuously absent" from the development of policies to address violence against women. Similarly, the Norwegian Equal Status Council, categorized as a high-access, high-policy-impact agency by Mazur and Stetson, has had little impact on policymaking with respect to abortion or crisis centers, two issues that have been very important to the women's movement (Van Der Ros 1994). Conversely, Canada's "low-influence" women's policy machinery played a critical role in developing policies to address violence against women. In Ireland, the women's policy machinery, although fragmented and somewhat haphazard, successfully promoted the issue of violence against women, resulting in major policy reform between 1994 and 1997. Yet Mazur and Stetson judge the women's policy machinery in Ireland to be among the least effective of the twelve cases. Similarly despite the "high-influence, high-access" machineries in Denmark and the Netherlands, these countries have adopted fewer policies to address violence against women. Thus, three of the four countries where Mazur and Stetson judge the women's policy machinery to be most effective—the Netherlands, Norway, and Denmark—are not the countries that are developing the most progressive and comprehensive policies to address violence against women. Of these three, the most responsive is Norway, but the very effective policy machineries in the Netherlands and Denmark have done very little to address violence against women.

Many of the women's policy agencies Mazur and Stetson identify are, in fact, equal opportunity offices within the ministry for employment. It is no wonder that offices designed to monitor equal opportunity have a greater impact on that specific policy area than offices that have a broader mandate. For example, it is not surprising that the Netherlands' Department for the Coordination of Equality Policy, situated in the Ministry of Social Affairs and Employment, had a greater effect on equal employment policy than did Status of Women Canada, which had the broader responsibility of developing Canada's plan of action for the Decade of Women (1975–85) By 1982, Status of Women Canada had partially or fully implemented 96 percent of the plan. The main complaint about Status of Women Canada was that women's groups had too little input into the process. Yet Mazur and Stetson characterize Canada's women's policy agencies as high access and low influence.

These discrepancies suggest that developing a typology of effectiveness based on examination of the impact of women's policy machineries on a single policy area is not a good way to gauge the general effectiveness of agencies across countries. Rather than reasoning backward from policy outcomes, it seems better to develop a theoretical account of institutional effectiveness—of what would make women's policy machineries effective—and then use that account to examine whether these institutions are in fact effective.

WHEN WOMEN'S POLICY AGENCIES ARE EFFECTIVE

Mazur and Stetson categorize women's policy agencies according to whether they have an impact on policy. They point out that the agencies that had centralized, cross-sectoral approaches to promoting gender equality into mainstream policy were the most effective (1995, 288). These agen

ies must be set up to coordinate women's policies in an authoritative man-
ner, that is, they must have the positional or institutional power to direct
policymaking across a number of departments; a subdepartmental desk in a
low-ranking ministry is unlikely to be an effective policy machinery. Similarly, an agency with few or no resources will be unable to carry out the
wide-ranging yet detailed policy analysis required. In her study of equal opportunity programs, Cockburn (1991, 234) argues that for policies in this
area to be effective, the administrators must be housed in a "high and secure
place" in the hierarchy. These observations suggest that a women's policy
machinery must have a degree of independence, some of its own resources,
and positional authority in order to be consistently effective.

Independence is also important in order for the women's policy agency
to be able to influence the government agenda. As long as the agency is
merely a subdepartmental unit, women's concerns will be represented only
as part of a laundry list of departmental activities, and there is no guarantee
that they will receive prominence in the overall government agenda. However, where a women's policy machinery is an independent body that can
put forward its own agenda for integration into the government agenda, the
exclusion of women's issues cannot occur accidentally in the aggregating of
ministerial preferences. For example, if a women's issue is in second place
on each department's agenda, and the overall decision agenda takes only the
first issue from each department, then women's issues will be excluded, even
though they were given relatively high priority within each department. If a
women's ministry or commission has equal stature with other departments,
then the most important issue to women might have a chance of getting on
the government's list.

Women's policy machineries improve government response to violence
against women because they make it possible to address women's issues as
such, rather than mainly as issues of health, labor, or criminal justice. This
benefit of a women's policy machinery is lost if it is merely a subdepartment,
since the women's issue must fit into the policy orientation of the rest of the
department in order to be addressed effectively.

Where women's policy agencies have the institutional power to review
and comment on government policies across sectors, they can provide an
important corrective to male bias in other areas of the institution by providing women's perspective on policies before they are enacted. In some
cases, a process for "gender-based" analysis can be incorporated into all
policy processes (Beveridge, Nott, and Stephen 1998). In Australia in 1976,
women's offices were set up in every department to analyze the gender impact of public policies, and these "satellite" offices were connected to a
powerful central "hub" in the prime minister's office. In Canada, similarly,

a guide for gender-based analysis of policy has been developed for general use within the government.

EFFECTIVENESS AND ACCOUNTABILITY

Mazur and Stetson (1995) as well as the neoinstitutionalists direct our attention to the relationship between political institutions and organized groups and activists. Above, we noted that access by women's movements would be key to an institution's effectiveness on issues of concern to women.

Malloy (1999) argues that state advocacy structures, or "agencies nominally designated to advance the status of collective social movements in public policy and society," (267) operate under unique criteria for effectiveness. Bureaucratic notions of effectiveness suggest the ability to influence policy and to compel compliance with policy decisions inside and outside bureaucracies (268). But state advocacy structures such as women's policy agencies also face considerable pressure from social movements to provide a voice for the movement inside government—to perform a representative function.

Indeed, many social movement activists express frustration that such structures do not reflect the "goals and diversity of the movement" (Malloy 1999; see also Sawer 1995; and Brownmiller 1999). One Canadian activist noted that many of the representatives on the federal government's Canadian Panel to Address Violence Against Women were "tokens" of region and race and that they thus did not provide real representation. She noted:

> The panel should be composed of representatives/delegates of women's groups but it isn't. Each of the members is on her and his own . . . the government announced them as members of groups and as tokens of certain groups of women. We insist on their accountability and we'll support them only to the extent that they exercise that responsibility. But how the hell can Mobina Jaffer be expected to represent both [British Columbia's] interests and the interests of immigrant women? (Lakeman 1991, 5)

Social movement activists and democratic theorists have expressed the concern that the institutionalization of movements in state advocacy structures necessarily results in co-optation and diffuses the movement (Dryzek 1990; Everett 1998; Gelb 1995; Naples 1998; Malloy 1999). Professionalization of activists, in this view, creates an elite class that quickly loses touch

vith its grassroots base (Everett 1998; cf. Sawer 1995). Ferguson (1984) argues that there are powerful forces that suppress dissent within bureaucracies. An internal agency whose role is to dissent and to criticize other
government agencies will face considerable pressure to support the existing
set of government priorities and policies. Many femocrats report feeling
caught in the middle between women's movement demands and the internal
demands of the bureaucracy (Sproule 1998; Sawer 1995).

Recent research suggests that it is possible to agitate for change within
institutions (Katzenstein 1998; Sawer 1995; Gelb 1995; Reinelt 1995).
Naples (1998) observes that antipoverty activists in the United States have
found that increasing opportunities for participation by grassroots activists
can counteract antidemocratic tendencies in a bureaucracy. Matthews
1995) argues that feminist movement organizations in the United States
avoided co-optation or deradicalization by building coalitions with other
groups, both across groups of women and with labor, antipoverty, and civil
rights groups. (See also Naples 1998; and Hoskyns 1996.)

Women's policy machineries must include mechanisms of accountability
to ensure that there is an independent source of pressure on the agency to
maintain a critical stance toward government policy (cf. Dryzek 1990).
Regular, public interaction between government officials and women's
movement activists may go some way toward counterbalancing internal bureaucratic pressures to limit participation by grassroots activists. Public
consultations, for example, can ensure that lines of communication between
professional and grassroots activists remain open. Such consultations have
become a routine part of environmental policymaking in the United States.
There is usually greater diversity among activists at the grassroots level than
there is among professionals, who are more likely to be middle class and
formally educated (Bystydzienski and Sekhon 1999, 385). Thus, consultative relationships can improve the representative function of the women's
policy machinery by keeping bureaucrats better informed about, and thus
better equipped to articulate, the goals and diversity of the movement. The
extra visibility that public consultations can give to women's movement demands can also strengthen the women's policy machinery internally in
terms of its dealings with other departments. They can refer to the demands
of their constituency as the reason for making certain types of requests or
demands themselves (Hoskyns 1996).

As noted, both Malloy (1999) and Mazur and Stetson (1995) identify
access by women's movements as an important aspect of the effectiveness
of women's policy agencies. In Costa Rica, the women's policy machinery
has been an important partner to the women's movement in addressing vi-

olence against women, helping to organize demonstrations and fund crisis centers. Indeed, such access can be both formal and informal. Where access is through informal channels, it usually depends on good relations between women's movement representatives and individual bureaucrats in the policy agency. Thus, at some times and in some areas, women's movements may be very effective because the individuals with whom they ally within the policy machinery feel responsible to women's organizations (Mansbridge 1995). But if these individuals are removed, the policy agency can suddenly become less responsive and less connected to women's groups (Mazur 1995b).

If consultation with women's groups is a formal part of the policy agency, then access is likely to be less capricious and more uniform across policy areas and over time. It may be more difficult for new administrations (who may be hostile to women's groups) to shut women's organizations out of the policymaking process when formal, regularized channels for consultation exist.

Thus, effective women's policy machineries have (1) the independence and resources needed to formulate and implement aspects of a women's agenda; and (2) formalized channels of access for activists and organizations. Note that these criteria concern the design of institutions, not policy impact itself. The hypothesis is that institutions with these characteristics will be more effective. Thus, they should have a greater impact on policy processes than institutions without resources and independence.

The women's policy agencies in the thirty-six stable democracies in this study are categorized according to these criteria in figure 5-2. Only eight of the thirty-four agencies meet both criteria for effectiveness: the policy machineries in Australia, Canada, Costa Rica, the Netherlands, Belgium, Venezuela, Portugal, and Germany.

We would expect that the countries having an effective women's policy machinery would have more comprehensive policies on violence against women. We can use statistical analysis to examine the relationship between the presence of an effective institution and responsiveness to violence against women, coding the governments in the top left-hand box 1 and the others 0.

The presence of an effective institution is associated with between two and four additional areas of government policy action (see table 5-1). Even in the context of a variety of other possible explanatory factors, an effective women's policy machinery stands out as the only one with a sizeable, significant association with a more comprehensive government response.

However, there is considerable variation in responsiveness among the countries in which an effective women's policy machinery has been established; the government of Venezuela failed to introduce even one initiative

	Formal Policy Access by Activists	No Formal Access for Activists
Institutional Power (Organizational Independence and Position Power)	Australia Canada Costa Rica Netherlands Belgium Venezuela Portugal Germany	France Austria New Zealand Trinidad & Tobago Spain Italy Colombia
No Organizational Independence or Resources	Luxembourg U.S. Denmark Iceland Ireland Bahamas U.K.	Botswana Norway Italy Sweden Finland Switzerland India Israel Japan Mauritius Greece Jamaica Barbados

Note: Nauru is not categorized here because there is no women's policy machinery in Nauru.

Fig. 5-2. Proposed Typology of State Feminist Offices, 35 Countries

by 1994, while Canada and Australia had introduced all seven possible policy initiatives. So although it appears that effective women's policy machineries significantly affect policy responsiveness to violence against women, it is not clear under what conditions they will have such an effect. I turn to this question in the next chapter.

INSTITUTIONS IN FEMINIST POLICY ANALYSIS

Feminist analyses of the welfare state have not adequately explored the effects of *variation* in political institutional structures on policy. One group of explanations are what Duncan (1995) calls "gendered welfare state models." These models complement the typologies of welfare state regimes developed by Esping-Andersen (1990) with gendered measures of welfare

Table 5-1: Coefficients, Dependent Variable = Scope of Government Response,
36 Countries, 1994

Model/ Independent Variables	B	Std. Error	Beta	t	Sig.	R-square
1/ Effective women's policy machinery	2.68	0.86	0.47	3.12	0.00	0.22
2/ Effective women's policy machinery	2.87	0.89	0.47	3.21	0.00	0.47
Strong, autonomous women's movement	1.17	0.58	0.30	2.00	0.05	
GNP per capita	0.00	0.00	0.34	2.23	0.03	
Number of women cabinet members	0.00	0.03	-0.02	-0.16	0.88	
3/ Strong, autonomous women's movement	1.43	0.56	0.36	2.57	0.02	0.42
Effective women's policy machinery	1.86	0.81	0.33	2.29	0.03	
Level of development	1.25	0.56	0.30	2.24	0.03	

state development, such as the degree to which women are able to establish households without a male present (Orloff 1993). The problem with these models, as feminist critics have noted, is that they are descriptive rather than explanatory (Duncan 1995; Lewis 1993). They are mostly aimed at typologizing welfare state impacts rather than at delineating the dynamics of welfare state development. Moreover, these approaches tend to equate the state itself with policy outcomes. The outcomes of policies, such as variations in the wage gap between men and women, are taken as indicators of the kind of welfare state one is examining. Taking this approach makes it impossible to separate political institutions and social policy analytically, and thus also makes it impossible to ask what impact change in political institutions has on social policy.

Feminist sociological approaches still appear to collapse the state and social policy, and to give little analytic attention to the state itself. For example, one major approach to analyzing the gender systems refers to "gender contracts": state policies are said to reflect historic compromises between gender groups. As Duncan (1995, 96) notes, "Rather than being a pre-eminent actor, the state reflects these contracts through its policies, rather than initiating them." But the process by which policy outcomes come to reflect these historic compromises is not at all clear. Somehow, the state (which is again equivalent to policy here) reflects a form of social organization. Similarly, Walby (1990) identifies the state as one of six mechanisms that create male dominance over women. Although specific state policies may appear to undermine gender oppression, overall the patriarchal state works as part of a gender system that subordinates women. But, as I have argued throughout this book, sometimes state agencies are important forces for undermining male dominance and reinforcing women's movements. Thus, feminist theorists need a more nuanced theory of public administrative structures and how they affect policies.

Recently, many feminist analysts have turned their attention to political institutions, providing us with important insights as to how institutions matter to women (Brown 1992; Duerst-Lahti and Kelly 1995; Staudt 1997; Stetson and Mazur 1995). This work explores, for example, the effect of committee structures and women's policy machineries on policy. Nevertheless, we still have no theoretical account of why some public bureaucracies are more responsive to women's concerns than others. Thus, feminist theory still cannot answer a key question raised by the results of this study: why do women's policy agencies make governments more responsive to violence against women?

I have argued that political institutions, unless they are reformed, tend to reflect the perspective and interests of historically dominant groups. This is because these political institutions have been designed and shaped by members of privileged classes or castes. But this bias is a contingent product of historical processes, not a necessary or permanent feature of political institutions. Biases can be at least partially ameliorated by changing the language and categories of government and the distribution of resources within government.

This possibility for change explains why the creation of effective women's policy agencies makes governments more responsive to violence against women. Women's policy machineries provide a base for policy research, for critical review of policy, and for administration of policy issues—such as violence against women—that would otherwise fall into the cracks between government departments. The establishment of women's policy machineries partially corrects for the organization of government around the priorities of historically dominant groups of men.

INSTITUTIONS MATTER FOR COMPARATIVE SOCIAL POLICY

Conventional explanations for the development of social policy do not appear to provide much insight into the important issue of government policy on violence against women. For example, as I noted in chapter 2, policy development in this area is not linear. Policies are adopted and then canceled. Legal reforms are revoked, and funding is withdrawn. In times of fiscal restraint and economic recession, policies on violence are expanded. This suggests that policy on violence against women is not a simple response to economic changes, and that it does not follow a universal pattern of convergence. Indeed, there is only a very weak relationship between level of development and government responsiveness to violence against women.

Nor is policy a direct product of conflict among social groups (Korpi 1978; Bock and Thane 1991). As we have seen, political institutions are critical to determining the scope of policies on violence against women. In Italy and the United States, a well-organized social group (women) agitated for national policy action on violence against women without much success for nearly twenty years. Similar action elsewhere produced policy responses much sooner. Thus, social conflict alone cannot explain policy development.

My analysis suggests that institutional factors made the difference. Changes in the structure of political institutions made some governments more responsive to women's movements than others. This suggests that the structure of public administration is of primary importance for understanding the development of social policy.

GENDER AFFECTS INSTITUTIONAL CAPACITY

Examining how social structures of gender shape institutional processes provides a more complete explanation for variation in policies on violence against women. Specifically, we understand that institutions are likely to be biased against women's issues and concerns unless they are reformed. This is true because social norms, practices, and laws regarding the relationship between the masculine and the feminine (gender) become reflected in the organization of political institutions. Where these relations are unequal, that inequality is also reflected in institutional structures that formalize, for example, the notion of a breadwinner (male) as distinct from a primary caregiver (female). Creating an effective women's policy machinery helps to ameliorate the bias in a public administrative structure that is not organized around women's concerns.

Note that this is not a question of the number of women in political office, nor is it a question of providing access points for social movements. Rather, the point is that the capacity of government to respond is curtailed in relation to a specific group—women. If the account I have provided is correct, it is likely that administrative structures are in some respects biased against other marginalized groups, such as the poor and ethnic or racial minorities. Historical and current relations among groups shape government capacities. The imprint of these group relations on political institutions creates group-specific institutional constraints. In other words, institutional effectiveness varies according to which group's concerns are being examined. This calls into question the neoinstitutionalist assumption that there are group-neutral institutional capacities (such as information gathering).

CONCLUSION

It appears that institutional reforms can greatly improve policy responsiveness to violence against women. Neither feminist theory nor neoinstitutionalist theories of policymaking alone can account for this finding. By combining and extending these bodies of theory, I have shown that political institutions are gendered, that is, they are implicated in creating and sustaining relations between the masculine and the feminine.

More importantly, institutional reforms can make political institutions more responsive to issues of concern to women and to social movements more generally. This suggests that political institutions ought to be given a more central place in feminist theory, and that theories of institutions ought to attend to the ways that gender and other axes of social stratification limit institutional effectiveness. If policy responsiveness to the most vulnerable groups (such as women, minorities, and the disabled) can be addressed by institutional reform, then we may have discovered a powerful new way to deepen democracy.

6

Social Movements, Political Institutions, and Public Policies on Violence Against Women

■We have seen that a particular type of institutional structure, an effective women's policy machinery, seems to improve government responsiveness to violence against women. However, an effective women's policy machinery does not, on its own, guarantee that there will be any government response to violence against women. We also know that although women's movements are the catalysts for government action in this area, they are sometimes unsuccessful in provoking government response. Thus, while both women's movements and political institutional structures are important, neither phenomenon alone seems adequate to explain the wide variation across countries in government responsiveness to violence against women.

In this chapter, I show that it is the interaction between women's movements and political institutions that best explains government responsiveness to violence against women. Both statistical analysis and historical accounts of policy development in Canada and Australia support this finding. The evidence also suggests that the argument holds, to some degree, for policy development as it affects marginalized subgroups of women.

THE LIMITS OF EFFECTIVE WOMEN'S POLICY MACHINERIES

When they provide access to activists and have sufficient resources, women's policy agencies can improve government responsiveness to violence against women. But sometimes, it appears, these agencies and offices have little or no effect on government responsiveness. Although eight national governments among the thirty-six stable democracies considered here have a women's policy machinery that meets the criteria for institutional effectiveness (outlined in chapter 5), only three of these (Canada, Australia, and Costa Rica) are among the most responsive countries, that is, those addressing five or more areas of policy (see table 6-1). Moreover, some national governments with effective women's institutions (such as Portugal and Germany) are addressing only two of seven areas of policy. Venezuela had not undertaken any action to address violence against women by 1994.

Venezuela, Germany, and Portugal are also characterized by the absence of a strong, autonomous women's movement. We know that women's movements are important for articulating the issue of violence against women but are, on their own, unlikely to produce a broad, multifaceted government response. We also know that the presence of an effective women's policy machinery is strongly related to the scope of government response. This suggests that the relationship between institutional structure and policy outcome may be an interactive one, that is, it may depend on the *interaction* between women's movements and institutional structure.

THE INTERACTION OF INSTITUTIONS AND WOMEN'S MOVEMENTS

Women's movements and effective women's policy machineries interact to improve government responsiveness to violence against women. Understanding the interaction between these elements is key to understanding the effect of each on violence-against-women policy, and to understanding their joint effect.

An effective women's policy machinery can strengthen a women's movement. By providing research support and opportunities for input on policy development, women's policy machineries can greatly increase the effectiveness of women's movement activists. In addition, by giving financial support for organizing and for independent research, women's policy machineries provide additional resources to women's organizations. These agencies also offer continuity over time for women's movement activists— sort of institutional memory. Instead of having to spend their energies re-

Table 6-1: Responsiveness of Eight National Governments with Effective Policy Machineries, 1994

Country	Strong, Autonomous Women's Movement	Percent of Women in Cabinet	No. of Policy Areas Addressed
Australia	Yes	12.9	7
Belgium	Yes	11.1	4
Canada	Yes	13.6	7
Costa Rica	Yes (after 1984)	9.5	5
Germany	No	5.2	2
Netherlands	Yes	10.3	3
Portugal	No	5.1	2
Venezuela	No	0.0	0

Source: UN 1995c.

educating each new policymaker about past efforts, activists can work to improve existing policies.

Duerst-Lahti (1989) has shown that the state commissions on the status of women in the United States played a very important role in the development of the women's movement, providing research, funding, and other organizational resources. The state commissions thereby strengthened the nascent women's movement, and they were especially critical in its transition from a loose collection of dispersed local movements to a national movement.

Conversely, strong, autonomous women's movements improve the institutional capabilities of government to address women's issues. When the women's movement is a significant political force, the women's policy machinery has more leverage over other government departments. Government departments will want to avoid conflict with activists and will want to be able to show that their policies take women's concerns into account; and bureaucrats inside the women's policy machinery can point to demands from the women's movement when asking for increased funding and other resources.

Increased leverage on the part of the women's policy machinery improves the institutional capability to coordinate policy action across departments and to revise departmental agendas to reflect women's priorities. Women's policy machineries can also provide the research support and analytic focus required for sound policy design and evaluation. A strong women's movement therefore improves the capacity of a set of political institutions to respond to women's concerns, when that set includes a women's policy agency.

Thus, strong, autonomous women's movements and effective women's policy agencies reinforce one another. This effect is not purely additive; it is interactive. Each factor magnifies the effect of the other.

POLICY DEVELOPMENT IN THE MOST RESPONSIVE GOVERNMENTS

Does the account developed above seem to explain the process of policy development in the most responsive countries? I focus on the most responsive countries as a form of plausibility probe: if the development of policy in these eight countries cannot be explained by the account I have developed, then it is possible that I am not accurately interpreting the relationships I have discovered, or that they are an artifact of the measurements I am using, or of the year on which I have chosen to focus. After establishing the plausibility of the theoretical account, I examine whether the statistical analysis supports the account.

I consider those governments addressing five or more areas to be the most responsive. There are eight governments in this category: Australia, Canada, the United States, France, Costa Rica, Israel, New Zealand, and Ireland. I focus both on explaining why these countries were more responsive and on accounting for the variation in responsiveness across these eight governments. Why are they more responsive than the other democratic governments identified in this study? Furthermore, why are Canada and Australia even more responsive than the others?

The process of policy development in these eight governments appears to conform to the hypothesized pattern. In every case, it was the women's movement that first articulated the issue of violence against women and pressed for government action. And every country had a strong, autonomous women's movement.

In all eight countries, powerful insiders who took up the demands of the women's movement placed violence against women on the government agenda. Strategically placed allies of the women's movement were also important in retaining the feminist content of legislation despite pressure to the contrary. In Ireland in 1987, for example, a submission by a rape crisis center to a nonpartisan committee of legislators resulted in a public report recommending policy reforms. Feminist bureaucrats inside the Irish government helped ensure that there was such a committee in the first place and that the final policy recommendations reflected the original ones from the rape crisis center (Mahon 1995). Following this report, there was a significant expansion in the Irish government's response to this problem. The government began addressing more areas after the publication of the report (with these new measures taking effect in 1990) and continues to improve its response (Ireland, Office of the Tanaiste, 1997c). Similarly, the response by the Costa Rican government appears to be a product of cooperation between feminists in a government agency (the Center for the Development of Women and the Family) and a variety of women's organizations. In the United States, the proposals of organized women's groups were taken up by sympathetic legislators both in the early policy initiatives of the 1970s and in the case of the Violence Against Women Act, passed in 1994. Although male legislators played an important role in the passage of the act, it appears that a feminist in the office of Senator Joseph Biden was key to retaining the feminist content of the bill despite pressure from Senator Orrin Hatch to the contrary. The women's caucus also seems to have played a role (Gelb 1998).

These examples illustrate the general pattern of policy development in this area: independent women's movements partner with feminist insiders to achieve policy change. This explains why some democracies with strong, autonomous women's movements have been able to procure government action on violence while others have not. I stress that it is feminist allies in influential positions, rather than simply women in government, who provide the window of opportunity.

In order to explain policy development in the two most responsive countries, however, we must examine the interaction of the institutional structure—the women's policy machinery—with the women's movement. Why did the government response in Canada and Australia not remain limited to a primarily criminal justice response, as it did in the United States? Why was the response not restricted to a focus on domestic violence, as it was in New Zealand and Ireland? Why did it go beyond the partial response of France and Costa Rica? In Canada and Australia, the relationship between women's movements and their internal allies was particularly effective because of the presence of an effective women's policy machinery. Feminist bureaucrats working inside the government worked with women's movements and with the resources of the women's policy machinery to get violence on the government agenda and to ensure feminist input into the policymaking process.

The national governments of Australia and Canada first began addressing the issue of violence against women in 1975. Since that time, there has been a proliferation of institutions designed to improve the status of women in both countries. This institutionalization has provided a permanent point of contact and an institutional memory that has strengthened both the women's movement and its allies within government. The institutionalization has made the difference between the fleeting window of opportunity provided by the election of legislative allies and the more long-term possibility of the ongoing development of government response with critiques and suggestions from the women's movement. It has also provided the institutional framework needed for a comprehensive, cross-sectoral response to violence against women.

Australia

Beginning Government Action on Violence Against Women (1973–1975)

Most discussions of the development of violence-against-women policy in Australia stress the role of the women's policy machinery, which has been very active in promoting a women's policy agenda but also in attempting to strengthen the women's movement (Sawer 1995; Eisenstein 1995). In 1973, the first women's advisor to the prime minister, Elizabeth Reid, was appointed in response to the demands of a strong, autonomous women's movement. Reid's role was "quasi-ministerial," and she announced that all policy and programs would henceforth be subject to a "gender audit" and that all cabinet submissions would have to include "impact on women" statements.

Reid was critical to the development of policies on violence against women in Australia. In her two years as head of the Women's Affairs Section, she was responsible for the initiation of federal government funding for women's refuges (for domestic violence) and for rape crisis centers (Sawer 1995).

Expansion of the Women's Policy Machinery (1976–1984)

In 1976, the Women's Affairs Section became the nucleus of a network of women's policy units that were established in each department. In the same year, the prime minister's advisor on women's issues formally attained ministerial status, with the appointment of a Minister Assisting the Prime Minister on Women's Affairs. The portfolio remains to this day, although in 1982 the Women's Affairs Section was renamed the Office of the Status of Women.[1]

The structure of the women's policy machinery was adopted on the recommendation of the Women's Electoral Lobby, which proposed the network, or hub, model in a 1974 submission to the Royal Commission on Australian Government Administration. Regular interaction with women's groups through a variety of formal mechanisms of consultation helped develop close relationships between women's organizations and government officials (Sawer 1995). For example, a federal advisory body, the National Women's Consultative Council, was established in 1984. This body (which is now defunct) was composed of women's organization representatives.

Expansion of Government Response to Violence (1987–1989)

In the late 1980s, the Office of the Status of Women housed the Commonwealth/State Domestic Violence Coordinating Task Force (which in 1990 became the Commonwealth/State National Committee on Violence Against Women). In 1987, the National Domestic Violence Education Programme was announced (Australia, Commonwealth Office of the Status of Women 2000c). This program articulated the feminist position that "the answer to the abuse of male power lay in the empowerment of women" (Sawer 1995, 86).

In addition, although criminal law is mainly a state responsibility, the national government has worked to ensure uniformity in statutes at the state level, and it has also worked to develop model legislation to address both domestic violence and rape. Women's organizations have been involved in consultations during the process of formulating these reforms. There have also been many public education initiatives to address violence against women. For example, the national government funded two major campaigns against domestic violence ("Real men don't bash and rape women") and sexual violence ("Read my lips—no means no") (Australia, Commonwealth Office of the Status of Women 1997).

Policy Agencies for Aboriginal Women (1984–1987)

Also in the late 1980s, government machinery for Aboriginal women expanded. From 1979 to 1983, Aboriginal women activists pressured the government to establish a task force on Aboriginal women that would recognize their importance in discussions of land rights, which were usually dominated by white and Aboriginal men (Bell 1994; Sawer 1995).

In 1984, the Aboriginal Women's Unit was established in the Commonwealth Department of Aboriginal Affairs (Australia, Commonwealth Office of the Status of Women 2000c; Sawer 1995). The Office of the Status of Women, responding to the pressure from Aboriginal women, helped initiate consultations with Aboriginal women on the issue of land rights (Sawer 1995). In 1987, the Aboriginal Women's Initiatives Programme was established in the Aboriginal and Torres Strait Islanders Commission (ATSIC) (Australia, Minister for Aboriginal and Torres Strait Islander Affairs 2000). However, these programs for Aboriginal women did not yet include measures to address violence against women.

Violence and Differences Between Women (1990–1994)

In the early 1990s, it became apparent that targeted programs were needed before general reforms on violence against women would have a positive effect for Aboriginal women. Research began to show that Aboriginal women were far more likely to be subjected to violence against women than were non-Aboriginal women. One government report claims that "in some areas the rate of family violence involving Aboriginal women is 45 times higher than for non-Aboriginal women and Aboriginal women are ten times more likely to be killed as a result of family violence" (Australia, Commonwealth Office of the Status of Women 2000b).Yet in 1991, there was only one all-Aboriginal refuge, and geographic barriers, cultural barriers, and racism among women meant that many Aboriginal women did not feel comfortable seeking refuge in general women's shelters. Moreover, government legal aid services for Aboriginal people only funded defendants in domestic violence disputes (usually men), leaving those placing charges (usually women) without funding for legal representation. In addition, legal reforms that focused on prosecuting male *partners* were of less help to Aboriginal women, who were often subjected to violence from family members other than their partners (Bolger 1991).

In 1989, the Remote Areas Domestic Violence project was set up with funding from the Department of Aboriginal Affairs. Under this project, two women would regularly visit remote communities to discuss problems (Bolger 1991). In 1991, the Office of the Status of Women began focusing on domestic violence in Aboriginal communities. In 1992, the ATSIC established the Family Violence Intervention Programme. In spite of these efforts, however, there was still great difficulty in the early 1990s in conducting public discussion of violence against women in Aboriginal communities (Bell 1994). In spite of the pervasiveness of violence against Aboriginal women and their widespread dissatisfaction with it (Bell 1994; Bolger 1991), there was little in the way of an organized effort by Aboriginal women to address the problem. Only a few Aboriginal women agitated against the violence at this time, and many white feminists were wary of speaking out for fear of appearing to impose their views on the Aboriginal community (Bell 1994).

During the same period, there was increased public attention to violence against women of racial and ethnic minorities. In 1993, the government undertook to study violence in ethnic communities (Australia 2000a), but Eisenstein (1995, 77) notes that issues of racial minority women were just being raised within the women's movement in Australia in the mid-1990s. Sawer (1995) points out that Aboriginal issues have been a traditional concern of the women's movement in Australia, but a government report on women published in 2000 states that discussion of family violence in Aboriginal communities is relatively new. In 2000, the Australian government announced a number of measures designed specifically to address violence against non-English-speaking women and indigenous women (Australia, Commonwealth Office of the Status of Women 2000b). The degree to which these initiatives will be implemented remains to be seen, but as of 1994, little action was being taken to address violence against Aboriginal and minority women—and, indeed, the need for government action was only beginning to be publicly articulated.

Continued Expansion of General Programs on Violence (1992–1994)

The Australian national government continued to develop and extend its general programming on violence against women throughout the early 1990s. In 1992, it launched a community education program called Stop Violence Against Women. In 1993, an integrated strategy known as the National Strategy on Violence Against Women was launched. By this time, the Australian national government was addressing all seven potential policy areas and was continuing to develop more policies and programs to improve government response.

This is not to say that national policy responsiveness to violence against women in Australia is perfect or complete. Certainly, there are many areas that remain to be addressed. More programming for minority and Aboriginal women is one obvious gap, but there are needs in many other areas as well. Indeed, as policy responses develop, there is increasing awareness of the need for better and more extensive programming in public education, training for police and social workers, advocacy programs, support services, funding for shelters and crisis centers, and so on. The point is that in 1994, the Australian government had adopted more policy initiatives in more areas than any other democratic government in the world except Canada.

Moreover, although much remains to be done, these efforts were far from symbolic. In 1992–93, the government was devoting $56 million for 263 refuges and shelters, between sixty and seventy crisis centers for sexual assault, and fifty counseling services (Government of Australia 1993; Sawer

1995; United Nations 1993). Sawer (1995, 86) notes that the majority of the government-funded refuges are "run in accordance with feminist collec- tivist principles." Several million dollars were also devoted to public educa- tion programs that put forth a feminist analysis of violence against women. This constitutes a significant amount of money devoted to feminist services for women and feminist analyses of violence against women.

In short, the national government of Australia is providing funding for shelters, crisis centers, public education, legal aid, housing assistance, coun- seling, and research on violence against women. National laws are being amended in attempts to better address the reality of violence against women. Some democratic governments are providing none of these services, and no government is providing services or programming in more areas. Even if these services are flawed or need supplementing, this difference in policy responsiveness is certainly worth explaining.

Explaining Policy Development in Australia

It seems that the women's policy machinery in Australia, particularly the Office of the Status of Women, was important not only in getting govern- ment action on the issue of violence against women, but also in ensuring that a feminist perspective was reflected in the policies that the office pro- duced. For example, a feminist bureaucrat, Helen L'Orange, in the Office of the Status of Women "played a key role in ensuring that feminist analysis re- mained central to government strategies on violence against women (i.e. that the root cause was gender inequalities in power)" (Sawer 1995, 34). In addition, feminists in the women's policy machinery (such as Elizabeth Reid) were crucial agents in getting violence against women on the govern- ment agenda and getting funding for shelters and crisis centers. Through consultative mechanisms set up by the government, women's movement representatives, including representatives from shelters and crisis centers, have had the opportunity to provide input into some important policy deci- sions.

The women's movement in Australia has been a key agent for articulat- ing the issue of violence against women and for creating political pressure for a policy response. But the Office of the Status of Women has also been important. It developed a women's policy agenda through a process that in- cluded extensive consultations with women's movement organizations. It worked to get issues of violence against women on the government agenda and eventually coordinated a national body on the problem. Bureaucrats in the office pushed for the framing of rape and domestic violence as issues of violence against women, and they were critical to the continued conceptualization of violence against women as a problem of gender inequality. This was particularly important at the stage of policy formulation and implementation.

Canada

Getting Violence on the Government Agenda (1967–1979)
Feminist activists and the women's policy machinery played a similarly critical role in the development of government response to violence against women in Canada. In 1967, the Royal Commission on the Status of Women was established in response to demands from the women's movement. Feminists criticized the report of the commission for not including discussion of violence against women, already an important issue for the women's movement.

In 1976, Status of Women Canada was established to "coordinate policy with respect to the status of women and to administer related programs" (Geller-Schwartz 1995). Other institutional mechanisms, such as the Women's Programme under the Secretary of State and the Canadian Advisory Council on the Status of Women (CACSW), were also created in the late 1970s. The Women's Programme provided funding to women's organizations such as independently run rape crisis centers and battered women's shelters (Gotell 1998). The CACSW is an independent, or "arm's-length," body funded by the federal government. Its mandate was to advise the government and inform the public on issues of concern to women (Burt 1998). It reported to the Minister Responsible for the Status of Women, and its members were appointed by an Order-in-Council.

Status of Women Canada had the broad responsibility for developing Canada's plan of action for the Decade of Women (1975–85). Increasing pressure from the women's movement for action on women's issues finally resulted in a general plan: *Toward Equality for Women,* released by the Office of the Status of Women in 1979. In this document, the government identified violence against women as one of its areas of concern. "The release of *Toward Equality for Women* . . . marked a tentative recognition of 'violence against women' as a site of policy intervention and began a decade that would see the development of a set of institutional responses to violence" (Gotell 1998, 42). The document made a number of commitments, one of which was to undertake a major study of violence against spouses and women, violence in the family, and crisis assistance in communities. This study was to be conducted as a cooperative effort involving at least three different departments.

In the same year, the CACSW decided to do its own research on the topic, and to focus specifically on wife battering. The result was the publication in January 1980 of *Wife Battering in Canada: The Vicious Circle.* This was the first Canadian book on the subject.

The CACSW developed a strategy to raise public awareness of the issue of battering and thereby to pressure other government agencies to act. As a follow-up to the book, the CACSW organized a series of consultations with the women's movement to allow battered women and the women who work with them to have a voice in the discussion. In the process, the council was able to fund women's organizations outside the state. In fact, during 1981–1982, nearly one-fifth of Women's Programme grants from the Secretary of State had violence against women as the primary issue. These efforts created a great deal of public awareness of the issue of wife battering.

In 1982, the report that came out of the consultations was published (Canada, CACSW 1982). Its recommendations for action on wife battering included special training for the RCMP (Royal Canadian Mounted Police); funding for shelters, research, and batterers' programs; programs to publicize the problem; and a federal-provincial conference on violence against women. The report encouraged the provinces to adopt mandatory arrest policies in suspected cases of wife abuse.

Government Action on Violence Against Women (1979–1986)

It appears that this report—the product of cooperation between women's groups and bureaucrats working in the CACSW—was successful in getting violence on the decision agenda and in provoking some government response. Over the next few years, the national government undertook more policy initiatives to address violence against women. Within a year, a national clearinghouse was established to disseminate information on family violence. In 1979 and 1983, the federal government enacted changes to the criminal code's rape provisions. The 1983 amendments criminalized a broader set of behaviors under the new heading of sexual assault, and marital rape and sexual touching without intercourse became criminal acts for the first time. The first rape shield provision and other evidentiary amendments were made in order to improve reporting and conviction rates (Gotell 1998).

By 1985, the women's movement had become so strong that one prominent journalist called it the most powerful lobby in Canada (Geller-Schwartz 1995). In that year, the main English-speaking national women's organization, the National Action Committee (NAC), established a set of policy committees, one of which focused on violence against women. Since

1985, the federal government has spent over $200 million on programs to address the issue of family violence. A significant proportion of this money was allocated to abused-wife shelter facilities through Project Haven, under the Canada Mortgage and Housing Corporation (CMHC).

In 1986, the Family Violence Prevention Unit was established in Health and Welfare Canada, charged with education and with coordination of federal activities in this area. In 1988, the government initiated the $40 million Family Violence Initiative to coordinate action on violence against women, children, and older adults by seven government departments. This initiative includes funding for shelters and second-stage housing for victims of domestic violence, legal reform, policy review, funding for community organizations, public education, service provider education, and community-based initiatives for the prevention of sexual assault. Status of Women Canada has responsibility for monitoring developments and making policy recommendations in the area of violence against women. It also has responsibility for coordinating funding for women's groups, for organizing consultations with women's groups, and for coordinating and consulting with the provincial ministers for the status of women.

Policies on Violence Against Aboriginal and Minority Women (1986–1989)

In the late 1980s, the federal government also began to get involved in some programming on violence targeted toward minority and Aboriginal women. The Family Violence Initiative included projects funded in Aboriginal communities starting in 1986. In addition, Health and Welfare Canada funded a pilot program run by Family Services of Greater Vancouver "to translate their present program and resources into other languages and to begin to bridge cultural gaps" (MacLeod and Shin 1990, 23). This mainly involved Spanish-language support groups for mothers, fathers, and children in families in which there had been wife abuse (23). In 1988, the CACSW published *Immigrant Women in Canada: A Policy Perspective.* This report was criticized by immigrant women's groups for its failure to consult with immigrant women, and it was eventually withdrawn from circulation in response to objections from these groups (Burt 1998, 134). Overall, by the end of the 1980s, the Canadian government had still done very little to address the distinct needs of minority women in Canada.

Expanding Government Response to Violence (1990–1994)

At the turn of the decade, however, the Canadian federal government response was expanded and revised further under pressure from women's movements in the wake of the 1991 Montreal Massacre. Women's organizations effectively presented a feminist interpretation of the event as a manifestation of the general problem of violence against women. As Gotell (1998, 51) notes, "The terror of the Montreal Massacre brought into stark relief feminist claims about the extreme consequences of 'violence against women.'" Feminists demanded that the government recognize December 6 as a national day of mourning for women victims of violence. Legislators ultimately did recognize the date as a national day of recognition of the problem of violence against women.

In 1991, a new Family Violence Initiative was established, which resulted in $50 million spent by seven departments over the years 1991–94. In the same year, the Status of Women Subcommittee of the Standing Committee on Health, Welfare, Social Affairs, Seniors and the Status of Women held hearings on violence against women. Its subsequent report, *The War Against Women,* described the phenomenon of violence against women as a war as a way of emphasizing the climate of fear that violence creates for women. This government report officially adopted the analysis and language of radical feminist groups and brought them into the mainstream of Canadian policy debates (Canada, Status of Women Subcommittee 1991; Gotell 1998). Other government action in the early 1990s included the 1992 reform of the rape shield law, the 1993 Violence Against Women Survey carried out by Statistics Canada, and the 1993–94 National Media Violence Strategy, developed together with the Canadian Broadcasters Association.

One of the most important (if controversial) developments of the early 1990s was the $10 million Canadian Panel on Violence Against Women. The panel, established in 1991, was a tribunal that traveled across the country hearing women's accounts of their experiences of violence. The panel came under fire from a wide variety of feminist organizations questioning its utility and protesting its structure. These organizations felt that it was not representative because it did not include independent representatives of women's organizations. Women's organizations were particularly exercised about the minimal representation of women of color and disabled women (Lakeman 1991; Gotell 1998; Molgat 2000). General women's organizations joined with organizations of women of color to denounce the panel, and the main women's groups refused to participate in the proceedings (Molgat 2000; Gotell 1998).

Nevertheless, the panel has proved to be an important milestone in the development of public attitudes toward violence against women. The final report (Canada, Canadian Panel on Violence Against Women 1993) was a "valuable chronicle" of the ubiquity and multiplicity of forms of violence against women, and it likely raised public awareness of violence against women as the stories of victims were recounted in daily newspapers (Gotell 1998).

In other respects, the 1990s saw a shift toward greater responsiveness to Aboriginal and minority women. In 1990, the National Clearinghouse on Family Violence published a report on abused immigrant and refugee women called *Isolated, Afraid, and Forgotten* (MacLeod and Shin 1990) that laid out the many gaps in government response to the needs of abused refugee and immigrant women in Canada. In 1993, the Clearinghouse put out an issue of its newsletter *Vis-à-Vis* devoted to discussion of the intersection of racism and sexism in violence, and the CACSW published a collection of the views of racial minority and Aboriginal women. The latter report, entitled *Sharing Our Experience,* was a "good, feminist-informed" publication, according to one critical observer (Burt 1998, 115). A report on violence in Aboriginal communities was also commissioned by the government in early 1990s.

There was also a proliferation of reports on violence in immigrant and minority communities and handbooks for service providers produced by specialized minority community groups themselves (Agnew 1998). These reports were "almost entirely produced with the financial support of government agencies," including Health and Welfare Canada, the Department of Canadian Heritage, the Secretary of State (both the Women's Programme and Multiculturalism), and the Research and Statistics Directorate (ibid., 123). These reports have "facilitated the provision of social services" and provided information about legislation and social assistance that "made some choices and alternatives available to abused working class women from Asia, Africa and the Caribbean if they desire to leave their abusive spouses" (141).

In addition to increased research and analysis, there were some concrete policy changes. Refugee policy was changed to acknowledge the violent experiences of refugee women. In 1993, the Canadian government published guidelines that took into account the specific ways in which women's experience of persecution might be different from that of men's and the importance of recognizing those differences in the process of determining refugee status; Canada may have been the first country in the world to do so (Abu-Laban et al. 1998).[2]

More funding was devoted to shelters operated by Aboriginal people in their own communities, although it appears there were only two in the entire Northern province of Nunavut. By 1994, 45 percent of all shelters in Canada had culturally sensitive programming for Aboriginal women (Transition Home Survey 1994–95, cited in Denham and Gillespie 1998). The problems of the Canadian Panel on Violence Against Women were avoided in a subsequent policy consultation process undertaken in order to formulate the "no means no" sexual assault law, Bill C-46. This consultation process, which began in 1994, was an important milestone for a number of reasons. First, the revised sexual assault law is judged by many feminist observers to be "the most significant criminal law reform introduced during the early 1990s" (Gotell 1998, 52; cf. Denham and Gillespie 1998). The second reason this legislation is important is that the inclusiveness of the consultation process, even for racial minority and Aboriginal women, was unprecedented (Denham and Gillespie 1998; Gotell 1998, 52). These consultations involved the administrative section of the Department of Justice that focuses on gender analysis of the law along with a coalition of more than sixty women's groups (Sproule 1998; Denham and Gillespie 1998). Perhaps the procedural criticisms raised in the context of the 1991 panel inspired efforts for greater inclusiveness in 1994.

In the 1990s, then, there was increased government action on a variety of fronts. Gotell (1998, 52) observes that by the early 1990s, the government explicitly recognized the category "violence against women." One statement from Health and Welfare Canada noted that "the social, economic and political inequalities experienced by women are linked to the violence perpetrated against them by men; violence against women must be examined within the context of a sexist society" (Canada, Health and Welfare Canada 1991, cited in Gottell 1998).

By 1994, the Canadian government had funded shelters and crisis centers, reformed laws to address sexual assault and domestic violence, developed training programs for the police and social workers, and worked to raise public awareness of violence against women in a variety of ways. The National Clearinghouse on Family Violence had been created to produce and coordinate information on violence. In addition, policy measures to address the needs of abused refugee, racial minority, and Aboriginal women had been undertaken. Canadian initiatives in research, training programs, and shelters for violence against women are seen as models by international experts (Kelly 1999; Connors 1989; Heise, Pitanguy, and Germain 1994). Many areas for improvement remain. Nevertheless, compared to other democratic national governments, the Canadian government has been particularly responsive to violence against women. Why is this so?

Explaining Policy Development in Canada

Throughout this story, we can see the importance of women's movements in articulating the issue of violence against women and exerting pressure on government to extend and improve policies in this area. As noted, feminist activists were responsible for the original public articulation of the issue in the course of their criticism of the Royal Commission on the Status of Women. The women's movement continued to press for a feminist framing of the problem of violence against women as a problem of gender inequality, and it was eventually successful in influencing public attitudes and government policy. The women's movement also pressed for greater inclusiveness and sensitivity to diversity in both the process and substance of making policy on violence against women, and may have won some victories there as well.

The women's movement activists were aided considerably in their efforts by the women's policy machinery at several crucial moments. First, government funding and other support for these groups facilitated the development of a network of women's organizations working on violence in the 1980s (Burt 1998, 138; Geller-Schwartz 1995). Indeed, in spite of recent cutbacks, government funding continues to be important in enabling the provision of services in hundreds of shelters and crisis centers across Canada. The women's policy machinery has been critical in providing and coordinating funding. In some cases, government funding can determine whether such services are provided at all.

In addition, government research and public consultations have proved critical to increasing public awareness and to informing policy action in at least two critical instances: the consultations on domestic violence in the 1980s and the consultations for the revised rape shield law in the 1990s. Government support has also been important for the development of research on, and services for, violence in immigrant and Aboriginal communities. Thus, the women's policy machinery has facilitated the women's movement efforts to publicize the issue of violence, provided money for organizing and service provision for feminist groups, and coordinated consultations and policy formulation on key occasions. Thus, both the women's movement and the women's policy machinery were key for the development of policies on violence against women in Canada.

Explaining Policy Responsiveness

In Canada and in Australia, the women's movement was responsible for articulating the issue of violence against women, but the presence of a women's policy machinery made it possible for femocrats inside government to push for the inclusion of violence against women on the decision agenda. Moreover, at the stage of policy formulation, the women's policy machinery has been key in providing the institutional support required for a comprehensive response to violence against women. This support has come in the form of funding for research and organizing as well as from providing a coordinating function for policy implementation and expertise on issues concerning women. It is clear that in both Canada and Australia, the strength of the women's movement has been vital to the success of the women's policy machinery. As one Canadian femocrat noted, "without external pressure, these structures have little hope of doing more than holding the fort or maintaining the status quo" (Geller-Schwartz 1995, 57). Similarly, the women's policy machinery has strengthened the women's movement by providing funding and access to the policymaking process.

In contrast, in countries without an effective women's policy machinery, policy development is partial or incomplete. For example, policy development in France was abruptly cut short in the late 1980s when the Socialists were voted out of power. The partnership between the women's movement and the feminists in the MDF broke down when the key feminists were removed from office and replaced with conservative-party faithful (Mazur 1995b). As a result, both the women's movement and the policy machinery were severely weakened. The case of France illustrates the importance of having formal mechanisms of accountability to women's movements. When the ranks of the MDF were purged of femocrats and filled with party faithful, women's movements had greater difficulty in obtaining access to the MDF. Because the bureaucrats in the ministry did not feel accountable to the women's movement, as many femocrats had, the influence of the women's movement on the MDF was greatly reduced.

In Ireland, policy development has depended on the reestablishment with each election of a standing committee on women's issues, and some elections have resulted in the removal of feminist allies within government. There is no permanent women's policy machinery with which the women's organizations are able to develop a partnership, and there is no institutional mechanism for ensuring that women's organizations have access to government (Mahon 1995). Similarly, policy responses in the United States and Israel depended on coalitions between temporary bureaucratic allies, feminist legislators, and women's organizations. At the time of key passage of the legislation in both the United States and Israel, there was no permanent institutional ally with whom women's organizations could partner to develop a more effective policy response.

In New Zealand and Costa Rica, a women's policy machinery was no established until the late 1980s, and partnerships between the permanent institutions and the women's organizations had only begun to develop by the early 1990s. Thus, there has been insufficient time for criticism and dialogue between government and women's groups to result in a more comprehensive policy. Of these two countries, only Costa Rica had an *effective* women's policy machinery in 1994.

Thus, the most comprehensive policy responses, adopted in Canada and Australia, occur as a result of the interaction between strong, autonomous women's organizations and an effective women's policy machinery. A noted, strong, autonomous women's organizations and their allies in government can create the insider-outsider partnerships that are the catalysts for policy development in this area. Importantly, however, such policy initiatives develop into broad, multifaceted government responses only when there is an effective, permanent institutional base for improving women's status—that is, when there is an effective women's policy machinery. Where both of these conditions obtain, critique and revision of policy result, over time, in a better response to violence against women. Where one of these conditions is missing, or where policy innovation is very recent, the government response is weaker.

The statistical analysis supports this argument (table 6-2). An indicator representing the interaction of the presence of a strong, autonomous women's movement and the presence of an effective women's policy machinery is a very strong predictor of comprehensiveness of government response being associated with more areas of government action than either of the two parts alone. The two-part interactive variable had a standardized Beta of .47, while an effective policy machinery and a strong, autonomous women's movement had standardized Betas of -.02 and .27 respectively (table 6-2, model 3). The two-part interactive term alone explained more than 30 percent of the variance. The interaction of a strong, autonomous women's movement and an effective women's policy agency is associated with an additional three or four areas of policy action (model 1). This is a significant effect, given a range of areas of possible action from 0 to 7.

This relationship holds even when controlling for other possibly intervening variables, such as level of development (model 2). The two-part interactive factor and GNP per capita together explain about 40 percent of the variance. The effect of the two-part interactive factor is still by far the more important of the two explanatory factors. It was as strong a predictor of government response when controlling for these variables as it was alone, still being associated with three or four additional areas of policy action.

Table 6-2: Coefficients, Dependent Variable = Scope of Government Response,
36 Countries, 1994

Model/ Independent Variables	B	Std. Error	Beta	t	Sig.	R-squared
1/ Effective women's policy machinery * strong, autonomous women's movement	3.50	0.89	0.56	3.93	0.00	0.31
2/ Level of development	1.21	0.56	0.30	2.18	0.04	0.40
Effective women's policy machinery * strong, autonomous women's movement	3.35	0.85	0.53	3.95	0.00	
3/ Effective women's policy machinery * strong, autonomous women's movement	2.94	1.95	0.47	1.51	0.14	0.37
Strong, autonomous women's movement	1.06	0.61	0.27	1.74	0.09	
Effective women's policy machinery	-0.11	1.70	-0.02	-0.06	0.95	

INSTITUTIONAL REFORM FOR MARGINALIZED WOMEN?

One question that might be raised at this point is whether the relationship identified above holds equally for all types of women's movements. For example, do movements aiming to speak for women of color or poor women benefit from the creation of women's commissions as much as do movements composed mainly of middle-class women and/or women of the dominant race or ethnicity? One Indian feminist charges that such agencies make the state women-organization friendly to but not women-friendly, meaning that one must be a "professional" feminist in order to access these women's commissions (Madhu Kishwar, cited in Everett 1998). In addition, some have raised questions as to whether all women are equally well served by these commissions. Groups organized by white professional women are more likely to be successful in accessing and influencing state policy because the language and procedures of policymaking will probably be more familiar to them (Bystydzienski and Sekhon 1999). This is likely to create a bias in policy outcomes. Thus, the most disadvantaged groups of women (such as poor and minority women) may not benefit from the creation of women's commissions to the degree that white middle-class women do. If this is true it suggests that a major qualification should be appended to the finding re ported above: women's policy machineries improve policy responsivenes for relatively privileged women, but not as much for women from disad vantaged or marginalized groups.

One way to explore this issue might be to examine whether women policy agencies were as likely to produce policies specifically focused on pre venting violence against marginalized groups of women as they were to ad dress violence against women in general. In some contexts, such targeted policies have proven necessary to reach vulnerable and marginalized group of women. In many countries, minority-ethnicity women are more likely to be confronted with violence against women than are women of the domi nant race or ethnic group (Tjaden and Thoennes 1998). A study in Indi suggests that low-caste women are more likely to be victims of domestic vi olence than are higher-caste women (Heise, Pitanguy, and Germain 1994).

Standard services provided to victims of violence (such as shelters an hotlines) are often more difficult for minority women to access because o geographical, language, and cultural barriers, as well as racism against thes vulnerable groups of women by women of the dominant race or class. In th United States, for example, shelters and crisis centers organized by whit women have often been established in predominantly white neighborhoods where they are less accessible to women of color. In addition, Hispanic an other minority women in the United States have sometimes been excluded from taking advantage of rape crisis and other hotline services because o language barriers. Finally, some women of color feel uncomfortable in envi ronments dominated by white women (Matthews 1995). Aborigina women in Australia and Canada report that racism from other womes makes it more difficult for them to use shelters and crisis centers organized by white women.

Aboriginal and minority women in Canada, Australia, and the Unitec States often see a relationship between violence that occurs because of eth nic or racist attitudes (such as lynching) and violence against women (Bel 1994; Bolger 1991; Davis 1990; Maracle 1988; LaRoque 1994; Agnew 1998). Women from marginalized communities feel that the violence the suffer by virtue of being women is inseparable from violence they suffer a members of disadvantaged ethnic or racial groups.

If women's commissions are as effective for women of systematically disadvantaged groups as they are for women of dominant ethnic or racia groups, then we would expect that the countries that are the most respon ive to violence against women in general would also be the most responsive o women of color, adopting policies targeted to the concerns of minority vomen. On the other hand, if they are not, we would expect to see a weaker elationship (or no relationship at all) between such institutional reforms nd policies aimed at assisting marginalized subgroups of women.

Conceptual problems and data gaps prevent a systematic cross-national xamination of this question for all thirty-six countries.[3] Another way of ;etting at this question is to ask whether the governments in the two most esponsive countries (Canada and Australia) appear to have been as re-ponsive to the needs of minority and poor women as they have been to the teeds of middle-class, Anglo, white women. Are these needs met at the same ime and to the same degree, or is there a difference in policy responsiveness .cross groups of women?

As noted, both the Australian and Canadian governments have under-aken to implement some sort of policy on violence that is targeted to mi-tority women. In neither case is government as responsive to women of olor and Aboriginal women as it is to white women, although improve-nents are being made. In both cases, responsiveness to Aboriginal women ppears to be somewhat greater than responsiveness to other racial minor-ty or immigrant women.

As one might have suspected, then, democratic governments appear to 1e more responsive to women of privileged groups than they are to women 1f marginalized subgroups. But this does not mean that independent organ-zation and women's policy machineries do not improve government re-ponsiveness for these disadvantaged women. On the contrary, an xamination of policy development on violence against women for Aborig-nal and minority women in Canada and Australia suggests that independ-nt organization and dedicated government offices may be even more mportant for these vulnerable groups of women than they are for women 1f the dominant race or ethnicity.

In Canada, the government began devoting some attention to the prob-ems of Aboriginal and racial and ethnic minority women after 1986. But acial minority and Aboriginal women had been voicing their distinct con-erns, and criticizing mainstream women's organizations for overlooking hem, since the early 1970s. NAC resisted attempts to raise these issues at hat time, but by the late 1970s it was beginning to take up the issues of acial minority and Aboriginal women.

Tension between Aboriginal and white women continued as NAC ought to respond to Aboriginal women's concerns. In the mid-1970s, NAC

became involved in a number of collaborative projects with a Native Cana
dian women's organization called Indian Rights for Indian Women. By th
end of the decade, the Canadian Congress of Black Women had joine
NAC, and an Aboriginal vice president was elected. In NAC meetings, sev
eral resolutions expressed interest in the issues confronting racial minorit
women, and some actions against racial discrimination were undertaken. *
Native Indian Women's Committee was formed within NAC in the lat
1970s, but it was not until 1985 that the Committee for Visible Minorit
and Immigrant Women was formed.

Government action for Aboriginal and racial minority women, whicl
had begun around 1986, expanded in the 1990s, with important improve
ments. These events paralleled increasing inclusiveness in the Canadia
women's movement and growing bonds of solidarity between minorit
women's organizations and more general women's organizations such a
NAC. In the 1990s, under the leadership of Judy Rebick and Suner
Thobani, NAC instituted affirmative action measures to ensure the presenc
of racial minority, Aboriginal, and disabled women on the executive coun
cil. NAC encountered great hostility as a result of its decision to oppose th
Charlottetown Accord in solidarity with the Native Women's Association o
Canada in 1993. Solidarity between general women's organizations and or
ganizations of women of color was also evident in the debate over th
Canadian Panel on Violence Against Women in the same year. This is not t
say that tensions disappeared, or that racism in Canadian women's move
ments ended, but merely that inclusiveness increased significantly over thi
period.

Government policy toward immigrant, refugee, and Aboriginal wome
also improved over the same period, although government policy lagged no
tably behind developments in independent women's organizations. It wa
NAC that was pressuring the government for greater inclusiveness in th
early 1990s, not the other way around. This suggests that increased gov
ernment responsiveness to violence against minority women at least par
tially reflected the increasing focus of the broader women's movement o
these issues.

The women's policy machinery in Canada was important in developin
policy responsiveness to violence against immigrant, refugee, and Aborigi
nal women. As noted, much of the research on women in ethnic minorit
communities was funded by government agencies such as the Women's Pro
gramme in the Department of the Secretary of State, Status of Wome
Canada, and the Department of Multiculturalism. The CACSW and Statu

of Women Canada commissioned important reports on violence against Aboriginal women, and with the Department of Multiculturalism worked to improve services for immigrant and refugee women. These departments also provided funding for shelters and crisis centers run by community groups through their various programs.

Because of the coalitional structure of NAC, minority women's organizations retained their independent organizational base even when they joined the coalition. NAC's internal committee structure also facilitated the articulation of the concerns of minority and Aboriginal women. Francophone women used this structure to leave or join NAC as they pleased when they had disagreements with the leadership. These organizational features meant that when governments consulted the main women's organizations, they also consulted organizations of minority and Aboriginal women. But the initiative for these issues came from the independent organizations of minority women. The white middle-class women who dominated NAC did not articulate (and initially even resisted efforts to discuss) the distinct needs of minority women confronting violence.

In Australia, the disparity between responsiveness to white Anglo women and to minority and Aboriginal women seems even greater. As late as 1994, there were few shelters offering culturally sensitive services to Aboriginal women. The government had done relatively little research on the issue and had not made much headway in publicizing it as a women's issue. Indeed, even current materials suggest considerable resistance to framing the issue as one of violence against women or as a gender issue, rather than as family violence and primarily an issue of healing the community. Certainly, the role of colonization in the creation of violent conditions in Aboriginal communities must be acknowledged. But many commentators have noted that the gender dimension of this phenomenon must also be acknowledged in order to permit an effective response (Bell 1994; Bolger 1991). By 1994, the government had also done little to address the problems of violence confronting women of a non-English-speaking background. The main women's organizations in Australia were also just beginning to address issues of the intersectionality of race and gender.

Sawer (1995) notes that Aboriginal women in Australia lack an independent organizational base. Bell (1994) similarly laments the inability of the male-dominated Aboriginal organizations to speak for Aboriginal women. Indeed, she attributes the difficulty of raising the issue of violence against women in Aboriginal communities to this lack of organization. Women of a non-English-speaking background formed a national organiza-

tion only in the early 1990s (Sawer 1995). Perhaps this relative lack of independent organizational structure explains the seemingly weaker policy response to the needs of minority and Aboriginal women in Australia.

This is particularly important to consider because Australia not only has
an Office of the Status of Women; it also has a unit and a program devoted
to the concerns of Aboriginal women in the ATSIC (not in the Office of the
Status of Women). But the ATSIC has done little to address the problem of
violence against women in Aboriginal communities. It may be that, as with
women's issues more generally, autonomous organizations devoted to Aboriginal women are necessary to provide the political pressure needed to gal-
vanize bureaucratic units into action.

Still, when such bureaucratic units exist, they can provide an additional
source of support and access for minority women's organizations. For example, agencies created to promote Aboriginal issues or multiculturalism
often helped provide funding for community groups or money to raise
awareness of an issue of importance to minority women, such as land
claims. There are specialized bureaucratic agencies to address Aboriginal
concerns in both Canada and Australia. This may be why in both Canada
and Australia, both women's groups and governments were more receptive
to the idea that Aboriginal women might have distinct issues and perspectives as women than they were to this argument when it was presented by
other ethnic or racial minority women. Perhaps such agencies give minority
women multiple points of access and thus improve their access to the state.
It might be that dedicated subunits, such as the Aboriginal Women's Unit in
Australia, would increase institutional effectiveness for minority women
where they were also organized and agitating outside government. In New
Zealand, the women's policy machinery includes a council of Maori
women; it would be interesting to explore whether this office has improved
policy responsiveness to Maori women with respect to violence or other issues.

For now, we can say that government agencies focusing on women are
not equally responsive to women of systematically disadvantaged groups
and women of dominant or privileged groups. But responsiveness to women
of disadvantaged groups, it would appear, is determined by the general
mechanism specified above. In the areas of violence against women, at least
policy responsiveness to such groups is improved where they are independently organized. Government agencies dedicated to improving women's status enhance policy responsiveness to these groups. In short, the interactive
relationship identified above appears to hold for minority women as well

The main difference appears to be that these groups must be organized separately from groups dominated by more privileged women in order to improve policy effectiveness to meet their distinct needs.

CONCLUSION

In summary, women's movements are always necessary for the initial articulation of violence against women as an issue. The initiative to address violence against women is always a response on the part of government to a demand that originates outside political institutions. However, women's movements alone almost never put the issue on the government agenda. Hence, a women's movement alone is not sufficient to produce a government response. Allies inside government are critical: when there are policymakers sympathetic to the women's movement, or even part of it, the issue of violence against women is more likely to be adopted as part of the decision agenda. Most policies to address violence against women are thus products of partnerships between women's movements and sympathetic insiders.

Such partnerships are much less effective in the absence of a women's policy machinery. In that case, the insider-outsider partnerships tend to produce partial, fragmented responses. In the presence of an effective women's policy machinery, they are more likely to result in broad, multifaceted policies to address violence against women.

A women's policy machinery, however, is not necessary for putting violence on the public agenda. It should also be noted that a women's policy machinery without a strong, autonomous women's movement will not articulate the issue of violence against women, so it is not sufficient, on its own, to produce a government response. It is only in the context of a strong, autonomous women's movement articulating the issue and pressing for government action that women's policy machineries have such a strong effect.

An effective women's policy machinery can strengthen a women's movement. Conversely, a strong women's movement improves the capacity of a set of political institutions to respond to women's concerns when that set includes a women's policy agency. Thus, strong, autonomous women's movements and effective women's policy agencies reinforce one another. This effect is not purely additive; it is interactive, meaning that each factor magnifies the effect of the other.

This argument also appears to hold for marginalized subgroups of women: policy responsiveness to the distinct needs of minority women is

enhanced by independent organization combined with some degree of soli
darity from the broader women's movement. When minority women are
organized independently of organizations dominated by white women or
minority men, the existence of government offices for women seems to im
prove policy response to minority women as well as to women in general. I
also seems that offices for multiculturalism or Aboriginal affairs may in
crease policy responsiveness to women of color.

These findings have important implications for theories of democratic
policymaking, as well as for feminist theory. They also suggest some con
crete ways of improving government responsiveness to violence against
women and to marginalized groups in general. I explore these implication
further in the following chapters.

7

Social Structures and Public Policy

■ I have argued that the impact of political institutions on policies to address violence against women observed in this study suggests some important revisions to both neoinstitutionalist and feminist conceptualizations of the policy process. In addition, it seems that comparative social welfare models also provide little explanatory leverage in this policy issue area (as we saw in chapters 2 and 5). But this analysis of policies on violence against women has even broader theoretical implications for the study of public policy. In the previous chapter, I demonstrated that effective women's policy agencies *interact* with independent social movements to improve government responsiveness to violence against women. In this chapter, I argue that the field of policy studies currently lacks a conceptualization of democratic policymaking that can adequately account for this finding. I join previous critics in arguing that both pluralism and corporatism, as models of the policy process, fail to adequately conceptualize the impact of social movements and political institutions. Approaches centering on subgovernments, policy entrepreneurs, and political opportunities are also likely to obscure significant effects of both social movements and political institutions. But most importantly, none of these approaches can account for the significant impact of the *interaction* between social movements and political institutions.

These problems are symptomatic of a tendency to ignore social structures in policy studies. We need to refocus our attention on these social structures. A structural approach is the only way of explaining the dynamic interaction between social movements and political institutions observed in the previous chapter.

By a structural approach, I mean a theoretical framework that examines social organization at a macrolevel and that asks which social values and groups are promoted by particular forms of organization. In this chapter, I focus mostly on structural analysis that attends to the relationships between social groups and uses standard social scientific techniques to identify those groups that are persistently economically, socially, and politically disadvantaged over time and across policy areas. When we disaggregate our analyses to examine policy processes and outputs with respect to such marginalized groups, we begin to understand the group dynamics that shape the policy process and that limit our efforts to democratize policymaking. Far from being impractical, efforts to develop this type of analysis have already been made by national, regional, and local governments, development agencies, and international organizations. Unfortunately, the dominant theoretical approaches to policy analysis still mostly fail to attend to the social structures of group disadvantage that confront democratic policymakers and citizens every day.

PLURALISM

Although the classical pluralist model is rarely explicitly invoked in policy studies today, the key assumptions of classical pluralism still influence policy scholars. In this model, citizens form groups based on their interests to advance those interests in the political arena. Truman (1953, 33) explains, "As used here, 'interest group' refers to any group that, on the basis of one or more shared attitudes, makes certain claims upon other groups in the society for the establishment, maintenance, or enhancement of forms of behavior that are implied by the shared attitudes." Through a somewhat chaotic but dynamic process of competition, these groups jostle and bargain with one another to exert pressure on policymakers (Dahl 1956, 146; Truman 1953). Although these associations vary in terms of the resources and organization they can command, there is a "high probability that any active and legitimate group can make itself heard effectively at some stage in the process of decision" (Dahl 1956, 150).

Although few recent analyses explicitly espouse a pluralist model in this classical sense, many contemporary accounts of policymaking implicitly employ a pluralist approach. The notion of policymaking as a process of competition among organized interests appears to remain particularly compelling. As Keeley and Scoones (1999, 14) observe:

This society-centred slant on the policy process remains influential, with the earlier language of interest groups finding echoes in concerns with civil society, NGOs and new social movements. Much of the environmental governance literature frames the difficulties within environmental policymaking in terms of the need to balance competing interests. So, whether the subject be genetically-modified food, transport policy, or climate change negotiations, it is often possible to identify core conflicts between environmental, business, consumer and local interest groups as central to the policy process.[1]

Problems in the Pluralist Conceptualization of Political Institutions

It might appear that classical pluralism offers the perfect starting point for considering the relationship between social groups and political institutions, since pluralism focuses on struggles between groups. In pluralism, a group's influence on policy is determined by the intensity of its commitment to the interest or issue in question. Those with a more intense commitment will devote more money, time, and energy to the cause than will those with a lesser commitment. Thus, "all other things being equal, the outcome of a policy decision will be determined by the relative intensity of preference among the members of a group" (Dahl 1956, 135).

Dahl contends that "constitutional rules are not crucial, independent factors in maintaining democracy: rather, the rules themselves seem to be functions of underlying non-constitutional factors" (1956, 137). Bureaucrats exert little independent effect, responding either to elected policymakers or to their "clientele" (147–48). Many scholars have pointed out that this way of characterizing the policymaking process reduces government institutions to a passive arena in which group competition takes place (Lake 1988; Skocpol 1979; Hill 1997). Institutional factors such as constitutions and bureaucracies have little effect on policymaking.

In pluralist theory, the state is understood as a neutral arbiter among social groups. But in practice, some groups may be systematically advantaged or disadvantaged by the institutional structure. The administrative structure reflects the priorities and perspectives of historically dominant groups. This creates a sort of bias in the institutional structure itself that makes it difficult for policymakers to address the problems of marginalized groups. Pluralist theory cannot account for this effect of political institutions.

Problems in the Pluralist Conceptualization of Social Movements

Nor is the impact of social movements well accounted for in pluralist models. In pluralism, interest groups represent shifting associations of individuals pursuing their interests. Following this mode of conceptualizing groups, analysts have tended to conceptualize social movements as interest associations formed to promote particular interests through a process of bargaining with other group representatives and through lobbying of policymakers.

But social movement organizations are only one manifestation of social movements. Understanding the broader, informal activities of social movements is critical for understanding their policy impact. The impact of lobbying or other forms of conventional political activity by representatives of social movement organizations depends for its effectiveness on the activities of the wider social movement (as we saw in chapter 3). If we ignore the activities of protest and public contention, we are likely to misunderstand the process by which social movements affect policy processes.

Moreover, neither social movements nor their organizations are equivalent to interest groups or associations. Social movements are inspired by claims of injustice rather than self-interest (Fuentes and Gunder Frank 1989). While social movements arise from broad cleavages in society, interest groups are purposeful organizations that people voluntarily join in order to promote some issue or interest they deem important. Social movements are said to arise from the experience of marginalization (Kitschelt 1993) or as movements against "encroachments by the state and capitalism" (Dryzek 1990). As Bashevkin (1996, 139) notes, "interest groups try to influence government decision makers, and social movements work to 'change the world.'" (See also Young 2000, 135–36; Dryzek 1996, 51; Fuentes and Gunder Frank 1989.)

As a result of this system-transforming perspective, social movements rarely focus on a single policy issue, although they may intervene in particular policy debates (Bashevkin 1996; Fuentes and Gunder Frank 1989; Dryzek 1990). Rather, they seek to propagate an alternative view or perspective on collective life, including but not limited to an alternative view of public policy. This is why social movements are often characterized as holistic, and why such a wide range of activities (cultural, social, personal) are included in their purview (Young 1990a; Dryzek 1990; Habermas 1987). Thus, social movements and interest groups differ in terms of their origins and objectives.

Social movements also employ a dazzling array of techniques for furthering their aims: sit-ins, marches, linguistic innovation (such as gender-neutral language), cultural events (such as benefits and festivals), and regular means of lobbying, such as producing policy briefs and meeting with policymakers. This "repertoire of contention" is much more varied for social movements than for interest groups or political parties, which as a rule shun illegal activities (Bashevkin 1996; Tarrow 1998).

When phenomena such as women's movements are understood as traditional interest groups, some of the most important political effects of these groups are likely to be obscured. As I explain below, social movements sometimes transform the context and process of policymaking. This effect is not primarily a result of traditional lobbying activities undertaken by social movement organizations. Thus, social movements and their organizations are not well conceptualized as interest groups. Since pluralist theory fails to conceptualize adequately the policy impact of both political institutions and social movements, it accordingly fails to conceptualize the impact of the interaction between these phenomena.

SUBGOVERNMENTS, POLICY NETWORKS, AND POLICY ENTREPRENEURS

It is common in contemporary policy studies to see policymaking as divided into subgovernments (see, for example, Sabatier 1999). National policymaking is viewed not as a single process, but as a cumulation of subprocesses that operate in each functional area (health, environment, and so on). In the classic approach to this kind of analysis, policymaking in each subgovernment is determined by bargaining among a tripartite set of actors who form "iron triangles": executive agencies, congressional committees, and relevant interest groups.[2] These subgovernments are called iron triangles because of their impenetrability; they are relatively closed to those outside the subsystem, including senior bureaucrats from other areas or programs. Policy is determined by a process of bargaining among these three types of agents. More recent approaches to policy analysis, such as the advocacy coalition framework and the notion of policy networks or communities, also employ the idea of subgovernments as an organizing concept.

Problems in the Subgovernmental Conceptualization of Political Institutions

A focus on subgovernments obscures the problems that arise in policy areas that involve more than one functional area. The issues of concern to marginalized groups often cut across the functional areas of government. Focusing on subgovernments takes the existing organization of government as given. But the overall structure of public administration itself is relevant to how policy issues fare in the process, as we have seen with respect to violence against women. This structure is not random and unpatterned, but rather is a reflection of historical priorities. New issues and priorities challenge the organization into subgovernments.

In contemporary analyses of subgovernments, the analytic focus is on individuals and the coalitions or networks they form in policy subsystems (Atkinson and Coleman 1992; Coleman, Skogstad, and Atkinson 1997; John and Cole 2000). Government agencies are understood as influencing the policy process through the individuals and organizations who are members of policy networks. These individuals and organizations are members solely by virtue of their focus on a specific policy issue. Their role as representatives of government more broadly is of minimal importance. As Heclo (1978, 106) observes, "In this situation any neat distinction between the governmental structure and its environment tends to break down." The individuals involved, and their beliefs and ideas, appear to be more important than institutional structure in determining policy outcomes. Thus, the significance of institutional changes, such as the creation of a women's policy machinery, seems to be underplayed in these models. Indeed, some scholars argue that institutional approaches and policy subsystem (or sectoral) approaches should be considered distinct and rival theoretical approaches (John and Cole 2000).

The Advocacy Coalition Framework (ACF) includes institutional change as an important factor affecting the policy subsystem. Institutional rules, appointments, and the like are together recognized as one element of a policy subsystem (Sabatier and Jenkins-Smith 1999). However, the issue here is not whether institutional change can be conceptually accommodated, but whether the framework helps us understand the role of political institutions in policymaking. For example, institutional rules are conceptualized as mostly stable parameters in the Advocacy Coalition Framework. Kingdon (1995) also conceptualizes political institutions mainly as constraints on policymaking, as establishing a set framework within which political events unfold (230). Political institutions offer venues for policymaking, or else procedures that constrain policymaking.

These conceptualizations certainly capture some of the ways that institutions affect policymaking. But we need a theory of political institutions that helps us understand how and when *changes* in the institutional structure affect policymaking. Why, for example, does the creation of a women's policy machinery improve government responsiveness to violence against women?

Institutional reforms that take place outside the subgovernment (such as women's policy agencies) may transform departmental priorities and create new subgovernments. For example, requirements to institute a gender audit or women's budget may change spending priorities. But such an impact cannot be explained by looking only at the subgovernment itself, in isolation. These institutional changes cannot be captured merely as the effects of agencies seeking to further their own preferences in bargaining with interest groups or congressional committees.

Problems in the Conceptualization of Social Movements

Subgovernmental analysis also provides little conceptual room for understanding social movements. In this understanding of policymaking, social movements influence policymaking through social movement organizations that participate as interest groups in iron triangles, as policy entrepreneurs, or as members of policy networks.

As I argued above, however, social movements are not well conceptualized as interest groups. Nor do the concepts of policy networks or policy entrepreneurs adequately capture the policy impact of social movements. Policy networks are "fairly open networks of people that increasingly impinge upon government" (Heclo 1978, 88). These networks have fuzzy boundaries. In fact, Heclo argues, "it is almost impossible to tell where a network leaves off and the environment begins" (102). In addition, participants move in and out of networks, and one group rarely has a lock on a policy issue area. Importantly, the members of an issue network—"a shared-knowledge group having to do with some aspect (or as defined by the network, some problem) of public policy" (103)—are seldom motivated primarily by direct, material interests. Rather, intellectual and emotional commitments are the main reasons people become members of issue networks (although after joining, they may redefine these interests in ways that reflect their participation)(102).

This fluid conceptualization of a loose web of committed individuals more closely approximates how social movements affect policy than does the notion of an interest group. It comes as no surprise, then, that policy networks have been a popular way of conceptualizing the impact of social movements on particular issues. For example, Keck and Sikkink (1998) argue that the international women's movement is better conceived of as an issue network. Hoskyns (1996) also conceptualizes transnational feminism as a policy network. Ryden (1997) employs the concept of a policy network to analyze sustainable development policies in the United Kingdom, and environmentalists are examined as participants in a policy community.

The problem with conceptualizing activists and other representatives of social movements and their organizations as "just another member of the issue network" is that it obscures the connection between these individuals and the broader social movement of which they are a part. The idea of policy networks conceptually detaches activists and organizational representatives from the broader movements. As Carroll and Carroll (1999) note, the concept of the policy network implies that members are focused mainly on the specific policy issue, as opposed to political and social transformation more generally.

This is also a problem with the concept of the policy entrepreneur when applied to social movement activists (Kingdon 1984). A policy entrepreneur is an advocate for a proposal or a particular idea. Policy entrepreneurs are distinguished by "their willingness to invest their resources—time, energy, reputation, money—to promote a position in return for anticipated future gain in the form of material, purposive, or solidary benefits" (179). Policy entrepreneurs "soften up" the political environment for their proposals by constantly pushing their ideas, and they wait for an appropriate opportunity or window. The presence of a skillful entrepreneur with persistence, good timing, and advocacy skills is a key factor in determining whether policy change will occur (182).

Activists or lobbyists are more likely to be successful when they are backed up by an active movement (Costain 1998; Stetson and Mazur 1995). In other words, their success depends on their embeddedness in a larger movement. If we detach these individuals from this broader context, it appears that they are particularly effective lobbyists or skillful policy entrepreneurs. We obscure important factors contributing to their success. If we adopted this perspective, we would marvel at the fortuitous combination of skillful individuals, institutional changes, and changes in public opinion, not perceiving the common cause of all three factors—the social movement of which the individual is a part. I am not trying to say that the skills and presence of these individuals are irrelevant, but rather that we cannot correctly assess their importance unless we perceive them as part of a broader movement, when that is the case.

This conceptual problem cannot be remedied by noting that social movements create "external shocks" to the policy subsystem (Sabatier and Jenkins-Smith 1999) or that they can change the national mood (Kingdon 1984). Social movements certainly do transform policy subsystems, in what might be characterized as an external shock. In some cases, they do change the national mood. But social movements are much more than just context for policy processes. They create new actors and institutions, and in doing so they create new subsystems or alter existing ones. They transform public opinion. They can represent the perspectives of politically excluded and marginalized groups. Thus, social movements can simultaneously alter recognition of a problem, the structure of political institutions, and the policy alternatives being considered. The common cause of these effects will not be noted unless we see the breadth of social movement activities and impacts.

Social Structures of Disadvantage

In addition, these approaches to public policy tend to ignore the consistent disadvantage that some groups experience across policy areas and stages of policymaking. Turning a blind analytic eye to disadvantaged groups results in underestimating the degree to which social structures order policy processes. This means that analysts do not detect connections between important political phenomena that shape policymaking, such as the relationship between social movements and institutional structure.

Kingdon (1995), for example, observes that some groups and classes have more political resources at their disposal and that this introduces class and other group biases into the policymaking system. These group privileges provide a structure to policymaking (223). Yet Kingdon's multiple streams model provides little insight into how such biases are introduced, how they affect the policymaking process, and how they might be eliminated. Sabatier and Jenkins-Smith (1999) characterize socioeconomic conditions, social movements, and social structures as relatively stable parameters that are external to political institutions and other aspects of the policy subsystem. Neither of these conceptualizations provides much insight into exactly how social structures affect political institutions and other aspects of the policy process.

Thus, these conceptualizations of policymaking do not illuminate the relationships between institutional structures, social movements, and the problems of disadvantaged groups. Pluralism offers little in the way of a conceptualization of political institutions, and indeed seems to assign them a secondary explanatory role. As a result, these conceptualizations fail to identify the theoretical and practical problem that group-biased administrative structures present for democratic politics. The same observation applies to the more important contemporary models of the policy process that have been influenced by the pluralist approach. These approaches treat all organized groups like interest groups and treat individual activists as lobbyists, technical experts, or policy entrepreneurs. As a consequence, important features of social movements are overlooked. Thus, these approaches do not adequately capture the dynamic relationship between social movements and political institutions observed in this study.

CORPORATISM

In classical corporatism, the state mediates between two key classes: business and labor. Policymaking is a tripartite negotiation between representatives of government, business, and labor. These negotiations are binding on the groups involved (Schmitter 1982). Corporatist models conceptualize the key groups in the policy process as groups founded to promote their interests in a process of bargaining.

Problems in the Corporatist Conceptualization of Social Movements

Social movement organizations are rarely in a position to engage in bargaining, because their organizational forms do not permit it (Peters 1991). Social movements command an allegiance beyond the formal membership of organizations, and many of their most ardent supporters are not members at all. In women's movements in the United States, for example, many feminists are not members of any of the many women's organizations (Ferree and Martin 1995). In addition, a social movement involves internally conflicting values and positions, and the boundaries of the movement are often unclear (Bashevkin 1996). Indeed, there may be significant disputes over values and policy within a social movement.

The social movement as a whole, then, is rarely identified with a single, hierarchical organization that can speak for the members and/or bind them in negotiations. There are certainly no spokespeople that can bargain on behalf of the movement as a whole. As Dryzek (1990, 49) notes, "This classical style in their internal workings means that no leadership can bind a movement's members to compromises with the state or other conventional actors. Thus, continued confrontation with such actors is to be expected, with demands made in stark, all or nothing terms." Indeed, many social movement organizations are unwilling to engage in bargaining at all, seeing such activity as compromising the total commitment to the movement's goals. Specifically, "the ends of new social movements have little to do with

promoting the interests of a particular class" (Dryzek 1996, 51). Thus, social movements are poorly conceptualized as interest groups engaged in bargaining, whether on behalf of a narrow interest (as in the pluralist view) or
on behalf of a class (as in corporatism).

More recent scholarship on corporatism, sometimes called neocorpo-
ratism, has broadened the concept to include sectors other than labor and
business; contemporary versions have a broader understanding of corporatism as a system of interest mediation. Schmitter (1982, 260) writes:

> The state may not be either an arena for which interests contend or
> another interest group with which they must compete, but a consti-
> tutive element engaged in defining, distorting, encouraging, regulat-
> ing, licensing and/or repressing the activities of associations—and
> backed in its efforts, at least potentially, by coercive claims to legiti-
> macy.

Corporatism, in this view, becomes a system of interest intermediation,
a "situation where the interest organizations are integrated in the governmental decision-making process of a society" (Ruin, cited in Lehmbruch
1982, 4). The participation of organizations in advisory committees and the
like is seen as one aspect of this corporatism. This model might seem to approximate some of the dynamics described in this book, as when women's
organizations participated in advisory committees on the status of women.
Neocorporatists argue that the state affects policy responsiveness to particular groups by recognizing and including them in policy processes, while
other groups are not so recognized or included. The latter do not enjoy the
same degree of policy access as formally recognized groups, and this is reflected in policy responsiveness. The creation of women's policy agencies,
recognizes or encourages the activities of women's associations. Hence,
such agencies enhance policy responsiveness to women's concerns.

Problems in the Conceptualization of Institutions
The description above captures something of the way that women's policy agencies improve policy responsiveness, but it still fails to capture important aspects of political institutions. Specifically, the corporatist
approach focuses too much on formal institutional structures and not
enough on the relationship between those formal structures and informal
social practices and norms. For example, in the United States, whites are not
officially organized as such by government institutions, and there are no
government agencies devoted explicitly to promoting white interests or so-

liciting input from white organizations. Yet African Americans in the United States feel that their perspectives and concerns do not receive an adequate hearing in the policy process. In the corporatist model, both white and African American interests are excluded or suppressed, since they are not formally recognized.

In the case of policies on violence against women, the broader context of inequality and systematic disadvantage explains why such special consultative measures are necessary to improve policy responsiveness to women: it is because informal social structures of gender inequality subtly advantage certain groups of men and disadvantage women in the policy process.

This suggests that the corporatist model is not fully capturing the dynamic by which the existence of women's policy agencies improves policy responsiveness to violence against women. The corporatist model fails to take account of the way that informal norms, historical institutional legacies, and social practices can influence policymaking to advantage or disadvantage particular groups. Thus, in some important ways, the corporatist model fails to function as an accurate model of the relationship between social structures and political institutions in policymaking.

POLITICAL OPPORTUNITY STRUCTURES

Institutional structure is sometimes considered to mediate the impact of social movements (such as women's movements) on policy processes by providing or blocking access for social movements (Skocpol 1992; Elman 1996a). These access points or opportunities are one key way that institutional structures mediate the impact of social movements on the policy process. The notion of a political opportunity structure is a common way of conceptualizing this interaction (Gelb 1989). The idea is that social movements confront, or arise in response to, opportunities that are presented by the political structure, broadly understood (MacAdam, Tarrow, and Tilly 1996). Political institutions are one aspect of this structure.

In this view, social movements are understood as external to administrative structures, rather than as contextual variables that affect the internal operation of institutions themselves. But this study has shown that social movements do both: they affect the broader political context, *and* they affect the internal structure and operation of political institutions themselves, thereby transforming political structure and creating opportunities (Tarrow 1998).

Social movements affect the structure and operation of political institutions in three main ways. First, they increase the political power of their allied constituencies within government. Social movements affect internal bureaucratic politics by providing external political support for agencies that might otherwise lack internal leverage. For example, strong women's movements provide political support for women's policy agencies, which increases the agency's influence vis-à-vis other government departments. This support affects the process of agenda setting as well as the policy capabilities of the administrative structure. Similarly, "the civil rights movement had a profound impact on political institutions, as in the increased assumption of authority by the federal courts, the altered filibuster rules of the Senate, changes in support for the political parties, and the use of executive power by the president" (Costain and McFarland 1998, 288). Thus, understanding the effect of social movements on political institutions is important for understanding the bureaucratic politics of policy development.

Second, social movements demand institutional reforms that alter the administrative structure of the state itself. Women's policy agencies, for example, are often created in response to women's movement demands (Stetson and Mazur 1995). Similarly, social movements of ethnic and racial minorities often demand changes in administrative structures that affect them. Inuit activists in the Canadian North demanded that a separate province (Nunavut) be constructed to facilitate self-government and the protection of Northern Native communities in a federal system (Arscott and Trimble 1997, app. B). The Muslim Personal Law Board in India was set up in response to demands from Muslim fundamentalist activists who demanded autonomous institutions to govern their religious personal law (Weldon 1992).

Third, social movements move inside political institutions themselves. For example, Katzenstein (1998) gives an account of how feminist movements developed inside the Catholic Church and the U.S. military. Sawer (1995) documents the way the women's movement in Australia consciously decided to begin working inside the state. Cockburn (1991) demonstrates that intraorganization feminist movements improve the success of organizational equality policies. Conversely, feminist bureaucrats, royal commissions, and women's policy agencies are elements of the women's movement. Thus, social movements and political institutions are, in practice, overlapping phenomena.

The concept of a political opportunity structure emphasizes factors external to the movement as being critical to the movement's origin, development, and success (Tarrow 1998; Gelb 1989). As Gelb (1989, 15) observes, "External factors help structure the type of group mobilization that occurs as well as the character and success of a movement." But social movements sometimes create their own political opportunities, as when women's movements obtain institutional reforms. Tarrow (1998, 72) notes that "once formed, movements *create* opportunities—for their own supporters, for others, for parties and elites." So the idea that social movements arise in response to political opportunities does not recognize the impact of social movements on the political opportunity structure itself.

The model of political change suggested by the concept of a political opportunity structure gives theoretical primacy to external factors such as institutional structure: political structure shapes social movements, but social movements do not shape political structure to the same degree. Although these external factors are important and certainly shape social movements to some degree, any model of the interaction between social movements and political institutions must recognize that they mutually influence each other, and that neither alone is determinative.

The notion of a political opportunity structure would suggest that once social movements exist, then a change in the structure of political opportunities should provide movements with the needed access. Analysis of political structure proceeds separately from an analysis of the movement itself. This model implies an additive interaction between existing social movements and political structure. Existing social movements, when confronted with political opportunities, affect policy processes. This model captures something of the dynamic between social movements and political institutions. But, as I have demonstrated, a multiplicative model better captures the interaction: social movements and political institutions have mutually reinforcing effects on policy outcomes. Social movements can strengthen and transform political institutions, and vice versa.

Thus, as Tarrow (1996, 874) argues, although the move toward a better conceptualization of the interaction between social movements and political institutions is much needed, the idea of political opportunity structure does not accomplish this goal. The complex interaction between institutions and social movements is not captured by the notion of social movements confronting (or arising in response to) a given political opportunity structure. As Costain and McFarland (1998, 288) observe in the context of American politics, "Evidence indicates an important two-way interaction between institutions and movements that sculpts many of the more visible pathways to change."

A STRUCTURAL APPROACH TO POLICY ANALYSIS

Conceptualizing the policy process as structured by social relations, such as the relations among social groups, provides a better understanding of political institutions, social movements, and their interaction. Below I explain what I mean by social structure and by a structural approach to public policy. Then I try to show how taking such an approach improves our understanding of political institutions, social movements, and policies on violence against women. Ultimately, I suggest, attending to such social structures will give us a better understanding of politics and policymaking more generally.

Comparative policy scholars, both feminist (Walby 1990; Duncan 1995, 1996) and otherwise (Ashford 1978; Skocpol 1979; Bobrow and Dryzek 1987; Dryzek 1996), have long advocated a structural approach to understanding public policy. Critical theorists have also advocated a structural approach to analyzing politics and policy (Young 1990a; Dryzek 1996). Social structural analysis of policy focuses on how the organization of politics at a macrolevel promotes some values or ways of life and obscures or represses others. Some structural theorists focus more specifically on how policies relate to the relationships among social groups. Bobrow and Dryzek (1987, 67), for example, argue that an analysis of social structures in policymaking "applies sociological reasoning to the content of public policies, with special reference to social consequences in terms of the distribution of goods (and 'bads') among individuals and groups."

But social structural analysis is not just distributive analysis (Young 1990a). *Social structure* refers to a mode of social organization, a set of relationships that position people relative to others. A social structure is composed of the norms, rules, and institutions that provide organization to everyday life and collective decisions (Giddens 1982; Young 2000).[3] Social structural analysis of how policy affects social groups, then, involves examining how policies determine, and are determined by, *relationships* among social groups. This involves discerning patterns in policymaking over time and across agencies.

Ashford (1978) argues that political institutional analysis is key to such an approach to policy. This is because political institutions constitute a critical component of social structures. Social structures are composed of combinations of social, political, and economic institutions and norms. For example, laws, market forces, public bureaucracies, and social norms combine to create a form of social organization that makes it difficult for workers to be simultaneously primary caregivers and primary breadwinners. Diverse norms and institutions all reflect (and thereby reinforce) the expectation that the primary breadwinner will be a man and therefore not a primary caregiver, who is usually expected to be a woman.

Gender is a social structure: various norms, institutions, and formal and informal rules construct relations between the masculine and the feminine, and thus between men and women (Walby 1990). The specific forms of these norms and institutions, and the relationships between them, vary considerably across social and political contexts. Nevertheless, we can think of these norms and rules as combining to create a political context that privileges men and the masculine and subordinates and devalues women and the feminine.

Race can also be thought of as a social structure. As Frederickson (1999, 333) argues:

> "Race" and all the ideas and attitudes associated with it are the product of social contexts that change over time and not the reflection of some "transhistorical" impulse that is rooted in objective human differences. . . . Race emerges from the interpretation or construction of such non-economic differences to create a sense of group solidarity or peoplehood that can provide the basis for a claim of dominance or privilege over those considered outside of the group.

Institutions, attitudes, and social norms about race position individuals and groups in relation to one another whether they like it or not. In the United States, residential racial segregation (the division into black and white neighborhoods) is one mechanism by which the structure of race relations is maintained (Massey and Denton 1993). Bias in the criminal justice system is another.

Similarly, class relations form a social structure.[4] *Class* can be used generally to mean any status group, but I use it here as Weber and Marx did: to refer to economic classes. Class in this sense is determined by relationship to economic structures. As Young (2000, 95) remarks, "Economic class is the paradigm of structural relations in this sense." Class analysis involves giving an account of the economic relations between groups. As class analysis has developed, scholars have recognized that the divisions between owners of capital and workers are overly simplified accounts of class. Some analysts have suggested including other distinctions, such as the division between professionals and nonprofessionals, as important class divisions (Young 1990a, 2000).

The impact of economic class is mediated by race, gender, and other structural social groupings. Sometimes gender or racial divisions impede class solidarity, as when African American workers were excluded from white unions in the United States and South Africa (Trotter and Smith 1997; Lipton 1988). The difficulty in unionizing part-time and contract workers, who are disproportionately women in most parts of the world, is an example of how gender can shape class relations.

Social structures that affect democratic policymaking include social structures that define social groups (such as gender, race, and class) and those that constitute an unsustainable and/or unjust form of political organization (militarism, technocracy, bureaucracy and centralization, and/or the domination of nature by humans). Some environmentalists argue that our current form of social organization is unsustainable because it depends on a model of the relationship between human beings and our natural surroundings that results in the destruction of nature. These forms of social organization are maintained by and reflected in political institutions (such as public bureaucracies and law), social institutions (such as the family), economic relations (the organization of work and markets), and cultural expression (movies, books, newspapers, and so on).

These social structures often combine or intersect to create a complex set of social relations with attendant policy problems (such as environmental racism). Structures can be discerned by asking how such patterns of social organization combine to affect the issue or context in question. Are some racial, ethnic, gender, or class groups disadvantaged or excluded by the prevailing ways of organizing public policy? Do current norms or practices in policymaking or public administration reinforce the subordinate position of some groups? How do norms and practices of policymaking relate to broader patterns of social relations? What values are embodied in the current way of organizing political and social life?

Note that although gender, race, and other social structures can be employed in cross-national comparisons, such comparisons need not assume that these structures are identical or that they work in exactly the same way across social contexts. As Frederickson (1999, 333) observes, "The construction of race can lead to secession in defense of racial slavery, the creation of social orders based on racial caste, or to gas ovens for stigmatized peoples." In a three–country comparison of racism, nation-building, and state policy, Marx (1998, 10) finds that "the modern house of race in each country was built on similar foundations of prejudice, but constructed according to various circumstances." Similarly, gender relations of male dominance vary cross-nationally in their form. Duncan (1996, 93) argues that "the six structures [of patriarchy] will be differentially developed as they interact with pre-existing situations, changes in other social structures (like capitalism) and each other. Historical and geographical outcomes will show considerable variation" (93).

A structural approach to public policy, then, asks how the norms, attitudes, and institutions of society as a whole affect the policy issue or problem in question. Such an approach would examine, for example, how social structures that create social disadvantage for marginalized and oppressed groups affect policy processes and outcomes (Bobrow and Dryzek 1987).

Staudt (1998, 14) defines a gendered policy analysis as one that focuses "on the ways that all policies—from tax, land, and labor to safety and health—differently serve and/or burden diverse men and women, including women who head households." Although gender analysis often does involve examining the differential impact of policies on men and women as groups, it is more than that.

A structural approach to the study of gender and politics suggests a reorientation away from the study of women as policymakers or social policy beneficiaries and more toward social and institutional structures and processes. As noted, the impact of gender on policy outcomes has often been conceptualized as the impact of differences between women and men on policy outcomes, particularly in American political science and policy studies. Specifically, much analysis of gender and public policy has focused on the impact of women (individual women leaders, feminist lobbyists, women in legislatures) on policy outcomes. But gender is not just about differences between men and women; it is a form of social organization that subordinates women and the feminine to men and the masculine.

A structural analysis of the impact of gender on policy, then, requires more than examining the impact of differences between men and women. It means analyzing social and political institutions and social movements in terms of whether they undermine or reinforce women's subordinate position. Depending on their design, administrative structures can facilitate or obstruct a government response to women's issues. Women's movements can be strengthened or weakened by variations in the structure of political institutions. Gender analysis should critically examine how policies are embedded in and reflect power relations, and not just differences, between the groups designated as "men" and "women."

A structural approach, then, is a framework for analysis rather than a grand theory of policymaking. It suggests some additional concepts and questions to add to traditional policy analysis in political science and sociology; it thus complements or extends, rather than replaces, these approaches.

I follow Duncan (1996) here in distinguishing such structural analysis from structuralism. Structuralism, as I understand it, holds that (among other things) the notion of a subject or actor independent of social structures is impossible. Rosenau (1992, 46) describes this position:

> Structuralists argued that the subject is a mystification because s/he is presumed to be an agent independent of social relations. Structuralists initiated the trend away from the author/subject by deemphasizing the individual and focusing on larger structures, on the formal laws of a system's functioning, on the linguistic construction of these structures, on the symbolic meaning they carry, and/or on change as manifest in structural transformations. Structuralism and systems analysis, then, deny the possibility of a subject with any personal capacity to maintain or change social relations. The subject was a "missing person" in the structuralist tradition. . . . Structuralists defined structures as beyond the reach of human intervention.

Although I do seek to emphasize social structures, I want to distinguish the structural approach I have outlined from structuralism as described above. A structural approach merely requires us to acknowledge that political life and political subjects make decisions in the context of social structures. Social structures are primarily the product of a cumulation of individual social actions. While it is usually true that individuals can do little to change social structures in the short term, they may lead movements (such as feminist movements) or undertake other forms of collective action (such as labor organizing) that change social structures, at least to some degree.

In addition, in the view of social structures I am advancing, social structures condition but do not determine action. As Young (2000, 101) puts it, "Subjects are not only conditioned by their positions in structured social relation; subjects are also agents. To be an agent means that you can take the constraints and possibilities that condition your life and make something of them in your own way." For example, norms of heterosexuality make it very difficult for gay men and lesbians to live openly as homosexuals and to form legal families. Nevertheless, many gays and lesbians do so, and this represents their choice about how to deal with the social and legal norms that condition their lives.[5]

Social Movements as Reactions to Structural Conditions

In policy scholarship, social movements are usually conceptualized as interest groups, policy entrepreneurs, or participants in advocacy or issue networks. These conceptualizations ignore or obscure important aspects of social movement activity. A better conceptualization of the impact of social movements on public policy is needed. Work from political sociology, feminist scholarship, and the comparative politics literature on social movements suggests that social movements are historically contingent reactions to social structures. Many social movements represent responses by marginalized groups to their structural position of disadvantage. Social movements usually seek to transform social structures, including changing institutions, everyday routines, and the very meaning of words and concepts that we use in writing and implementing policy. Such a structural conceptualization of movements provides a better understanding of the impact of social movements on public policy.

Tarrow (1998) provides a compelling synthesis of the literature on social movements. Sociologists distinguish between isolated acts of protest and the sustained mobilization of political contention that constitutes a social movement. Protests arise in response to the perception of improved political opportunities—for example, a lessening of state repression or improved access to institutions. Such acts of mere protest are likely to develop into full-fledged social movements, into "national struggles for power," when a number of conditions obtain. Protests develop into a social movement when they "revolve around broad social cleavages in society, when they bring people together around inherited cultural symbols, and when they can build on or construct dense social networks and connective structures" (19).

Some social movements are reactive in that they arise in response to social change, seeking to transform society in order to *undo* social changes. Other social movements, such as the environmental and peace movements, focus on transforming social values and structures in new ways. Finally, many social movements aim to transform society in order to liberate oppressed groups. These latter movements, I propose, are of particular interest to those concerned with democratic policymaking because they express the perspectives of systematically marginalized social groups.

Let me explain exactly what I mean by oppressed or marginalized social groups. Social groups are collectives of people that are demarcated by social norms and institutions, by tradition or by law (Young 2000, 90). The "markers" of such groups are socially constructed—that is, the product of cumulative social practice—as opposed to natural (in the sense of biological or inevitable). Although the characteristics that define such groups tend to be involuntary, ascriptive characteristics, such as biological sex or ethnic lineage, the meaning of the characteristics varies over time. Polish workers in the United States, for example, struggled to be designated as white so they could belong to the white unions (Blee 1998).

Social groups are not intentionally or purposefully formed, but rather emerge from interaction with, and in relation to, other social groups. Young (2000, 90) explains:

> Before the British began to conquer the islands now called New Zealand, for example, there was no group anyone thought of as Maori. The people who lived on those islands saw themselves as belonging to the dozens or hundreds of groups with different lineage and relation to natural resources. Encounter with the English, however, gradually changed their perceptions of their differences; the English saw them as similar to each other in comparison to the English, and they found the English more different from them than they felt from one another.

Williams (1998, 16) distinguishes marginalized ascriptive groups from other social groups according to four characteristic features:

> 1) patterns of social and political inequality are structured along the lines of group membership 2) membership in these groups is not usually experienced as voluntary 3) membership in these groups is not usually experienced as mutable, and 4) generally, negative meanings are assigned to group identity by the broader society or dominant culture.

Importantly, Williams emphasizes that patterns of social and political inequality persist over time, and continue into the present. In other words, marginalized social groups suffer current as well as past disadvantage.

Such systematic marginalization constitutes a social cleavage of the sort that often produces social movements. As noted, social movements originate as expressions of protest against structural inequalities or injustices, or in defense of perceived threats to privilege. They often arise when members of oppressed groups identify some injustice that they suffer and when these claims resonate to some degree within and beyond their social group (Young 2000, 92). Members of marginalized social groups tend to have some networks of connection with others within their group and to have some shared symbols or history, even if only as a product of their common exclusion. For example, in the United States, the Confederate flag has a very different meaning for African Americans than it does for many white Southerners.

Social groups have distinct perspectives on public issues. A social perspective reflects the vantage point of the social position in which a group finds itself (Young 1994, 1996). As Williams (1998) observes, members of the group have the experience of being marked by society as members of a particular class. As members of the group, they may confront obstacles and issues that others need not confront.

When groups are marginalized, their distinct voice or perspective is excluded from politics (Williams 1998; Young 1990a, 2000; Phillips 1995; Mansbridge 1999). Social movements of marginalized groups seek to make this excluded voice heard. As Rochon and Mazmanian (1993, 77) note, social movements produce "social interests that are newly defined as legitimate."

Social movements represent attempts to transform the organization of political life and are thus reactions to social structures. They often express the perspective of otherwise marginalized groups and seek to give them some kind of a voice in the policy process. Sometimes, however, they represent a conservative backlash against changes in social structures, in defense of group privilege. Reactions to structural conditions or to changes in structures are often expressed through existing social networks and institutions. However, a movement is not reducible to any particular network or institution.

Understanding social movements as collective mobilizations aimed at transforming social structures helps us to understand their impact on policy. Social movements are aimed primarily at social transformation, and only secondarily or instrumentally at policy change. Thus, they have both direct and indirect impacts on the policy process (Rochon and Mazmanian 1993). The main ways that social movements affect policy processes are indirect— specifically, by changing social meanings or values and demanding institutional or procedural changes.

Indirectly, social movements act to diffuse new interpretive frameworks to the public, engaging in "discursive politics" (Fraser 1989; Katzenstein 1995; Stone 1997). Sometimes this can result in dramatic shifts in public perceptions of events, for example, changing public attitudes toward domestic violence (Gelb 1998; Gotell 1998). Social movements affect the policy process by transforming social values (Rochon and Mazmanian 1993, 77). Changing the very meanings of words (such as "citizen" or "person")

r "equal treatment") is one of the most important ways that social move-
nents affect policy change.

Social movements engage in "discursive politics" in a number of ways.
)ne distinct mode of political mobilization, personal politics, consists of an
ndividual's range of everyday activities aimed at changing others' attitudes,
ncluding challenging assumptions in discourse, changing behavior and lan-
;uage, and the like (Molyneux 1998; Mansbridge 1995; Katzenstein 1995).
\ second form of political mobilization used by social movements is cul-
ural politics, expressed through cultural productions such as books,
novies, magazines, and theater. A third type is regular organizing and ac-
ivities, such as forming networks to exchange information and to conduct
liscussions, letter writing, street protests, petitions, lobbying, and so on.

All these forms of political activity involve a struggle over meaning (cf.
Katzenstein 1995; Fraser 1989; Stone 1997). Most social movements strug-
;le over the meaning of key political concepts (such as justice, basic needs,
ind equality) central to their activities (Fuentes and Gunder Frank 1989;
Fraser 1989; Tarrow 1998). Social movements for the emancipation of his-
orically disadvantaged groups work to diffuse publicly the previously sup-
)ressed or ignored perspective of their group.

When social values or frameworks change, new problems and issues are
recognized, and new speakers are acknowledged as legitimate. Long-stand-
ng situations are defined as "problems," as in the case of violence against
women. Thus, these efforts to change social practice and public opinion can
iffect agenda-setting processes by producing public pressure to address new
)roblems or issues. They can also affect the process of policymaking by de-
nanding new procedures or the inclusion of new groups.

This study of policy on violence against women illustrates how women's
novements influence public discussion by advancing moral and political ar-
;uments to create public support for their claims and to exert pressure on
policymakers. Women's movements work to diffuse a women's perspective
or agenda throughout society. For example, in places where there is a strong
women's movement, most people have a sense that there are some issues
that are "women's issues," and they can identify some of them. When
women's movements are extremely effective, they can affect the legitimacy
of a democratic government by creating a broad groundswell of support for
their policy issue that politicians ignore at their peril (Walker 1991).

Social movements also affect policy processes by transforming the political institutions that make policy. Theories of political institutions usually
conceptualize social movements as entirely external to administrative structures, as inputs or stimuli (for example, Skocpol 1992; Immergut 1992).

However, women's policy agencies are often created in response to women's movement demands (Stetson and Mazur 1995). Moreover, the activities of women's movements can increase the influence of a women's policy agency vis-à-vis other government departments. This affects the process of agenda setting and the policy capabilities of the administrative structure.

Rochon and Mazmanian (1993) argue that social movements often aim to gain participation in the policy process. Social movements result in the inclusion of new groups and interests in the policy process by "the creation of new mechanisms for dialogue and collaboration between government and political organizations" (75).

Costain and McFarland (1998) contend that the fundamental structure of policymaking in the United States was profoundly altered by the civil rights movement. Rochon and Mazmanian (1993), similarly, note that the Equal Employment Opportunities Commission and the Environmental Protection Agency were created in response to protests by movements. These agencies have both become more important over time. Thus, this type of institutional change can have ramifications far beyond the original aims of reformers and may impact a diverse group of policy areas (ibid., 87). Social movements are more than "inputs" for institutions: they shape institutions themselves.

Social movements also have more direct effects on the policy process by demanding particular policy changes or raising specific issues through directed protests and lobbying. But these direct measures depend to a large degree on the existence of a broader movement. Although social movement organizations can achieve an effect on policy through lobbying, the main way that movements influence public policy is through the more diffuse strategy of transforming the public agenda, political institutions, and policy context through discursive politics. Interpretations are advanced in cultural productions, protest politics, and everyday politics as well as through formal channels of "professional politics," such as the production of policy briefs. It is through these mechanisms that the social movement agenda or perspective enters the public policy arena.

Social movements, then, bring previously ignored perspectives and excluded groups into the policy process. These perspectives and issues are often those of groups that are systematically disadvantaged economically, socially, and politically and, as a result, excluded from meaningful participation in the public institutions of democratic society (such as the political parties, parliament, or congress).

When social movements provide a voice for systematically marginalized groups, they represent an important force for democratizing policymaking (cf. Dryzek 1990; Young 1990a). Of course, social movements are imperfect representatives of marginalized groups. An internal lack of structure makes it hard to know who can legitimately speak as a member of the movement, and internally disadvantaged subgroups often must struggle to obtain representation within the movement. Nevertheless, there may be potential benefits for the further democratization of policymaking that are obscured by collapsing social movement organizations with traditional interest groups, activists with lobbyists or policy entrepreneurs. I discuss these possibilities more in the next chapter.

This account of social movements is structural in that it relates the development of social groups and movements to persistent patterns of social organization. Doing so helps us to appreciate the broader impact of social movements on policy processes, because we better understand the origins, objectives, and organization of social movements. The impact of social movements on the policy process is only superficially similar to the impact of interest groups or policy entrepreneurs, and cannot be reduced to these concepts. In the sections below, I turn to providing a structural account of political institutions, showing how examining social structures illuminates the powerful interactive effects between social movements and political institutions observed in this study.

Political Institutions and Social Structures

The movement toward a "new institutionalism" has produced a great deal of theoretical and empirical work on the impact of political institutions on policymaking (for example, March and Olsen 1989; Skocpol 1979, 1992; Weaver and Rockman 1993; Weir, Orloff, and Skocpol 1988; Orloff 1993). In addition, feminists and critical theorists have been theorizing the relationship of social structures of gender and class to the state. However, neoinstitutional studies have not systematically considered the effects of social structures that privilege some groups and disadvantage others with respect to policymaking. On the other hand, most feminist and critical-theoretic scholarship on social structures has not adequately specified the relationship among those social structures and the institutions of public administration (cf. Ashford 1978).[6] Thus, in spite of the important contributions of this newer scholarship, we still lack an adequate conceptualization of the relationship between social structures, political institutions, and policy outcomes. Although each of these approaches offers important insights, none of these literatures can adequately account for this study's finding that women's policy machineries combine with social movements to greatly improve policy responsiveness to violence against women.

Social structural analysis helps us to identify and understand the barriers to and possibilities for further democratization that political institutions present. The conceptualization of political institutions I am advancing in this book sees them as both reflecting and shaping struggles among social groups. When dominant groups design institutional structures, they leave the imprint of their perspective (for example, their priorities). Unless administrative structures are reformed, their design both reflects and rein forces the historical influence of dominant social groups, such as privileged men, or dominant races (Staudt 1998; Marx 1998). The creation of specialized agencies is one way of correcting for such institutional biases.

Note that it is not the bureaucratic nature of the state per se that results in biases against disadvantaged groups (contra Ferguson 1984). Nor can bias in the state be traced to its functional relationship to social structures, as in some feminist accounts (Brown 1981; MacKinnon 1989; Abramovitz 1988) and Marxist theories (Offe 1984; Gough 1979). Rather, institutional biases against women and other disadvantaged groups are the product of historically contingent processes. It is said that victors write history; victors also create political institutions. But reform of these institutions is possible, and it may remove or at least partially correct for biases against disadvantaged groups.

Depending on their design, then, administrative structures can facilitate or obstruct government response to women's issues and issues important to other marginalized groups. For example, policies on issues that require coordination across many departments are more difficult to design and implement than policies that can be made in a single department. Women's policy issues tend to require such coordination, since the administrative priorities that shaped current administrative structures were not chosen with an eye to promoting the status of women. Women's policy agencies can help overcome this male bias in institutional structures by performing the critical function of coordination.

The Interaction Between Social Movements and Institutions

A social structural approach helps us understand the powerful, interactive effect of social movements and institutions on policymaking. Unless institutional reforms are undertaken, democratic political institutions are likely to remain biased against the priorities and perspectives of marginalized groups. The social movements of these groups confront a state that is ill equipped to respond to their concerns even when the political will exists to introduce well-designed policies. As noted, cross-sectoral coordination problems and entrenched priorities often bedevil attempts to introduce policies to address the concerns of marginalized groups.

Social movements create the political will, and institutional reform creates the institutional capacity to respond to the concerns of marginalized groups. Institutional reform in the absence of social movements is unlikely to have much effect. Bureaucrats in newly created agencies and commissions must argue for the importance of their proposals in an administrative system that has traditionally given these issues little attention. But a social movement that transforms social attitudes and values covers bureaucrats in its wake. Attitudes begin to change inside and outside political institutions. Thus, the combination of autonomous social movements and reform of political institutions is powerful.

Social movements represent a broad effort to change dominant interpretations of public problems, to articulate previously suppressed or ignored perspectives. In many cases, these movements are working to displace the interpretation of problems reflected in the existing structure of institutions. Institutional reform to correct these problems can facilitate policy response to the demands of social movements. The interaction between institutional reform and a strong, autonomous social movement can have dramatic effects: as I have shown here, the creation of effective women's policy agencies significantly improved government response to violence against women. Similarly, one might expect that creating a "racial equality policy agency" might improve policy responsiveness to demands from movements of African Americans and other minorities.

The social structural approach reveals the connection between institutional and other social changes: When we perceive the initial institutional bias against marginalized groups, we expect institutional change to improve responsiveness to marginalized groups as institutional obstacles to government response are removed. But we also notice that other, noninstitutional barriers may remain and obstruct or mitigate the impact of institutional reform. Social movements are working to change social structures and to transform society as a whole, including policy, political institutions, attitudes, language, and everyday routines. When we recognize that these social structures order policy processes, we can begin to explore how such structures create barriers to a deeper democratization of policymaking.

Common Criticisms of a Structural Approach

Social structural analysis is sometimes criticized for being deterministic and for ignoring the importance of human agency. The conceptualization of social structures presented in this chapter is not deterministic. Social structures are seen merely as the cumulation of human actions over time and across society (Giddens 1982). Like social norms, they can be changed through organized, coordinated efforts and campaigns. Individuals on their own can do little to change social norms or structures, except as catalysts to group campaigns or other social trends. Social structures are made up of human actions and are the results of human actions. So social structures are not opposed to individual or group agency, and they do not determine political outcomes.

Nor does the notion of social structure imply that all members of marginalized groups have the same experience or identity. The members of marginalized groups are positioned by social structures, but individuals do not experience or react to this positioning in the same way (Young 2000). Moreover, social structures interact to create marginalized subgroups, such as African American women. I say "interact" here to emphasize that these groups are not defined in an additive way. The position of African American women cannot be understood merely by adding the problems or experiences of African Americans to the problems or experiences of women. Race refracts gender for both white women and African American women, and gender refracts race for African American women and men.

Social structures such as gender have some broad similarities across and within countries (Duncan 1995; Walby 1991; Beckwith 2000). Race may also be conceptualized for cross-national comparison (Marx 1998). These similarities are what makes it possible and interesting to ask about lessons for women in the United States from women in Scandinavia or India, or to ask about lessons for racial minorities in the United States from South Africa or Brazil. Such questions do not assume that the United States and India and Sweden are the same, but rather that there are some similarities and differences from which we can learn. These similarities and differences must be established empirically, rather than assumed.

Bobrow and Dryzek (1987) note that structural approaches sometimes appear to lack clear policy implications. This may raise concerns that the approach I recommend is fine for policy scholarship but will create a greater gulf between policy academics and practitioners. In fact, the opposite is true. Adopting a structural approach will bring policy scholarship into better contact with the practice of policymaking. For example, there is plenty of evidence that policymakers are currently struggling to devise ways to take account of marginalized social groups. For example, methods for gender-based analysis, including specific guidelines for how to proceed, have been developed by a variety of national and local governments. The European Union even commissioned a study of the different methods of "gender mainstreaming" employed by member governments in order to develop a model that all governments could use (Beveridge, Nott and Stephen 1998). The Canadian national government has also developed guidelines for gender-based analysis (Status of Women Canada 1995). Development agencies such as the World Bank, the Organization for Economic Cooperation and Development, and the Canadian International Development Agency have developed kits and workshops that train policymakers to take gender into account in their analyses and recommendations (World Bank 1995, 1998; Organization for Economic Cooperation and Development 1995; Canada, CIDA 1999).

Government agencies have developed useful but nuanced guidelines to distinguish disadvantaged groups from privileged groups. For example, in the United States, national government transportation policy requires that a certain proportion of contracts go to enterprises owned by members of disadvantaged groups (U.S. Department of Transportation 2000). Similar policies exist at state and local levels. In order to justify policies targeted at particular groups, governments in the United States must demonstrate that the groups suffered disadvantage historically and that this disadvantage continues into the present. Sophisticated social scientific techniques, both qualitative and quantitative, have been developed to establish the existence of such disadvantage.

Thus, governments and activists use the language of group disadvantage and marginalization, but policy scholars have for the most part eschewed such talk. Acknowledging and studying the social structures that create marginalized groups would permit policy scientists to examine critically and perhaps improve this talk about disadvantage, as well as to deepen our understanding of how such social structures continue to limit our progress toward more inclusive democracy.

This project began with the important subject of violence against women. In the next chapter, I return to my focus on this problem and ask what this study suggests we should do to improve government responsiveness to violence against women. I also suggest some practical implications for democratizing policymaking more generally.

8

Responding to Violence Against Women

Practical Lessons for Democrats, Feminists, and Policymakers

Violence against women is a manifestation of historically unequal power relations between men and women, which have led to domination over and discrimination against women by men and to the prevention of the full advancement of women . . . violence against women is one of the crucial social mechanisms by which women are forced into a subordinate position compared with men.

UNITED NATIONS, 1993

The feminist political position insists that confronting violence against women is fundamental to the struggle for democracy. . . . Only by incorporating the struggle against violence can the movement extend democracy. . . . Democracy . . . cannot continue to be a space of power and domination of one sex over another.

VIRGINIA VARGAS, 1997

■Violence against women constitutes a violation of women's human rights (U.S. Department of Labor 1996; Nelson 1996). It is a serious public policy problem in all stable democracies. Although virtually all stable democratic countries take some action to address violence against women, there are only two cross-national analyses of government response to the problem: one compares policies in the United States and Sweden (Elman 1996a), the other compares policies in the United States and India (Busch 1992). Policies to address violence against women thus constitute an important but understudied area.

This study employs an original cross-national data set on government response to violence against women. This rich data set provides a new empirical basis for evaluating competing approaches to explaining cross-national policy variation. Multivariate statistical analysis is combined with an examination of the process of policy development in a few countries in order to test the plausibility of the various explanations.

What does this analysis tell us about how democratic governments respond to this important and pervasive problem? What additional policy demands should women's groups and other community groups incorporate into their agendas in order to obtain a better government response? What lessons does this study offer to those seeking to improve policymaking and make it more democratic? Finally, what questions remain to be answered regarding policies on violence against women and regarding women's issues and democratic policymaking more generally?

A BRIEF REVIEW OF THE FINDINGS

The global approach used in this study permits us to examine the impact of level of development and cultural differences on government responsiveness to violence against women. Although these factors are usually assumed to be fundamentally determinative of national policy outcomes, they appear (at least in this issue area) to be relatively unimportant. Measures of national and regional cultural differences offer little insight into government responsiveness to violence against women. Level of development appears to have some relationship, but it is a weak, nonlinear one that is far from determinative. Thus, these concepts leave unexplained the bulk of the variation in government response to violence against women.

Strong, independently organized women's movements improve government responsiveness to violence against women. In fact, women's movements are a *necessary* condition for the initial articulation of this issue. It is women's movement activists who work to get violence against women recognized as a public problem rather than a private affair and thus put it on the public agenda. Women's movements are most effective in this respect when they are organized independently of political institutions and parties.

But articulation of an issue is not sufficient to produce a government response. How does the articulation by the women's movement of the issue of violence against women get taken up by government and translated into policy action?

The received wisdom in the study of women and public policy is that a greater proportion of women in the legislature leads to more women-friendly outcomes. One might think, therefore, that large numbers of women in the legislature increase the likelihood that government will take up the issue of violence. This expectation is not borne out by this study. There is only a very weak, nonlinear relationship between number of women legislators and policy outcomes on violence against women. This pattern would be consistent with the pattern of a "point of diminishing returns" only if the threshold point were a very small number of women. It may be that individual feminist women are important in getting policies passed as policy entrepreneurs. Indeed, it may be that the presence of at least one woman in the legislature is a necessary condition for policy development in this area. But there is no linear relationship between the overall number and proportion of women in government and government responsiveness to violence against women.

However, when there are policymakers who are sympathetic to the women's movement, or even part of the women's movement, the issue of violence against women is more likely to be adopted as part of the decision agenda. Allies inside government are critical to providing the political will to take up an issue that is always articulated outside government institutions. Most policies to address violence against women are products of such partnerships between women's movements and sympathetic insiders.

These partnerships are much less effective in the absence of a women's policy machinery. Where there is no effective women's policy machinery, the insider-outsider partnerships tend to produce partial, fragmented responses where there is such an agency, the partnerships are more likely to result in broad, multifaceted policies to address violence against women.

A women's policy machinery, however, is not *necessary* for putting violence on the public agenda. Nor is it sufficient to produce a government response: a women's policy machinery, in the absence of a strong autonomous women's movement, will not articulate the issue of violence. It is only in the context of a strong, autonomous women's movement articulating the issue and pressing for government action on violence against women that women's policy machineries have such a strong effect.

An effective women's policy machinery can strengthen a women's movement. Conversely, a strong women's movement improves the capacity of a set of political institutions to respond to women's concerns when that set includes a women's policy agency. Thus, strong, autonomous women's movements and effective women's policy agencies reinforce each other. This effect is not purely additive; it is interactive. Each factor magnifies the effect of the other and this interaction produces the broadest government responses to violence against women.

THE ARGUMENT FOR A STRUCTURAL APPROACH

I have demonstrated that standard comparative social policy and public policy explanations are inadequate for explaining cross-national variation in policies on violence against women (chapters 2 and 7). Perhaps more surprisingly, feminist and neoinstitutionalist approaches, by themselves, also fail to provide a satisfying explanation of policies on violence against women. These models are incomplete because they offer an inadequate account of (or fail to take any account of) the way that gender, race, class, and other social structures order policy processes. Even feminist, critical theorist, and neoinstitutionalist accounts, I have argued, are flawed because they do not adequately specify the relationship between public administrative bodies and social structures. Feminist and critical theoretic explanations devote insufficient attention to variation in administrative structures, while neoinstitutionalists fail to attend to the social structural aspects of social groups.

A structural policy analysis asks how social relations affect the policy issue or process in question. For example, a structural approach would take gender into account by considering the pattern of social norms and practices that determines the relations between and among men and women. How do changes or continuities in gender relations affect the operation of political institutions, political deliberations, and policy implementation, and vice versa? A structural approach also suggests the converse question: How do changes or continuities in the organization of political life and public policy affect gender relations?

Some have suggested that structural analyses rarely have specific policy implications. But I offer some below, drawing them out from this analysis by returning to the question with which I began this study: How can we improve government responsiveness to violence against women?

RESPONDING TO VIOLENCE AGAINST WOMEN

Most women's groups are already demanding government action in the seven areas I mentioned at the outset of this study:

(1) legal reform to address wife battering;

(2) legal reform to address sexual assault;

(3) funding for shelters or other forms of emergency housing provision for victims of wife battering;

(4) funding for crisis centers for victims of sexual assault;

(5) government-sponsored programs providing training for service providers and other professionals dealing with violence against women, such as police, judges, and social workers;

(6) government-sponsored public education initiatives; and

(7) a central agency for coordinating national policies on violence against women.

Activists and policymakers should also attend to the different ways that violence afflicts disadvantaged subgroups of women, such as minority, disabled, or lesbian women. These women are often at even greater risk of violence than white, able-bodied women. There may also be geographic, language, and other barriers that prevent certain subgroups of women from accessing services provided to women in general.

WORKING FOR INSTITUTIONAL REFORM

The findings of this study suggest ways of changing the policy process to make it more responsive to violence against women, and perhaps to women's issues more generally. Women's groups should demand institutional reforms to promote women's status. Ideally, such reforms should include the creation of the following:

A women's bureau: A women's bureau or agency should have plenty of resources and a head with the status of a cabinet-level appointment. This bureaucratic unit should be charged with overseeing policy research, policy formulation, and policy evaluation as they pertain to women. The bureau would also have administrative functions, coordinating policies that affect women where appropriate. This women's bureau should be a separate agency—not a subdepartment of tourism, recreation, family concerns, or even justice or health. Well-designed policies to address women's concerns usually require coordination across such divisions, so the women's bureau should not be positioned "beneath" these other administrative units in the bureaucratic hierarchy. However, a central women's bureau can be complemented by departmental women's units, as in the Australian "hub and spoke" model (Sawer 1995). Also, administrative subunits or committees focusing on marginalized subgroups of women may improve government responsiveness to violence and other issues as they affect these groups, although (as noted below) this likely depends on the existence of an autonomous social movement made up of these women.

An advisory council: An advisory council or body provides a mechanism by which women's groups may access government and express their concerns about policy. It is also a way for the government to consult women's organizations. This advisory council can be a part of the women's bureau or separate from it. Again, the council should certainly include substantial representation of marginalized subgroups of women. This could be accomplished by instituting a review of all council recommendations by subcommittees focusing on the concerns of specific marginalized subgroups.

Advocacy structures for other marginalized groups: The brief overview of government responsiveness to minority women in Canada and Australia that was presented in chapter 6 suggests that government commissions to address other axes of disadvantage may improve responsiveness to violence against minority women. Women's groups should push for similar administrative agencies and commissions for racial minority groups, the disabled, gays and lesbians, and so on.

A government commission on women: The case studies suggest that such institutional reforms can be catalyzed and legitimated by a government commission on women. Women's groups facing considerable opposition to their demands for reform may wish to demand a comprehensive presidential, royal, or other prestigious national commission to review progress on women's status and to lay out specific policy recommendations in a number of policy areas. Such commissions in India, Canada, and the United States were very successful in influencing public opinion and provided a unified program around which diverse women's organizations could unite.

Institutional reforms to provide public access to policymakers and accountability: Women's movements and other social movements will provide stronger checks on government action if they have better information and access to policymakers. In addition, advisory councils and bureaucratic organizations may become somewhat closed or elitist or may even be co-opted over time. Also, as noted, marginalized subgroups are sometimes dominated within social movements. General provisions requiring public consultations, public notification, and access to information can provide a check against such co-optation by ensuring that those who feel unrepresented by the formal organizations involved have an opportunity to voice their dissent and challenge the legitimacy of those who claim to speak for them. Since groups may need to go to court to demand enforcement of laws guaranteeing them access to information, funding for such legal action should be provided.

Such efforts to reform government institutions should greatly improve government responsiveness to violence against women. They should provide the administrative capacity necessary to design, formulate, and perhaps even implement policies on violence against women. These benefits will likely extend to other women's issues as well, especially those that do not fit neatly into current administrative structures. Such issues might include reproductive freedom and breaking down the gender division of labor (reorganizing both paid and unpaid work). The benefits of institutional reform, however, depend on the ability of the women's movement to maintain its independent organizational base.

MAINTAINING INDEPENDENT WOMEN'S MOVEMENTS

These institutional reforms are unlikely to have the intended effect un-less they are (at least to some degree) supported by and connected to inde-pendent women's movements. Thus, in order to improve responsiveness to violence against women, governments and activists should also work to maintain the independent base of women's movements. Government fund-ing has sometimes strengthened a women's movement that is critical of gov-ernment. This criticism improves the policy responsiveness of government. Of course, governments will periodically seek to eliminate this funding as a way of silencing their critics. For this reason, funding for women's organi-zations should be administered by an arm's-length body, whose members are appointed and retain their positions across administrations. Of course, the elimination of this body itself cannot be prevented, but a strong women's movement can protest such cutbacks and thus limit their impact. In Canada, feminists rallied to protest the Mulroney government's funding cuts to women's centers, and this funding was partially restored as a result. Against this background, I recommend the following:

Government funding for women's civil society: Government funding should be provided for independent women's organizations, newspapers, bookstores, and other women's movement institutions. This initiative should include funds targeted to marginalized subgroups of women, such as lesbian, minority, and disabled women. Where possible, women's groups re-ceiving government funding should seek to diversify the sources of their funding in order to avoid relying too heavily on a single source.

Forming a united women's coalition independent of government: Au-tonomous women's movements are stronger if united. For this reason, they should create a coalition or peak body of women's organizations that pro-vides an independent forum for articulation of and deliberation on the pri-orities of women. This body should, of course, include substantial representation of women from marginalized subgroups.

Separate nongovernmental organizations or caucuses for women from marginalized subgroups: Many women's groups in Canada have adopted a form of organization in which marginalized subgroups of women form cau-cuses within larger women's organizations and/or develop separate organi-zations that cooperate with more general women's organizations. It may be that such independent organization contributed to greater policy respon-siveness to minority women in Canada vis-à-vis Australia.

Although women's organizations should maintain independence, it should be done with an eye to improving cooperation between diverse women's groups and government agencies. In other words, autonomy should not be interpreted to mean that women's groups should refuse to interact with bureaucrats, or that those inside government should be seen as co-opted or "outside the movement." Rather, autonomy is a means of retaining a focus on women and on marginalized subgroups of women, and of helping to reorient women's movement goals and government policy.

The relationship between the National Action Committee (NAC) in Canada and the Native Women's Association of Canada (NWAC) exemplifies this model of separate organization and solidarity among women. These groups agitated to change government policy, and they participated in government consultations with great effectiveness. Although the NAC and NWAC received some government funding, they were vociferous critics of government on key issues. For example, in the early 1990s, they strenuously opposed the Charlottetown Accord, a proposal for constitutional reform that the Mulroney government had hoped to make its crowning achievement. This is not to suggest that NAC, NWAC, or the Canadian women's movement in general is perfectly inclusive. I only mention this example to suggest that there is the potential for combining separate organization, solidarity, and independence from government with engagement in policy processes.

MARGINALIZED GROUPS, SOCIAL STRUCTURES, AND DEMOCRATIC POLICYMAKING

This study suggests new ways to think about democratizing policymaking more generally, not just with respect to women's issues. Many studies have identified the normative and practical problems that marginalized groups present to modern democracies. In the United States, both Democrats and Republicans talk about the need for creating a "big tent," meaning a more inclusive polity. In Canada, the very existence of the state has been threatened by problems of inclusion, such as the possible secession of Quebec. In India, efforts to include oppressed castes by creating reserve seats for "backward castes" in Parliament resulted in riots and backlash. In Australia, the issue of reconciliation between Anglo or European Australians and indigenous peoples is also pressing.

Without suggesting that all of these situations are the same, I want to point out that there is a "family resemblance" among the problems of marginalization and political inclusion. Many scholars have argued that the inclusion of a greater variety of perspectives would enrich democratic policymaking (Phillips 1995) and improve public trust in political institutions (Mansbridge 1995). Many attempts to include the distinct voices or perspectives of disadvantaged groups have focused on getting more minorities or women into policymaking positions (Young 1996; Mansbridge 1996; Williams 1998; Phillips 1996).

One underexploited avenue for improving the representation of such perspectives in policymaking lies in the creation of administrative agencies whose job it is to liaise with autonomous social movements and develop policy research on issues of importance to disadvantaged groups. In the United States or Canada, for example, a bureau of racial equality could institute a "racial equality audit" program similar to the gender audit procedures developed in Australia and the European Union. Under such a procedure, departments would submit all policy proposals to the racial equality bureau for an evaluation as to whether the program had taken racial equality adequately into account. Alternatively, departments could be required to publish information on how the concerns of disadvantaged groups have been taken into account. For example, the state government in Texas requires government agencies to report the proportion of contracts that have been awarded to minority-owned businesses (Texas, General Services Commission 2000). Such measures permit active rights organizations, such as the NAACP (National Association for the Advancement of Colored People) in the United States, to monitor government departments and call them to account. In other words, there may be ways of changing institutional rules and structures that are as important to the political representation of women and minorities as is their actual physical presence.

These proposals are not meant to imply that the inclusion of minorities or women as policymakers should be abandoned as a goal. Rather, I suggest that recognizing and altering structural constraints on reform-minded policymakers and providing access and resources to citizen's groups and activists can make government responsiveness to social movements of disadvantaged groups more likely.

The institutional reforms described above are unlikely to have much effect unless they are (at least to some degree) supported by and connected to autonomous social movements. Again, women's policy agencies had an impact on violence-against-women policy only where there were strong, autonomous women's movements to articulate the issue of violence against women and keep up political pressure for an effective government response. If the experience of women's movements can be generalized to other social movements, autonomous organizing by social movements improves government responsiveness to their concerns.

Such organizing is likely to be the most effective mode of articulating policy issues of concern to disadvantaged groups. For policymakers inside the state, there will be pressure to shape social movements' demands so that they fit into preexisting priorities more easily. This may distort or suppress some issues of importance to disadvantaged groups. Autonomous social movements have the independence and critical distance needed to point out such difficulties and to maintain a direct focus on the key issues of concern to the movement.

Democratic governments should encourage autonomous movements by funding organizations, newspapers, bookstores, cultural festivals, and other activities that facilitate the development of autonomous networks among the members of marginalized groups. Democratic governments should also enact reforms that permit citizens to spend time participating in such groups. Such reforms would include government support for child care and elder care, a shorter workday (women in Norway are demanding a six-hour workday), and stronger protections for union organizers and other activists in their workplaces.

The vision of democracy that informs these recommendations is one in which both civil society and government institutions celebrate group difference and work to eliminate group-based oppression. Equal citizenship cannot be attained by pretending that we are all the same, or that group affiliations do not matter, when those group affiliations fundamentally determine the life chances of citizens. Insisting on a superficial group neutrality when none is actually possible disadvantages groups that are already defined as "different" from the norm: women in the paid workplace appear "different" from "workers in general" because of their child care responsibilities; Jews and Muslims in Christian-dominant societies appear "different" because of different customary practices and holidays. Recognizing such differences allows us to ensure that members of disadvantaged groups are merely different, and not also disadvantaged because of that difference.

Some worry that official recognition of group difference increases conflict and "balkanizes" the polity. Some states in the United States have a women's commission, a Mexican American commission, and a Native American commission. The Trudeau government in Canada was noted for creating commissions to "speak for" women, aboriginal Canadians, and cultural minorities. The European Union has a women's bureau and an office focusing on immigrants. While a proliferation of such commissions and agencies can be merely symbolic, I believe that this impulse is a positive one for democracy, and not a sign of increasing balkanization. Political inclusion must not require assimilation (Young 1990a, 2000).

Of course, one problem with the model I am suggesting here is that social movement organizations are not perfect mechanisms for representing marginalized groups. The lack of formal organization that is so characteristic of these movements makes it difficult to establish firm lines of accountability (Freeman 1975; Dryzek 1990). In addition, the many criticisms of racism and heterosexism within the women's movement in Canada and the United States make it plain that women's movements are not free from relations of domination internally (Davis 1989; hooks 1981). It is important to avoid romanticizing social movements.

In spite of these problems, social movements are the best mechanisms for articulating the views of marginalized groups. Formal mechanisms for special representation of marginalized groups, such as quotas or reserved seats, would offer clearer relationships of authorization and accountability.[1] But even in this case, marginalized groups would need to form a public of their own, to discuss issues and alternatives that are important to them. In addition, the administrative reforms I have suggested would still be needed to improve administrative capacity and to improve policy research and formulation. So the recommendations I advance here are intended to indicate just one way in which government responsiveness to marginalized groups could be improved. Administrative reforms of the type I have suggested would not, on their own, solve the problems of political exclusion and marginalization. But they might help.

DIRECTIONS FOR FUTURE RESEARCH IN WOMEN AND POLITICS

This study indicates many new directions for research on women in politics and on democratic policymaking more generally. First, if my analysis is correct, the establishment of women's policy agencies should improve policymaking in some (but not necessarily all) other areas of concern to women besides violence against women. Women's policy machineries are likely to have the greatest impact on those policy issue areas that do not tend to be conceptualized in gender-neutral terms. Violence against women, for example, is a problem that requires targeting policies to women and thus is not framed in gender-neutral terms. We might also expect women's policy agencies to effect dramatic improvements on issues such as reproductive freedom and breaking down the gender division of labor (reorganizing both paid and unpaid work). On the other hand, women may sometimes benefit from universal income assistance or employment policies that are not designed particularly to help women. Similarly, one might expect universal income assistance policies or attempts to establish a living wage to reflect the efforts of labor unions, community organizations, and like-minded groups.

Although women's policy agencies may improve the formulation of policies on poverty or minimum wages, we would not expect this impact to be as dramatic as in the case of policies that require an explicit focus on women.

Second, although I attempted a brief investigation of how the arguments in this book apply to disadvantaged subgroups of women, more research in this area is clearly needed. There is little work in feminist comparative policy analysis that focuses on the conditions of disadvantaged subgroups of women. To be sure, such projects are difficult to undertake, partly because data are scarce and partly because of concerns that concepts such as "women of color" do not "travel" across national boundaries. Still, I think that comparative feminist policy scholars should be careful not to take the easy way out on this issue (Beckwith 2000). After all, gender structures vary quite a bit cross-nationally and even within countries, but cross-national studies of gender politics and policy are becoming almost routine. In addition, there are certainly cross-national studies of race and politics outside the field of women and politics (for example, Marx 1998).

Analysts and policymakers should work to develop concepts and data that permit cross-national comparison of the situation of marginalized subgroups of women, such as disabled women, racial and ethnic minority women, immigrant women, indigenous women, lesbians, and so on. At the Fourth World Conference on Women in Beijing, governments agreed that

> Many women face particular barriers because of various diverse factors in addition to their gender. Often these diverse factors isolate or marginalize such women. They are, inter alia, denied their human rights, they lack access or are denied access to education and vocational training, employment, housing and economic self-sufficiency and they are excluded from decision-making processes. Such women are often denied the opportunity to contribute to their communities as part of the mainstream. (UN 1995a, Platform for Action, para. 31)

The Declaration also called on governments to

> Intensify efforts to ensure equal enjoyment of all human rights and fundamental freedoms for all women and girls who face multiple barriers to their empowerment and advancement because of such factors as their race, age, language, ethnicity, culture, religion, or disability, or because they are indigenous people. (UN 1995a, Beijing Declaration, para. 32)

This language suggests that policymakers are finding ways to address intersectionality in practice. Feminist comparativists should be able to develop ways to do this theoretically (Beckwith 2000).

Third, this study focused on the role of women's movements and agencies in affecting policy responsiveness. The question remains as to whether the argument applies to other aspects or "stages" of policymaking. For example, does a women's policy agency improve policy implementation or effectiveness in dealing with violence against women or similar women's issues? Many questions remain as to the impact of both political institutions and women's movements on policymaking.

Fourth, I have not addressed the impact of women's transnational organizing. It seems to me that over the period examined here (1974–1994), the impact of this networking came through national women's movements. In other words, feminist activists were inspired by and learned from their contacts with women in other parts of the world. After the Fourth World Conference on Women in Beijing in 1995, though, this international organizing seems to have had some independent effects on the formulation of policies that affect women. For example, it appears that the conference may have inspired some Latin American governments to adopt quotas to increase the number of women in government (Htun 1999). Thus, the question of how a growing international women's movement affects democratic policymaking processes also remains to be investigated.

We need both qualitative and quantitative work on these questions. For example, the ministry for women's affairs in New Zealand established mechanisms for the special representation of Maori women. Has this improved government responsiveness to violence against women in Maori communities? Has it improved responsiveness on other issues of importance to Maori women?

Studies of particular policies or policy contexts (countries, states or provinces, or cities) could explore the issues of policy effectiveness and implementation more effectively than is possible in a cross-national study of this scale. Of course, even more focused studies have had difficulties in measuring implementation, but this is one area where more work is needed. Studies of particular countries, states, or cities could also ask whether the general argument about policy responsiveness developed here seems to apply to that context.

Cross-national studies could examine other policy areas of concern to women in general, or could focus on marginalized subgroups of women. For example, a study might examine policies that affect disabled women cross-nationally. Parental leave policies, policies providing freedom of access to abortion and other reproductive technologies, and policies to address gender discrimination in the workplace would also be interesting to explore cross-nationally. What determines policy responsiveness in these areas? Do women's policy agencies and women's autonomous organizing have a similar effect in these other policy areas?

Another direction for cross-national policy research involves contrasting states' responsiveness to violence against women with the more conventional areas of gendered policy analysis, such as income assistance or employment policy. My findings suggest that focusing on violence yields a very different picture of which states have the most progressive policies in regard to women. To take the most striking examples, Ireland looks much more progressive than many feminist accounts would allow, and Sweden looks much less feminist. The United States, Canada, and Australia are not "residual" welfare states in this model, but rather are among the most developed when it comes to social policies that focus specifically on the subordination of women. This may suggest that welfare state typologies based on policies that do not explicitly challenge gender roles (such as state provision of benefits to stay-at-home mothers or to part-time workers) examine a different dynamic than that which underlies welfare policies aimed explicitly at changing gender roles (such as nontransferable paternity leave or policies to address violence against women) (cf. Gelb and Palley 1982).[2] In any case, these findings reinforce a growing body of literature that questions the accepted typologies of states and the developmental assumptions that undergird them (cf. Skocpol 1992; Elman 1996a; Duncan 1995). The usual groupings may be missing important aspects of the development of social policy. These missing pieces are likely to be particularly important for those interested in the study of gender and social policy. Further research should investigate these questions.

To sum up, the impact of gender on policy processes cannot be captured by looking only at individual-level variables. How policy affects and is affected by social relations between men and women cannot be determined by examining only the policy preferences or leadership styles of individual legislators. Nor can the impact of gender be understood through an analysis that assumes that states can be subsumed as functional parts of structures of male dominance. Policies, states, and gender structures must be conceptually distinguished before we can map the relations between them. Gender-based policy analysis must include an examination of institutional structures. Feminist policy scholars must examine whether political institutions facilitate or obstruct the articulation and enactment of policies addressing women's issues. Similarly, examination of women's movements that press for policies to undermine women's subordination must be part of a gendered analysis of policy. In other words, the organization of political life matters for gender politics.

DIRECTIONS FOR FUTURE RESEARCH IN PUBLIC POLICY STUDIES

One key question raised by the argument in this book is whether the conceptual analogy I have drawn between women's movements and movements to eliminate poverty, racism, homophobia, environmental degradation, and so on makes any sense. Do other social movements affect democratic policymaking in the way I have suggested? Specifically, do social movements transform political institutions and processes through discursive politics? The theoretical approach I am advocating here suggests that they do. Although we have some empirical studies of the effects of social movements such as the civil rights and environmental movements on policy processes (for example, Costain and McFarland 1998; Rochon and Mazmanian 1993), more empirical investigation of exactly how social movements transform political institutions is needed.

Similarly, would institutional reforms creating agencies analagous to women's policy agencies improve government responsiveness to other disadvantaged groups and social movements? I have argued that they should do so when there is a strong, autonomous social movement to support them. Again, this remains to be examined empirically.[3] The U.S. state of Maryland, for example, has a governmental department of minority affairs. Has this improved policymaking for minorities in Maryland vis-à-vis U.S. states that do not have such an agency? Did the creation of the United States Department of the Environment improve government responsiveness to the environmental movement?

It would also be interesting to examine the impact of such institutional reforms on areas that are not thought particularly to be women's issues or minority issues. For example, in Australia, each department had to submit its budget for evaluation as to whether it had taken women's concerns into account. How, if at all, did this affect transportation or economic development policy?

International institutions and transnational social movements appear to be playing a bigger role in democratic policymaking. In Canada, for example, a Native Canadian woman appealed to the International Court of Justice about a law that discriminated against Native women in determining who had a right to live on reserve. This law was supported by the main Native Canadian organizations at the time. The international court ruled against the law, and the law was changed (Whyte 1984). Similarly, international activism on sweatshops and human rights issues raises the question of how transnational activism affects democratic policymaking, particularly as it affects marginalized groups. This is largely uncharted territory.

CONCLUSION

In this book, I have demonstrated that greater policy responsiveness to the problem of violence against women is a product of the mutually reinforcing interaction between women's policy agencies and strong, autonomous women's movements. This analysis suggests a number of theoretical insights for the study of democratic policymaking, particularly as it pertains to women and other disadvantaged groups. If this analysis is sound, it points to some ways to further gender equality and to democratize policymaking. Institutional reforms aimed at providing an intra-institutional base for policy research and coordination on issues of importance to disadvantaged groups may provide a new way to ensure the representation of previously excluded perspectives. For example, institutional reform may be a relatively unexamined strategy for challenging gender inequality and for including women's perspective in policymaking. The effectiveness of democratic governments may also be improved by encouraging the mobilization of independent social movements. Government funding and other support for women's movements, for example, can strengthen the movement and thereby indirectly improve government responsiveness to these groups.

Thus, this study of policymaking on violence against women indicates many avenues for improving both scholarship and practice with respect to social movements, political institutions, and democratic public policy. I hope that these insights will help improve government responsiveness to violence against women and to other important problems confronting oppressed groups in modern democracies.

Appendix A
Compilation of Studies and Reports of Violence Against Women in Stable Democracies

This appendix is intended only to provide evidence that rape and domestic violence are problems in all stable democracies. Most of the data presented here are not comparable across countries because of differences in legal definitions and differing rates of reporting and awareness. Please see United States, Bureau of Justice Statistics (1988) for further discussion of the limited comparability of crime statistics. Publications are indicated by author and date; see the bibliography for the complete reference. Interpol statistics for 1988 are reported in Kurian (1991) and for 1984 they are taken from BJS (1988). UN statistics for 1980 are also reported in BJS (1988). For all other sources, note that the date of publication does not always correspond to the date of the data provided (for example, a report published in 1994 may contain data from 1992 or 1988).

COUNTRY	OVERALL VIOLENCE AGAINST WOMEN	RAPE REPORTS	WIFE BATTERING REPORTS
Australia		Sex offenses rate per 100,000 pop., 1988: 77.23 (Interpol)	Government reports it is a significant problem. (UN 1991)
		Sex offenses rate per 100,000 pop., 1984: 13.8 (Interpol)	
		2,806 rapes, 1990 (UNCJIN 1996)	
Austria		Sex offenses rate per 100,000 pop., 1988: 43.91 (Interpol)	Government reports it is a significant problem. In 1985, domestic violence was cited as a contributing factor to the breakdown of marriage in 59% of 1,500 divorce cases. Of those cases, 38% of working-class wives, 13% of middle-class wives, and 4% of upper-class wives called police. (UN 1991)
		7.5 rapes per 100,000 pop., 1980 (UN)	
		949 rapes, 1990 (UNCJIN)	
Bahamas	Increase in violence against women in the form of physical and sexual assault, including rape, incest, child abuse, and neglect.(CARICOM 1995, cited in Babb 1997)	Sex offenses rate per 100,000 pop., 1988: 66.37 (Interpol)	436 cases of domestic abuse, 1991–93 (Clarke 1997)
Barbados		71 rapes, 1990 (UNCJIN)	30% of women battered as adults; 50% of women and men report that their mothers were beaten. (Island-wide national probability sample; 264 women and 243 men aged 20–45). (Heise, Raikes, Watts, and Zwi 1994)

Continued

COUNTRY	OVERALL VIOLENCE AGAINST WOMEN	RAPE REPORTS	WIFE BATTERING REPORTS
Belgium	A random sample of 1,000 women in 1987 and 1988 found that 50% had been confronted with violence of one kind or another: 21.7% had experienced both sexual and physical violence by intimate partner. (Belgium 1994)	Sex offenses rate per 100,000 pop., 1988: 35.28 (Interpol) Government reports it is a significant problem. (UN 1991, 19) 14.9% report experiencing sexual violence in 1988 and 1989. (Belgium 1994)	25% of adult women have been physically assaulted by an intimate partner in 1989 (Belgium 1994) 21.3% of women reported experiencing physical violence. (Belgium 1994)
Botswana	Violence against women is a serious problem. (U.S. Department of State 1995, *Botswana Country Report*)	614 rapes, 1990 (UNCJIN)	The problem of spousal abuse is beginning to receive increased attention. (U.S. Department of State 1995, *Botswana Country Report*)
Canada	51% of women have experienced male violence, defined as physical or sexual assault considered an offense under the criminal code. (Statistics Canada 1993)	Sex offenses rate per 100,000 pop., 1988: 58.88 (Interpol) 14.1 per 100,000 pop., 1980 (UN) 27,842 rapes, 1990 (UNCJIN) 23.6% of women surveyed reported being victims of sexual assault in their lifetime (1993 study based on 420 randomly selected women). (Statistics Canada 1993) Of college-age women, 8.1% reported completed rape while 23.3% reported completed or attempted rape. (DeKeserady and Kelly 1993, cited in Heise, Pitanguy, and Germain 1994)	25% of adult women have been physically assaulted by an intimate partner. (Statistics Canada, 1993)
Colombia		4.4 per 100,000 pop., 1984 8.6 per 100,000 population, 1980 (UN)	46% of battered wives report marital rape. (Heise, Raikes, Watts and Zwi 1994) 20% physically and 33% psychologically abused; 10% raped by husband (1990 national random sample of 3,272 urban and 2,118 rural women). (Heise, Raikes, Watts, and Zwi 1994)
Costa Rica		9.9 per 100,000 pop., 1980 (Interpol) 13.5 per 100,000 pop., 1980 (UN) 256 rapes, 1990 (UNCJIN) 7% of women reported being sexually assaulted in a 5-year period; 5% of women reported being victims of sexual incidents in the past year (random stratified sample of 983 people; national survey). (UNICRI 1996)	54% of women attending child welfare clinics reported being physically assaulted by an intimate partner. (UN 1995c)

COUNTRY	OVERALL VIOLENCE AGAINST WOMEN	RAPE REPORTS	WIFE BATTERING REPORTS
Denmark		7.7 per 100,000 pop., 1984 (Interpol) 6.3 per 100,000 pop., 1980 (UN) 486 rapes, 1990 (UNCJIN)	About 4,000 women stay in domestic violence shelters each year. (LOKK 1996)
Finland		Sex offenses rate per 100,000 pop., 1988: 42.86 (Interpol) 7.7 per 100,000 pop., 1980 (UN) 381 rapes, 1990 (UNCJIN) Government reports it is a significant problem. (UN 1991)	Government reports it is a significant problem. (UN 1991)
France		Sex offenses rate per 100,000 pop., 1988: 32.14 (Interpol) 3.5 per 100,000 pop., 1980 (UN)	Government reports it is a significant problem. (UN 1995c)
W. Germany		9.7 per 100,000 pop., 1984 (Interpol) 11.2 per 100,000 pop., 1980 (UN) 5,112 rapes, 1990 (UNCJIN) Government reports it is a significant problem. (UN 1991)	Government reports it is a significant problem. (UN 1991)
Greece		0.9 per 100,000 pop., 1984 (Interpol) 5.3 per 100,000 pop., 1980 (UN) Government reports it is a significant problem. (UN 1991)	Government reports it is a significant problem. (UN 1991)
Iceland	Discussion at CEDAW suggests that violence is a serious problem, but little is known about the precise extent. (UN, CEDAW 1996a)		
India		0.7 per 100,000 pop., 1980 (Interpol) 10,068 rapes, 1990 (UNCJIN) 2% of women reported being victims of sexual assault in the past 5 years; 0.5% of women reported being victims of	4,835 women killed as victims of dowry deaths 75% of scheduled- (lower-) caste men reported beating their wives; 22% of higher-caste men reported beating; 75% of scheduled-caste wives reported being beaten frequently (1990, 50% sample of

Continued

COUNTRY	OVERALL VIOLENCE AGAINST WOMEN	RAPE REPORTS	WIFE BATTERING REPORTS
India *(Cont.)*		sexual incidents in the past year (random stratified sample of 1,000 people; survey of Bombay). (UNICRI 1996)	all scheduled-caste households and 50% of all non-scheduled-caste households; 109 women and 109 men from Jullunder Dist., Karnataka). (Heise, Raikes, Watts, and Zwi 1994)
			22% of women reported being "physically assaulted" by husbands; underreporting suspected (1993; 100% sample of a potter village in Karnataka). (Heise, Raikes, Watts, and Zwi 1994)
Ireland	8,000 calls per year to women's aid 6,000 calls per year (1996) to domestic violence and sex assault unit of police Multiple forms of abuse are common. (Ireland 1997c)	Sex offenses rate per 100,000 pop., 1988: 7.70 (Interpol) 14 per 100,000 (UN) 6,100 calls to Dublin's rape crisis center in 1995 (Ireland 1997c)	18% of women reported domestic violence in 1996. 7% of women in a national survey were abused by a partner or ex-partner over the previous year. (1996) 2,000 barring orders granted in 1996.
Israel		Sex offenses rate per 100,000 pop., 1988: 48.86 (Interpol)	Government reports it is a significant problem. (UN 1991)
Italy		5.3 per 100,000 pop., 1983 (Interpol) 3.3 per 100,000 pop., 1980 (UN) 687 rapes, 1990 (UNCJIN) Government reports it is a significant problem. (UN 1991)	There are about 100 centers serving victims of domestic violence. They are not funded by the federal government. (Italy 1997)
Jamaica	Increase in violence against women in form of physical and sexual assault, including rape, incest, child abuse, and neglect (CARICOM 1995, cited in Babb 1997)	Government reports it is a significant problem. (UN 1991) 1,297 reported cases of rape and carnal abuse (Clarke 1997)	Government reports it is a significant problem. (UN 1991) 2,176 reports of domestic abuse, 1991 (Clarke 1997)
Japan		Sex offenses rate per 100,000 pop., 1988: 3.57 (Interpol) 1.6 per 100,000 pop., 1984 (Interpol)	59% of adult women reported being physically assaulted by an intimate partner (based on a limited 17% return of questionnaires distributed nationally). (Heise, Raikes, Watts, and Zwi 1994)
Luxembourg		Sex offenses rate per 100,000 pop., 1988: 26.50 (Interpol) 2.8 per 100,000 pop., 1984 (Interpol) 28 rapes, 1990 (UNCJIN)	There are government-funded shelters for victims of domestic violence providing refuge to about 65 women each year. They receive 40–45 calls per day. (U.S. Department of State 1997, *Luxembourg Country Report*)

COUNTRY	OVERALL VIOLENCE AGAINST WOMEN	RAPE REPORTS	WIFE BATTERING REPORTS
Mauritius		Sex offenses rate per 100,000 pop., 1988: 6.88 (Interpol) 38 rapes, 1990 (UNCJIN)	Between 1989 and 1995, there were 1,500 reported cases of wife battering. (UN, CEDAW 1995, *Concluding Observations, Mauritius*) From 1993 to 1994, there was a 43% increase in spousal abuse. (U.S. Department of State 1995, *Mauritius Country Report*)
Nauru	Human rights reports indicate that violence against women occurs but is rarely dealt with by police. (U.S. Department of State 1996d)		
Netherlands		7.2 per 100,000 pop., 1984 (Interpol) 5.6 per 100,000 pop., 1980 (UN) 1,321 rapes, 1990 (UNCJIN)	21% of adult women reported being physically assaulted by an intimate partner. (Heise, Raikes, Watts, and Zwi 1994)
New Zealand		Sex offenses rate per 100,000 pop., 1988: 100.35 (Interpol) 14.4 per 100,000 pop., 1984 (Interpol) Of college-age women 14% reported completed rape while 25.3% reported completed or attempted rape. (Gavey 1991, cited in Heise, Pitanguy, and Germain 1994)	17% of adult women reported being physically assaulted by an intimate partner. (UN 1995c)
Norway		Sex offenses rate per 100,000 pop., 1988: 21.73 (Interpol) 4.2 per 100,000 pop., 1984 (Interpol) 3.2 per 100,000 pop., 1980 (UN) 376 rapes, 1990 (UNCJIN)	25% of adult women reported being physically abused by an adult partner. (UN 1995c; survey only in Trondheim)
Portugal	Government reports that violence against women is a serious problem. Many cases are not reported at all. (Portugal 1994)	2.0 per 100,000 pop., 1984 (Interpol) 1.2 rapes per 100,000 pop., 1980 (UN) 315 rapes, 1990 (UNCJIN) In 1993, 174 rapes were reported to police. In addition, 86 cases of sexual abuse were reported. (Portugal 1994)	60 women were killed by men and 75 women were victims of manslaughter by men in 1993. 1,904 women were victims of bodily harm. (Portugal 1994)

Continued

COUNTRY	OVERALL VIOLENCE AGAINST WOMEN	RAPE REPORTS	WIFE BATTERING REPORTS
Papua New Guinea		Sex offenses rate per 100,000 pop., 1988: 31.36 (Interpol) 14% of women reported having been sexually assaulted in a 5-year period; 11.8% of women reported being victims of sexual incidents in the past year (random stratified sample of 1,583 people representing three cities). (UNICRI 1996)	67% of rural, 56% of low-income urban, and 62% of urban elite women "beaten by husbands" (sample of 736 rural men, 715 rural women; urban low-income: 368 men and 298 women; urban elite: 178 men and 99 women). (Law Reform Commission 1986, cited in Heise, Raikes, Watts, and Zwi 1994)
Spain	10% of women suffer one form of violence or another. (Spain 1997b)	Sex offenses rate per 100,000 pop., 1988: 12.52 (Interpol) 3.6 per 100,000 pop., 1984 (Interpol) 2.5 per 100,000 pop., 1980 (UN) 1,790 rapes, 1990 (UNCJIN) 1,863 rapes reported in 1995. Police received 16,000 calls about abuse, but experts estimate only 10% are reported to police. Women's groups estimate 600,000–800,000 cases of abuse each year.	16,378 "marital problems, up 3% from 1996" (Spain 1997b) 47 women killed by partners (U.S. Department of State 1997, *Spain Country Report*)
Sweden		Sex offenses rate per 100,000 pop., 1988: 46.10 (Interpol) 11.9 per 100,000 pop., 1984 (Interpol) 10.6 per 100,000 pop., 1980 (UN) 1,410 rapes, 1990 (UNCJIN)	A study of 82 battered women found that 76% had also been subject to forced sex. (Elman and Eduards 1991)
Switzerland		Sex offenses rate per 100,000 pop., 1988: 57.65 (Interpol) 5.8 per 100,000 pop., 1984 (Interpol) 428 rapes, 1990 (UNCJIN)	There are centers to assist victims of domestic violence, but no official statistics about how many cases. (U.S. Department of State 1995)
Trinidad & Tobago	Increase in violence against women in form of physical and sexual assault, including rape, incest, child abuse, and neglect (CARICOM 1995, cited in Babb 1997)	Sex offenses rate per 100,000 pop., 1988: 10.21 (Interpol) 220 rapes, 1990 (UNCJIN) Government reports it is a significant problem. (UN 1991) Charges of rape, attempted rape, and serious indecency rose from 185 to 250 between Sept. and Nov. 1995 (Babb 1997)	Government reports it is a significant problem. (UN 1991) Jan. to Oct. 1995, 12 women murdered by husbands. Between Oct. 1991 and Apr. 199? a total of 8,297 applications were made for protection orders. (Clarke 1997)

COUNTRY	OVERALL VIOLENCE AGAINST WOMEN	RAPE REPORTS	WIFE BATTERING REPORTS
United Kingdom		Sex offenses rate per 100,000 pop., 1988: 41.14 (Interpol) Of college-aged women, 11.7% reported completed rape while 19.4% reported completed or attempted rape. (Beattie 1992, cited in Heise, Pitanguy, and Germain 1994)	Government reports it is a significant problem. (UN 1991)
United States	Women experienced over 1 million violent victimizations per year committed by an intimate. Nearly 30% of female homicide victims were killed by their husbands. (Department of Justice 1996) Women with incomes below $10,000 were more likely to be attacked (1994–95) (Department of Justice 1998)	Sex offenses rate per 100,000 pop., 1988: 35.67 (rape only) (Interpol) 1 in 5 to 1 in 7 women will be a victim of a completed rape in her lifetime (legal definition of rape) (six studies based on random probability samples). (Heise, Raikes, Watts, and Zwi 1994) Of college-age women, 15.4% reported completed rape while 27.5% reported completed or attempted rape. (Koss, Gidyoz, and Wisniewski, cited in Heise, Pitanguy, and Germain 1994) A study of 137 battered women found that 73% had also been pressured to have sex by their batterers. (Frieze 1983)	28% of adult women reported being physically assaulted by an intimate partner. (UN 1995c)
Venezuela		Sex offenses rate per 100,000 pop., 1988: 45.89 (Interpol) 2,928 rapes, 1990 (UNCJIN) Government reports it is a significant problem. (UN 1991)	About two-thirds of women asking for help at shelters have problems with violence in the family. (Marin 1997)

Appendix B
Notes on Method and Measurement

This appendix is intended to supplement the discussion of methods and measurement provided in the preceding chapters. Some basic concepts are explained for those less familiar with regression analysis, and some more technical details about measurement choices and analysis are included.

The statistical analyses reported in this study use a single cross-section of countries in the year 1994, a total of thirty-six cases. Although data exist for all the countries from 1974 to 1994 for most variables, for several key variables (women's policy machinery, women in cabinet, and women subministers) data are available only for the 1990s, so cannot use the full pooled time series data set for the statistical analysis. I should note however, that preliminary analyses using the whole data set were completed for variable for which data were available (such as GNP per capita, number of women in the legislature, and the presence of a women's movement), and the results were consistent with those using the single cross-section. This preliminary analysis of the full pooled time series data set used a special version of ordinary least squares that adjusts for autocorrelation in times series data, called estimated generalized least squares (EGLS). See Gujarati 1995 for a fuller discussion of this method.

Analysis of Data Using Ordinary Least Squares Regression

Ordinary least squares (OLS) regression is a statistical technique that examines whether a given data set shows a linear relationship between variables. A linear relationship is one that can be described using a straight line. This means that the value of the dependent variable (y) can be calculated given the value of the independent variable and the y-intercept. Those who remember their high school algebra will recall that the formula for a straight line is $Y = bX + c$, where c is the y-intercept (the value of y when x is o) and where there is one independent variable. In this formula, the coefficient of x (which we are calling b) describes the amount of change in Y we can expect for a one-unit change in X—the slope of the line.

Coefficients and Standard Errors

OLS is a technique that tries to fit a number of formulas to a data set to see which one best describes the relationship. OLS identifies the equation that results in the smallest errors in predicting Y using X. Like the coefficient B described above, the value of the coefficients in the equation calculated using OLS can be interpreted as the amount of change in the dependent variable (Y) associated with a one-unit change in the independent variable (X). The standard error is the average amount of error associated with prediction of y using x that arises from using the x coefficient in the linear equation derived using OLS. When errors are large compared to coefficients, the usefulness of the independent variable as a predictor of the dependent variable is minimized. Large errors in prediction may make it more reasonable simply to guess the mean (or average) of the dependent variable.

Standardized Betas

Sometimes we wish to know which of a number of independent variables is the best predictor of the dependent variable. But the raw coefficients (b's) in the regression equation can be misleading, since the change in the dependent variable for one unit of change in the independent variable is not always a good comparison. For example, a change in one unit (one dollar) of GNP per capita will not be as important as a one-unit change in the number of women in cabinet. GNP per capita can range from zero to twenty-five thousand dollars, and a one-dollar change is a very small proportion of this variation; but the number of women in cabinet may only range between zero and eight, so an increase of one woman may be important. In order to compare the strength of association of the independent variables with the dependent variables in one regression equation, we must standardize the coefficients to adjust for the difference in units for different variables. We can do this by using a measure of variability (the standard deviation) of the independent variable and comparing it to the variability of the dependent variable. Coefficients that have been adjusted for different levels of variability are called standardized coefficients, or standardized Betas.

The Assumptions of Ordinary Least Squares Regression

Before a multiple regression can be used, several conditions, or assumptions, must be met (Gujarati 1995; Berry and Feldman 1985). Here I list these assumptions and show how the data set I have created measures up.

1) The relationship is linear and additive.

Linearity: As explained above, OLS identifies the equation for the line that best describes a relationship. Nonlinear relationships (for example, those that are curvilinear, or exponential) will usually not be detected using OLS. However, nonlinear relationships can sometimes be captured by transforming the relevant variable. For example, exponential relationships can be captured by transforming the variable using a log transformation and then using the transformed variable in the regression equation. In this study I use a log transformation for two variables: GNP per capita and number of women in the lower house of the legislature. So some nonlinearity can be accommodated by OLS.

Additivity: In its usual mode of application, multiple regression allows us to see how much variance is associated with an explanatory factor X compared to other explanatory factors. This allows us to evaluate how much additional explanatory leverage is gained from adding that factor, X, to other explanatory factors.

For most of the analysis presented here, this additive version of the relationship can be assumed to capture the theoretical model underlying the statistical test. Some hypotheses, however, involve testing interactions that could have a multiplicative effect. In order to take this into account, I employ techniques that allow me to use regression to assess whether the specific type of multiplicative relationship I propose is supported in the data. An example is multiplying the factors together and then treating them as a single variable that has a linear relationship with the dependent variable.

(2) The values of the factors are fixed in repeated sampling, that is, x is assumed to be non-stochastic.

This assumption is not relevant for studies that do not involve sampling, such as this one.

(3) The number of observations must be greater than the number of independent/explanatory variables (that is, parameters to be estimated).

Multiple regression examines how the value of the dependent variable changes as a result of changes in an explanatory factor, x, when other explanatory factors are at constant levels. In order to allow for this kind of controlled comparison, there must be a sufficient number of cases or observations to allow observation of variance in the independent and dependent variables. With only one observation, this is impossible. In addition, the smaller the number of observations and the greater the number of cross-tabulations that must be done to carry out the regression, the greater the risk of error in generalizing from a small number of cases to the whole population. The latter rationalization is of less importance for population studies than it is for studies that involve sampling. As noted above, the number of observations in this study (thirty-six) is greater than the number of independent variables (three or four at most in each equation).

(4) There must be some variability in the value of the explanatory variable.

If there is no variability, it is difficult to assess how different levels of the explanatory variable affect the dependent variable. This study involves considerable variation in the dependent variable, government response to violence against women; it ranges from o (no response) to 7 (the best response).

(5) The regression model is correctly specified.

The regression model tests how well a straight line can capture the relationship between the dependent and independent variables. If the relationship is not linear, the method of multiple regression can sometimes be adjusted to take this into account. If no adjustments are made, however, regression can be a poor method for examining nonlinear relationships (such as parabolic or exponential relationships).

In addition to misspecifying the form of the relationship, regression can result in inaccurate assessments of the relationship between dependent and independent variables if irrelevant variables are included in the relationship, or if relevant variables are excluded from the equation.

In this study I have taken care to specify the relationships so as to best capture the meaning of the theoretical arguments I am testing. Where the theoretical arguments suggest a nonlinear relationship (as in my own hypothesis), I employ techniques to take this into account. There are methods for testing for both types of errors, and I employ them in this analysis to check the assumptions in the model.

(6) All variables must be measured at the interval level and without error.

Interval-level measurement: Multiple regression usually requires that all variables be measured at the interval level of measurement—that is, not only do the values dictate a particular order, but the difference between the values (for example, between 1 and 2 or between 3 and 4) must be of the same significance. In this study, some of the variables are measured at the interval level, such as GNP and number of women in the legislature. However, some of the factors we are interested in, such as religion and region, are categorical variables, that is, they are variables for which the answer can only be categorized, not ranked. There is no obvious order, for example, Catholic–Protestant–Hindu–Jewish–Buddhist–Greek Orthodox, or to Latin America–Europe–Oceania. In general, using categorical data in combination with continuous data in a regression equation is acceptable as long as the dependent variable, or the outcome one is trying to explain, is measured at the interval level and is continuous.

The measure I have constructed for scope of government response to violence against women is not, strictly speaking, continuous, since the meaning of "half a policy area" is not immediately obvious. But conceptually, government response can be conceived of as continuous: that is, a partial response can be understood conceptually; initiatives may be partially implemented, or partially adopted, or overturned. Theoretically, we could also have "negative" responsiveness to violence against women. I am coding policies as responses to violence against women only when they explicitly (not accidentally or incidentally) aim to prevent violence against women. Policies that explicitly aim to promote violence against women (such as a formal policy advocating rape or honor killings of women) are the exact opposite of responsiveness to violence and therefore should be coded negatively. To my knowledge, none of the countries in this study has adopted such explicit violence-promoting policies during the study period, but it is at least conceptually possible that a government could do so. Since the dependent variable can be conceptualized as continuous, then, the fact that the measure itself is not continuous is not a serious threat to the validity of the process.

In addition, it is important to note that the continuous nature of variables really only requires the distribution of values over a sizeable range. As Aldrich and Nelson (1984, 12) note, the dependent variable in theory must be free to take on any value, from negative infinity to positive infinity. In practice, though, the dependent variable will take on only a small set of values in the data. For example, family income for the year is likely to fall only within a small range of the possible set of values from negative infinity to positive infinity. Nevertheless, since the assumption of continuity for family income holds, interval measurement will not be a bad approximation for the continuous variable. If the dependent variable can only take on two values, however, this is too severe a restriction on the assumption of continuity. But variance across eight categories (0–7), as in this study, is sufficient to warrant use as a dependent variable in a regression equation.

Measurement Error: In practice, measurement error is unavoidable. The main concern here is whether we are really measuring the concept in question, that is, a concern about validity (Berry and Feldman 1985). In this study, of course, I strive to choose good measures of the concepts I am using. Some individual indicators are discussed below.

(7) For each set of values for the k independent variables $(x_{1j}, x_{2j}, \ldots x_{kj})$, the mean value of the error term is zero.

This assumption merely requires that factors not included in the model, and therefore subsumed in the error term, do not systematically affect the mean. The positive errors should cancel out the negative errors so that their mean is zero and they have no effect on the dependent variable. (This assumption is important only when the analyst is interested in the precise value of the intercept.) As I mentioned above, I examine the residuals to check whether factors not included in the model are systematically affecting the mean.

(8) For each set of values for the k independent variables, the variance of the error term is constant (no heteroscedasticity; that is, variability is constant in Y for each value of X).

Heteroscedasticity affects the estimates of the standard error and thus affects the accuracy of tests of statistical significance. In most cases, heteroscedasticity has only small effects on the coefficients, but in other cases it can be a problem.

Certain types of variables are more likely to result in heteroscedasticity than others. Variables that are thought to be necessary but not sufficient to affect the dependent variable are likely to interact with other variables, meaning that they have differential amounts of effect on the dependent variable at different levels. This means they are not homoscedastic. In order to detect such heteroscedasticity, it is usual to plot the residuals of the regression equation against the suspect variable in order to see if there is any relationship. I plot the residuals against the indicators for women's movement, women's policy machinery, and number of women in elected and appointed public office in order to check for heteroscedasticity. As noted, I use these variables in a multiplicative fashion in my own hypothesis, which eliminates some of the problems associated with necessary but not sufficient conditions.

(9) For any two sets of values for the k independent variables, the error terms are uncorrelated; thus there is no autocorrelation.

Omitted factors can result in autocorrelation. I check for omitted factors using an examination of residuals and by paying close attention to the theoretical basis for the hypothesis.

(10) Each independent variable is uncorrelated with the error term.
Again, the correlation of independent variables with the error term is a result of specification error—in this case, excluding relevant variables from the analysis that are correlated with one of the independent variables in the equation. As I mention above, I check for excluded variables by examining the relationship between the residuals and the individual independent variables.

(11) There is no perfect collinearity. No independent variable is perfectly linearly related to one or more of the other independent variables in the model.

I have regressed each of the explanatory factors here on the other explanatory factors and have not found any levels of association even close to .70. I have also examined bivariate correlations and have found only low levels of association. I therefore conclude that I have no problems with collinearity.

(12) For each set of values for the k independent variables, the error term is normally distributed.

This assumption is necessary only for tests of statistical significance and thus is of little importance here. However, residuals appear to be normally distributed.

Notes on Operationalization and Measurement of Selected Variables

These notes are intended to supplement the discussion of selected variables provided in the previous chapters. For this reason, not all variables are discussed below.

Scope of Government Response (Dependent Variable)

Scope is a variable that measures how many areas of policy on violence against women a government addresses; it ranges from 0 (no areas) to 7 (seven areas). A coefficient *(b)* of 1.00 for an independent variable means that a one-unit change in the independent variable is associated with one additional area of policy action.

Note that scope is not an event count. All seven areas can be addressed in one piece of legislation, or in a number of different pieces of legislation. In addition, if a government addresses the same policy area with two different legislative measures or programs, this is counted as one policy area, according to my coding rules. Thus, this dependent variable violates the assumptions required for doing an analysis using a Poisson distribution (sometimes used for dependent variables that are event counts). Fortunately, regression using the dependent variable appears to meet the minimal requirements for analysis using OLS. Since violations of regression analysis using the normal distribution are less serious than violations of the assumptions of regressions using the Poisson distribution, the former is used in this analysis.

All seven policy areas are equally important for addressing violence against women, oth symbolically and substantively. This means that governments sometimes obtain the ame score by enacting different policies. Policy experts and activists argue that there is o single policy solution and that an appropriate response is one that attacks the prob- m on all fronts (Busch 1992; UN, CEDAW 1998b; Chalk and King 1998). For this rea- on, the dependent variable is measured in terms of the number of different sorts of things lat governments are doing (which I am calling scope) rather than by which of the seven olicy areas they address. By this measure, a government that undertook only a criminal istice response or only public education initiatives would receive a lower score than one lat undertook both types of response.

Because this measure is a straightforward measure of scope, rather than an index, it not appropriate to evaluate whether action in one of the seven areas is correlated with ction in the others, as is often done for composite indices. Each area is a distinct type of olicy action, and there is no a priori reason to think that action in one area would be re- ted or unrelated to action in another area. Although such relationships may be inter- sting to explore in future research, they are not relevant for this study, which focuses on cope of government response.

Nevertheless, some readers will insist that this measurement constitutes an index. or these readers, I report that Chronbach's alpha for these seven items exceeds .7, al- lough I maintain that alpha is inappropriate for evaluating the measure presented here.

egion (Independent Variable)

Region is coded as a dummy variable, that is, each category is coded as applying (1) r not (0) for each country. For example, we would create the variable "Latin America" nd code Latin American countries 1 and all other countries 0. Since there are six regions f the world, we use five dummy variables to categorize the dimension of region (the mitted variable is the variable signified by all zeros—in this case, Europe). If a particu- ir region is associated with greater responsiveness, then we would expect a score of 1 to e associated with a sizeable change in scope.

Since Europe is the omitted category, the coefficients for countries in a particular re- ion should be interpreted as estimating the difference in scope of government response ssociated with being in that region rather than in Europe. A positive coefficient means lat governments are more responsive than European governments, and a negative coef- cient means they are less responsive. The omitted variable is generally the one that is of le most theoretical significance. Europe is chosen here because most of the cultural ex- lanations of policy variation take European countries as their referent.

eligion (Independent Variable)

Like region, religion was measured using a dummy variable. In this case, Catholicism the omitted category, since it is the only religion about which there are specific hy- otheses. Data on dominant religions are taken from the CIA *World Factbook* (U.S. Cen- ral Intelligence Agency 1993).

Vomen's Movements (Independent Variable)

Women's movement activity is often operationalized as the number of women's or- anizations or as the number of women belonging to such organizations. Comparable, eliable data on women's organizations and their membership are not available for all the countries in this study. While the numerical nature of these data makes it easy to use them in regression equations as measures of women's movement activity (no doubt one reason for the popularity of these measures), there are several drawbacks.

The number of women's organizations may be a poor indicator of the importance of the women's movement in a country. There may be many traditional women's organizations and auxiliaries that predate the feminist movement and remain completely removed from it. In addition, it is not clear that one influential, encompassing organization is less important than several fragmented or weak organizations. Using organizational membership figures does not resolve these problems. Because of many feminists' opposition to bureaucratic forms, some women's groups eschew formal organization and formal membership requirements. Many feminist activists are not members of any large organization, although they participate in demonstrations, write letters and petitions, and work for reform in their workplaces and other institutions. This is particularly a problem in cross-national studies, where membership in feminist organizations may tell us more about people's predilection to join organizations than it does about the women's movement. For example, in Norway, about 80 percent of the general population belongs to an organization of some kind.

As I argue in chapter 3, looking only at women's organizations misoperationalizes the source of the influence of a women's movement—namely, the broader activities of the movement. Costain (1998) operationalizes this activity by coding accounts of feminist activities reported in newspapers and finds that the influence of women's groups depends on these less government-oriented activities. Unfortunately, such a coding project is impractical for this study.

Fortunately, better indications of women's movement activity are possible. In cross-national comparative studies of women's movements, which tend to be historical narrative accounts, women's movement activity is usually taken to be indicated by accounts of feminist demonstrations, petitions, conferences, and other events; feminist newspapers and publications; the development and decline of women's organizations and coalitions and the like. The strength of a women's movement is often taken to be indicated by public support for the movement as expressed in public opinion polls, newspaper editorials, number of signatures on petitions, size of demonstrations, behavior of public officials, and so on.

The existence of women's movements can be studied cross-nationally based on coding of historical and other narrative accounts of the women's movement in each country. Women's movements can be coded as autonomous if they have an organizational base outside political parties, unions, and other political institutions. Movements can be coded as strong if they are described in narrative accounts as strong, influential, powerful, mobilizing widespread public support, or the like. Where the women's movement is both strong and autonomous according to these criteria, the country is coded 1; where either strength or autonomy is absent, the country is coded 0. (For a summary of coding by country, see table 3-1.)

This limited "on-off" coding for strength and autonomy was the only possible way to consistently and reliably code movements across countries; the data did not permit more refined coding of either strength or autonomy. Conceptually, it is hard to think how one would rank countries according to variations in autonomy. How would we classify one women's movement as slightly more autonomous than another? The bigger differences I have identified (for example, whether the women's movement is organized inde pendently of the state) are a less refined categorization, but an easier one to explain and defend. Thus, it is not clear that, even if data did exist to create more refined categories for strength and autonomy, the costs in persuasiveness would be worth having this more refined coding scheme. The classification developed here, while broad, has the advantage of being clearly conceptually based on the discussion of women's movements in the literature and of also being relatively easy to apply to a variety of contexts.

Women Policymakers (Independent Variable)

Several different measures of women's impact as policymakers are employed in this study. Data on the number and proportion of women in the legislature are taken from the Interparliamentary Union's 1995 report. The number, proportion, and logged number of women in legislature are used in regression analyses. In addition, in order to test for a critical mass, countries with legislatures containing a critical mass were coded 1, while those without were coded 0. This was done to test for critical mass effects at two levels, 10 percent and 30 percent.

The proportion of women in cabinet and the proportion of women subministers were also employed as indicators of women's influence as policymakers. These data were taken from *The World's Women* (UN 1995c). Of course, these measures were run in separate models to avoid problems with multicollinearity.

Women's Policy Machinery (Independent Variable)

A women's policy machinery is a set of one or more government institutions (for example, an office, department, commission, or ministry) whose main purpose is to promote the status of women. Listings are taken from the United Nations' directory of women's policy machineries (UN, Division for the Advancement of Women 1993).

Most countries now have women's policy machineries. More important for this study than their mere existence is the distinction between effective and ineffective women's policy machineries. Effective ones have (1) formalized channels of access for women's organizations; and (2) the independence and resources needed to formulate and implement aspects of a women's agenda.

Formalized channels of access are taken to be indicated by the existence of a formal consultative body of independent women's organizations, by the existence of a liaison office for women's organizations, or when formal meetings with women's organizations are part of organizational procedures. An agency is judged to be independent when its head has cabinet status or when it is a completely separate agency that reports directly to the head of government. Arm's-length bodies are also taken to be independent. Adequate resources to implement a women's agenda include staff and resources to do research and organizational work.

Organizational charts for many women's policy machineries are provided in the UN directory (UN, Division for the Advancement of Women 1993). In addition, historical accounts of the development of the women's policy machinery are available for many of the countries studied here (Stetson and Mazur 1995; Staudt 1997; Tremblay and Andrew 1998; Nelson and Chowdhury 1994). Based on information in these sources, countries are coded 1 if they meet both conditions for an effective women's policy machinery, and 0 if they do not. The results of this coding are reported in chapter 5.

The machinery is coded 1 only if both conditions are met because neither condition alone is theoretically sufficient for policy influence. If women's movements have access to a women's policy machinery but the machinery does not have the resources to do research or analysis or to organize consultations with important policymakers, then this access is unlikely to result in policy influence. If the policy machinery has plenty of resources and influence but excludes women's organizations, then it is unlikely to articulate a women's agenda. Under the latter circumstances, the women's policy machinery is more likely to function as a public relations body than as a mechanism for improving responsiveness to women's issues in political institutions. So in order for the women's policy machinery to have an impact on policy, both conditions specified above must obtain.

Appendix C
List of Sources by Country

In this listing, sources are given by name and date. See the bibliography for the full citation.

Global Documents

These documents have data on all or almost all of the countries in the study, so they are listed here to avoid repetition.

Barrett 1993
Connors 1989
Heise, Pitanguy, and Germain 1994
Heise, Raikes, Watts, and Zwi 1994
Randall 1982
Schrier 1988
Seager 1997
Stetson and Mazur 1995
UN 1993, 1995c

Australia

Bell 1994
Bolger 1991
Commonwealth Office of the Status of Women 1997, 2000a, 2000b, 2000c
Eisenstein 1995
Minister for Aboriginal and Torres Strait Islander Affairs 2000
Sawer 1994, 1995
U.S. Department of State 1997, 1996 *Human Rights Report: Australia*
Women's Electoral Lobby 1994
Yeatman 1990

Austria

Federal Minister for Women's Affairs and Consumer Protection 1998a, 1998b, 1998c
Kaplan 1992
U.S. Department of State 1995, *Austria Country Report, 1994*

Bahamas

Babb 1997
CAFRA Bahamas 1998
Clarke 1997
Crisis Centre 1998
Ortiz 1997

U.S. Department of State 1997, *1996 Human Rights Report: Bahamas*
Vargas 1997

Barbados
Babb 1997
Bureau of Women's Affairs 1998
Clarke 1997
Ortiz 1997
UN, CEDAW 1994, *Barbados Praised;* 1994, *Concluding Observations, Barbados;* 1994,
    Press Release
U.S. Department of State 1995, *Barbados Country Report, 1994;* 1997, *Barbados
    Country Report, 1996*
Vargas 1997

Belgium
Belgian Co-ordinating Committee 1994
Conseil de l'Égalité des Chances entre Hommes et Femmes 1997
Lovenduski 1986
Ministère de l'Emploi et du Travail 1997
Ministère de la Justice 1998
Paternottre 1998
Secrétaire d'État à l'Emancipation Sociale 1987
U.S. Department of State 1995, *Belgium Country Report, 1994*

Botswana
Human Rights Watch 1994
U.S. Department of State 1995, *Botswana Country Report, 1994;* 1997, *Botswana
    Country Report, 1996*
Women's Affairs Division 1995

Canada
Andrew 1995
Arscott and Trimble 1997
Bashevkin 1993; 1994; 1998
Begin 1997
Belanger and Regehr 1998
Canadian Advisory Council on the Status of Women 1982
Canadian Council on Social Development and Native Women's Association of Canada
    1991
Canadian Panel on Violence Against Women 1993
Denham and Gillespie 1998
Department of Justice Canada 1995
Family Violence Prevention Division, Health Canada 1996a, 1996b
Family Violence Prevention Unit, Health Canada 2000
Geller-Schwartz 1995
Gotell 1998
Health and Welfare Canada 1992

House of Commons, Standing Committee on Health, Welfare, Social Affairs, Seniors
     and the Status of Women 1982
House of Commons, Status of Women Subcommittee of the Standing Committee on
     Health, Welfare, Social Affairs, Seniors and the Status of Women 1991
Sproule 1998
Statistics Canada 1990, 1993
Status of Women Canada 1991, 1995
Tremblay and Andrew 1998
U.S. Department of State 1997, *Canada Country Report, 1996*
Vickers, Rankin, and Appelle 1993
Walker 1990, 1993

Colombia
Babb 1997
Colombia 1996
Marin 1997
Ortiz 1997
UN, CEDAW 1994, *Concluding Observations, Colombia;* 1994, *Experts at Committee
     on Elimination of Gender Discrimination;* 1995, *Concluding Observations,
     Colombia*
U.S. Department of State 1995, *Colombia Country Report, 1994;* 1997, *Colombia
     Country Report, 1996*
Vargas 1997

Costa Rica
González-Suárez 1994
Ortiz 1997
Sagot 1994
U.S. Department of State 1997, *Costa Rica Country Report, 1996*
Vargas 1997

Denmark
Bergqvist 1999
Borchorst 1995
Centre for Women and Gender Research 1995
Danish Equal Status Council 1995
Haavio-Mannila 1985
Kaplan 1992
Kvindecenterfonden, Dannerhuset 1998
Landsorganisation af Kvinderkrisecentre (LOKK), 1996, 1998
Lovenduski 1986
Ministry of Foreign Affairs 1994, 1996
Ministry of Foreign Affairs and the Equal Status Council Secretariat 1996
Ministry of Justice 1998
Ministry of Social Affairs Denmark 1998
UN, CEDAW 1994, *Concluding Observations, Denmark*
U.S. Department of State 1995, *Denmark Country Report, 1994;* 1997, *Denmark
     Country Report, 1996*

Finland
Bergqvist 1999
Finland 1889, 1997a, 1997b
Haavio-Mannila 1985
Kaplan 1992
Lovenduski 1986
Ministry of Justice 1998
UN, CEDAW 1995, *Report on Status of Finland's Women*
U.S. Department of State 1997, *Finland Country Report, 1996*

France
Hantrais 1993
Jenson and Sineau 1994
Kaplan 1992
Lovenduski 1986
Mazur 1995a, 1995b
Le Ministre Chargé des Droits des Femmes 1997
U.S. Department of State 1996, *France Human Rights Practices, 1995*

Germany
Federal Ministry for Family Affairs, Senior Citizens, Women and Youth 1995
Germany 1996
Kaplan 1992
Lemke 1994
Lovenduski 1986
Permanent Mission of Germany to the United Nations 1998

Greece
Cacoullos 1994
General Secretariat for Equality 1998
Papageorgiou-Limberes 1992
U.S. Department of State 1996, *Greece Human Rights Practices, 1995*; 1997, *Greece Country Report, 1996*

Iceland
Bergqvist 1999
Haavio-Mannila 1985
Kaplan 1992
Lovenduski 1986
UN, CEDAW 1996, *Concluding Observations, Iceland*; 1996, *Iceland's State Treasury*
U.S. Department of State 1996, *Iceland Human Rights Practices, 1995*; 1997, *Iceland Country Report, 1996*

India
Busch 1992
Desai and Krishnaraj 1987
Everett 1979, 1998

Forbes 1979
Forum Against the Oppression of Women 1994
India 1974
Jaising 1995
Jayawardena 1986
Katzenstein 1991
Kishwar and Vanita 1984
Krishnaraj 1991
Liddle and Joshi 1986
Swarup et al. 1994
U.S. Department of State 1997, *India Country Report, 1996*

Ireland
Mahon 1995
Office of the Tanaiste 1997a, 1997b, 1997c
UN, CEDAW 1989a, 1989b
U.S. Department of State 1995, *Ireland Human Rights Practices, 1994;* 1997, *Ireland Country Report, 1996*

Israel
Prime Minister's Advisor on the Status of Women 1997
Shaler 1995
Sharfman 1994
Yishai 1997

Italy
Beckwith 1987
Guadagnini 1995
Hellman 1996
Italy 1996
Kaplan 1992
Lovenduski 1986
Ufficio del Ministro per le Pari Opportunita 1997
U.S. Department of State 1997, *1996 Human Rights Report: Italy*

Jamaica
Babb 1997
Bureau of Women's Affairs 1998
Clarke 1997
Ortiz 1997
Smith 1994
UN, CEDAW 1988, *Concluding Observations, Jamaica*
U.S. Department of State 1997, *1996 Human Rights Report: Jamaica*
Vargas 1997

Japan
Ling and Matsuno 1992
Office for Gender Equality 1998a, 1998b, 1998c
UN, CEDAW 1994, *Concluding Observations, Japan*
U.S. Department of State 1995, *Japan Country Report, 1994;* 1997, *Japan Country Report, 1996*
Yoko, Mitsuko and Kimiko 1994

Luxembourg
Ministère de la Promotion Féminine 1995
UN, CEDAW 1995, *Contribution Luxembourgeoise;* 1997, *Concluding Observations, Luxembourg*
U.S. Department of State 1997, *Luxembourg Country Report, 1996*

Mauritius
UN, CEDAW 1995, *Concluding Observations, Mauritius;* 1995, *Statement by Honourable Mrs. Sheilabai Bappoo;* 1995, *Women's Integration in Mauritius's Development*
U.S. Department of State 1995, *Mauritius Country Report, 1994;* 1997, *Mauritius Country Report, 1996*

Nauru
UN, CEDAW 1995, *Statement by Ms. Marlene Moses*
U.S. Department of State 1996, *Nauru Human Rights Practices, 1995*

Netherlands
Kaplan 1992
Leijenaar and Niemoller 1994
Lovenduski 1986
Outshoorn 1995, 1996, 1998
Randall 1987
UN, CEDAW 1994, *Concluding Observations, Netherlands;* 1994, *Initial Report of the Netherlands*
U.S. Department of State 1996, *Netherlands Human Rights Practices, 1995;* 1997, *1996 Human Rights Report: The Netherlands*

New Zealand
Ministry of Women's Affairs 1997, 1999
Non-governmental Organization Coordinating Committee 1996
UN, CEDAW 1988, *Concluding Observations, New Zealand;* 1989, *Concluding Observations, New Zealand*
U.S. Department of State 1997, *1996 Human Rights Report: New Zealand*

Norway
Bergqvist 1999
Bystydzienski 1988, 1992a, 1995

Gender Equality Ombudsman 1978, *Gender Equality by Law*
Haavio-Mannila 1985
Kaplan 1992
Karvonen and Selle 1995
Lovenduski 1986
Mørkhagen 1991
Permanent Mission of Norway to the United Nations 1998
Royal Ministry of Foreign Affairs and Royal Ministry of Children and Family Affairs 1994
U.S. Department of State 1997, *1996 Human Rights Report: Norway*
Van der Ros 1994

Papua New Guinea
Bradley 1994
UN, CEDAW 1995, *Statement by Ms. Felicia Dobunaba*
U.S. Department of State 1997, *1996 Human Rights Report: Papua New Guinea*
Wormald 1994

Portugal
Commission for Equality and Women's Rights 1994
Council of Ministers 1997
Kaplan 1992
Lovenduski 1986
UN, CEDAW 1995, *Address Given by the Head of the Portuguese Delegation*
U.S. Department of State 1995, *Portugal Country Report, 1994*

Spain
Astellara 1992
Instituto de la Mujer 1992, 1996, 1997a, 1997b, 1998
Lovenduski 1986
Mendez 1994
U.S. Department of State 1995, *Spain Country Report, 1994;* 1997, *Spain Country Report, 1996*
Valiente 1996

Sweden
Bergqvist 1999
Elman 1993, 1995, 1996a
Equality Affairs Division 1998
Gelb, 1989
Haavio-Mannila 1985
Heise, Pitanguay, and Germain 1994
Kaplan 1992
Lovenduski 1986
Ministry of Justice, Ministry of Health and Social Affairs, and Ministry of Labour 1998
Ministry of Labor 1997

Switzerland

Kaplan 1992
Stämpfli 1994
Switzerland 1994
UN, CEDAW 1995, *Swiss Confederation Statement*
U.S. Department of State 1995, *Switzerland Country Report, 1994;* 1997, *1996 Human Rights Report: Switzerland*

Trinidad and Tobago

Babb 1997
Marin 1997
Ortiz 1997
U.S. Department of State 1997, *1996 Human Rights Report: Trinidad and Tobago*
Vargas 1997

United Kingdom

Lovenduski 1986, 1994, 1995
United Kingdom, Women's Unit <http://www.womens-unit.gov.uk>
U.S. Department of State 1997, *1996 Human Rights Report: United Kingdom*

United States

Department of Justice 1996, n.d.
Department of Justice, Bureau of Justice Statistics 1994
Department of Justice, Violence Against Women Office 1998, n.d.
Elman 1996a
Elperin 1998
Gelb 1998
Gelb and Palley 1982
Matthews 1993, 1995
National Institute of Justice 1998
National Organization of Women 1998
Nelson and Carver 1994
President's Interagency Council on Women 1996
Stetson 1995, 1998
Tjaden and Thoennes 1998

Venezuela

Babb 1997
Marin 1997
Ortiz 1997
UN, CEDAW 1995, *Examen de los Informes Presentados*
U.S. Department of State 1995, *Venezuela Country Report, 1994*
Vargas 1997

Notes

Chapter 1

1. The 1983 law was struck down in 1991 in *Regina v. Seaboyer.* In 1992 the criminal code was changed, and the new rape shield provisions were ruled constitutional by a unanimous Supreme Court in October 2000 ("Rape Shield Protections Upheld" 2000).

2. The 1998 act (H.R. 3514; S. 2110) was popularly known as VAWA II, because it built on the success of the 1994 Violence Against Women Act (Erickson 1998).

3. For evidence that violence against women inhibits economic development and is an important public health problem, see the special World Bank publication on this topic (Heise, Pitanguy, and Germain 1994). For additional evidence on the impact of violence on these problems, as well as on women's employment and the well-being of children, see the comprehensive report of the U.S. National Research Council (Chalk and King 1998). For evidence of the problems violence presents for welfare reformers in the United States, see Raphael 1996a and Brush 2000.

4. Connors (1994) gives a summary of government response to violence against women worldwide and offers an expert commentary on violence-against-women policy and its development, although her commentary is not (and was not intended to be) based on systematic comparative analysis. The Ford Foundation's *Violence Against Women* (Bunch 1992) also offers a general introduction to the issue, but it is an anthology of national perspectives on various aspects of violence against women and community response rather than an analysis of policy variation.

5. Of course, the difference between government responsiveness to "problems" and responsiveness to citizen articulations should not be understood as a difference between responding to objective conditions on the one hand and ideas or socially constructed problems on the other. Whether driven by changes in routinely gathered indicators, social movements, or cataclysmic events, problems are always socially constructed in the sense that our understanding of them always depends on our conceptual frames, values, and the like. Still, government responsiveness to problems can be driven either by technical processes internal to government or by external demands made by citizens. This is the sense in which I distinguish between government responsiveness to problems and government responsiveness to citizen demands.

6. Similarly, understanding violence against women as linked to male dominance does not mean that all men are violent, that all women are direct victims of violence, that women are nonviolent, or that maleness itself is sufficient to explain any individual act of violence. Rather, this study sees violence against women as part of a social relationship between groups. This relationship provides the frame of reference in which in-

dividual interactions take place, but it does not determine the specific outcomes of those interactions.

7. International agreements prohibiting violence against women, including the Convention on the Elimination of All Forms of Discrimination Against Women (CEDAW) and the International Convention on Civil and Political Rights (ICCPR), preceded the Beijing agreement. In 1994, the UN Commission on Human Rights appointed the first Special Rapporteur on Violence Against Women (UN, CEDAW 1998b).

8. See appendix A for evidence that sexual assault and wife battering are serious problems in the thirty-six countries considered here. *Wife battering* is defined to include battering of any intimate female partner, not just women who are married. *Wife* is used here instead of *partner* to indicate both the femaleness of the victim and the intimate nature of the relationship (something that *woman battering* does not capture).

9. For a summary of the literature, see Heise, Pitanguy, and Germain 1994, which describes thirty-four studies documenting domestic violence in twenty-four countries. These studies include both developed countries (for example, Canada, Belgium, and New Zealand) and developing ones (for example, Korea, Malaysia, and India). Studies of the incidence of rape between 1991 and 1993 that use questions from the Sexual Experiences Survey (SES) are also described for four Anglo-American countries (the United States, Canada, Britain, and New Zealand). For further documentation on sexual assault and wife battering, see appendix A.

10. Such policy action can be contained in one policy or piece of legislation or in several. Areas can be addressed all at once or at different times.

11. Chronbach's alpha for these seven items exceeds .7. For further discussion, see appendix B.

12. I am grateful to Jenny Nedelsky of the University of Toronto for this observation.

13. Of course, if they are targeted only toward immigrant women, for example, this could constitute evidence that the government is denying the importance of the problem for women generally but accepting that certain "backward" communities might have the problem of violence against women. In this case, targeted services follow from a logic of racial, cultural, or ethnic superiority (unsupported by the data) rather than from a concern that some groups of women are not well served by shelters run by and for white women. See chapter 5 for further discussion.

14. For an excellent discussion of the problems confronting comparative research that seeks to take account of differences among women, see Beckwith 2000. Beckwith's suggestions as to how scholars might find a way around these problems are also instructive.

15. Countries that the Freedom House survey classified as "free" continuously throughout the study period were included. Countries that were classified as "not free" in any year in the study period were eliminated from the population. States that were "free" for most of the time but had a brief period (less than three years) in which they were classified as "partially free" were also included. Only eight states fell into this category, but eliminating them would have meant excluding some countries that are generally considered relatively stable democracies (e.g., Spain, Portugal, Luxembourg, Venezuela, and India). It also would have reduced the number of developing countries in the study population, which might have limited my ability to draw conclusions about the relationship between level of development and government response to violence against women.

16. Note that qualitative and quantitative do not map onto the categories of case studies and large-N studies, as is often assumed. Case studies may employ both quantitative and qualitative methods. For example, Robert Putnam's book *Making Democracy Work* (1993) reports on a case study of Italy that uses both methods of analysis. Similarly, large-N studies (studies of twenty units or more) may be either qualitative or quantitative. Sandra Halperin's excellent book *In the Mirror of the Third World* (1997) is an example of a global study using historical methods to analyze quantitative and qualitative data. LeDuc, Niemi, and Norris (1996) use quantitative methods to investigate issues in the study of comparative democratic electoral systems.

17. Mazur (1999) delineates the field of comparative feminist policy studies and reviews the many works in this field.

Chapter 2

1. There are, of course, exceptions. To cite a few: Stetson and Mazur 1995 analyzes a number of advanced industrialized countries of North America and Europe; Koven and Michel 1993 also focuses on advanced industrialized countries; Lewis 1993 develops a comparative framework for gender and social policy in Europe; Charlton, Everett, and Staudt 1989 develops a global framework for analyzing the relationship between women, the state, and development; Nelson and Chowdhury 1994 takes a global perspective on women and politics, reviewing forty-three countries; O'Connor, Orloff, and Shaver 1999 examines four "liberal" countries (Australia, Canada, Great Britain, and the United States). Even these multi-authored volumes are based on chapters that are single-country studies, currently the dominant approach to the comparative study of gender and social policy.

2. A few works do compare across levels of development. Busch 1992 compares India and the United States; Charlton, Everett, and Staudt 1989 compares a variety of states from a number of regions; Nelson and Chowdhury 1994 compares forty-three countries at different levels of development.

3. On income assistance policies, see, for example, Gordon 1990; Gelpi, Hartsock, Novak, and Strober 1986; O'Connor, Orloff, and Shaver 1999; Skocpol 1992; Orloff 1993; and Weir, Orloff, and Skocpol 1988. For a comprehensive review of the literature on maternalism, see Brush 1996. The literature on abortion policy is extensive; a few of the explicitly comparative studies are Diamond 1983; Glendon 1987; and Shaver 1993. For comparative studies of the U.S. states, see Goggin 1993.

4. As noted, the study by Heise, Raikes, Watts, and Zwi is more descriptive than analytical in its discussion of policy.

5. Of course, as with many social programs, much of this money goes to administrative costs and professional salaries. The same is true for the "welfare" programs (Aid to Families with Dependent Children, or AFDC) that were under attack during this time period and subject to deep cuts in 1996. It is notable that one of the few exemptions to the time limits and other conditions placed on aid recipients under the new welfare program (TANF) was for domestic violence. This exemption provided some (minimal) financial support to women attempting to leave abusive relationships, which further supports my argument that something changed in the United States between the mid-1980s, when President Reagan argued that domestic violence shelters were antifamily, and 1994, when bipartisan legislation made federal funding for such shelters available.

6. Note that this discussion undermines the relatively common practice of using a nation-state variable as a proxy for culture: in other words, whatever is not attributed

to specified explanatory variables can be attributed to "country effects" or national culture. As Pfau-Effinger (1998) points out, culture ought not to be treated as such a "residual" category.

7. Europe is the omitted category in the dummy variable. For further explanation, see appendix B.

8. For a comprehensive review of this literature, see Brush 1996.

9. For a discussion of such attitudes in the Japanese workplace, see, for example, Knapp 1995; and Saso 1990.

10. For recent discussions of convergence in social policy, see Castles and Pierson 1996; Overbye 1994; Bonoli 1997; and Boyd 1996.

Chapter 3

1. Vargas and Wierenga (1998, 9) define women's movements to include "the whole spectrum of conscious and unconscious action of individuals, groups or organizations with the aim of combating gender subordination." I find this definition too broad. Although many people unknowingly perpetuate the ideas and practices of the women's movement, this is an effect or impact of the women's movement, rather than part of the movement itself. The movement that focuses on women mostly involves people who consciously focus on improving the lives of women. So action that unconsciously or unintentionally promotes the status of women cannot be included among the activities of the women's movement.

2. I take this definition to exclude what Molyneux (1998) calls "directed" mobilizations, where women's organizations are formed by state authorities and women are directed to join them.

3. For example, Gonzalez-Suarez (1994) describes a very active radical women's group in Costa Rica that evolved from an all-women union. Apparently, until a few years ago, many members of the group were unwilling to call themselves feminists because "they felt the term overlooked the fact that women's struggle was immersed in an even larger battle for social justice" (183).

4. See also Ortiz (1997) for a broad discussion of women's mobilizing around violence across Latin America and the Caribbean; and Heise, Pitanguay, and Germain (1994) for a general review of the situation in developing countries.

5. This model of women's group influence as mainly a product of lobbying is usually implicitly coupled with a pluralist model of the state as a gender-neutral environment. Vargas and Wierenga (1998, 9), for example, describe women's groups as "special interest groups in society," where "competing interest groups, with unequal resources, vie for influence in the government and the state."

6. There is a vast literature on the reasons for considering even the category "women" problematic; see, for example, Spelman 1988; Butler 1990; and Epstein and Straub, eds. 1995 (especially the chapter by Marjorie Gerber).

7. As Collins (1994, 61–62) notes, black women's experience of motherhood is much different from that of white women.

8. Lugones does not see herself as a postmodernist, but I see her critique as similar enough to the postmodern line of argument I want to explicate that I use her as an example here.

9. Kaplan (1992, 6, 282), for example, argues that women's movements do not affect policies determining the status of women when structures of socioeconomic inequality persist. Similarly, some feminist state theorists whose orientation is Marxist

(for example, Abramovitz 1988) or radical (for example, MacKinnon 1989) find that capitalist and/or patriarchal social structures determine policy outputs. Hernes (1987) focuses on the structural changes associated with development of the welfare state, arguing that the welfare state is a form of social organization that is "woman friendly" and that women benefit disproportionately from welfare state development. For these theorists, the presence or absence of a women's movement does not enter into the equation determining policy outputs.

10. Call, Nice, and Talarico (1991) find that socioeconomic factors (urbanization, racial composition, and level of education) are better predictors of state-to-state variation in policies on rape than a number of other factors, but they do not even consider the women's movement as an important variable.

11. I take this sense of the term *autonomy* to incorporate both independent and associational forms of women's movements, as described by Molyneux (1998, 70).

12. This is important because it shows that the strength of a women's movement is logically separable from policy influence, thus avoiding what would otherwise be a tautological claim: that women's movements influence policymaking when they are influential in policymaking. Instead, I am arguing that when women's movement pronouncements and actions command public attention, they are more likely to have an influence on policymaking, because public opinion and attitudes force politicians to pay attention to them. Of course, sometimes policymakers are unable or unwilling to translate these pressures into policies. So we can distinguish conceptually between women's movement strength and policy outcomes affecting women.

13. Note that I am never coding a women's movement as strong simply because it appears to have influenced policies on violence against women. I am usually using general assessments of the strength of the women's movement or its influence on public opinion, mass attitudes, public discussions, and so on.

14. Elman's positive assessment (1996a) of the impact of the women's movement in the United States on violence-against-women policies refers to policy at the state and national level and examines policy adoption, implementation, and revision. In spite of the broader empirical focus of that work, I examine Elman's theoretical arguments here as they apply to policy responsiveness at a national level.

15. The critical mass effect has been observed in a variety of forums (classrooms, academic programs, and other groups); the literature referred to here mostly replicates this finding for women in political bodies, such as legislatures (Etzkowitz et al. 1994; Bystydzienski 1992a; Berkman and O'Connor 1993; Thomas 1994; Dodson and Carroll 1991; Dodson 1991; Darcy, Welch, and Clark 1987).

16. Policy development in the United States looks very different when examined at a national, rather than state, level. But even at a local level, the United States was not the first country to implement legal reforms regarding violence against women. It was in Australia, that such policies were first implemented at a state level in the English-speaking world.

Chapter 4

1. Of course, as I discuss in chapter 3, there are many studies of the importance of women's movements for policy change. The point I am making here is that studies of differences between male and female legislators have not adequately taken into account the impact of the women's movement.

2. Davis's cross-national study (1997) of women in cabinets finds that women are

more likely to be found in areas such as social welfare policy and less likely to hold positions with responsibility for defense.

3. Other studies in the context of the United States include Dodson and Carroll 1991; Dodson 1991; Hansen 1993; Tamerius 1995; and Kathlene 1995.

4. The twelve states included in the study were Arizona, California, Georgia, Illinois, Iowa, Mississippi, Nebraska, North Carolina, Pennsylvania, South Dakota, Vermont, and Washington.

5. Murphy's study does not include the District of Columbia.

6. Hansen (1993) is somewhat of an exception, since she conceptualizes the number of women in the legislature as one aspect of women's political mobilization. Other indicators of women's political mobilization include percentage of women in the labor force, women's lobbyists as a proportion of all lobbyists, a public commission on women, number of women in the state executive, and membership in NARAL (National Abortion Rights Action League). The analysis collapses three variables of interest—women's autonomous organizing, women as policymakers, and the structure of political institutions—by considering them all to be indicators of women's political mobilization. This makes some sense in the context of Hansen's argument but leaves a key question (for our purposes) unanswered: With respect to policy outcomes, is there an interactive effect of women's autonomous organizing and women in government?

7. For an example of such a directory, see Barrett 1993.

8. An individual's gender can, however, sometimes undermine position power, as shown by a case study of women who are chairs of congressional committees (in Kathlene 1995). In this study, women chairs enjoyed less power than did men in a similar position. Congressmen interrupted and challenged women chairs more than they did men chairs. Nevertheless, women chairs did have more influence on their committee than did other women on the committee. Thus, gender does not negate position power, but it may mitigate it.

9. Tamerius (1995), for example, finds that women are more likely than men to provide leadership for feminist policies in the United States. She notes that party affiliation is insignificant in determining whether women take on this role. Cf. Thomas 1994.

10. Papua New Guinea might appear to be an exception, but it is not. The one policy initiative on violence against women there was undertaken and spearheaded by the sole woman legislator, who was later voted out of office.

11. This point-of-diminishing-returns interpretation could be seen as consistent with a critical mass theory (cf. Berkman and O'Connor 1993). The small numbers of women present in many important cases of policy development in this area suggest that the point of diminishing returns would have to be a very small number of women (as few as four) for this argument to hold (see table 4-1). This number would be much smaller than any previous studies of critical mass have indicated (10 to 40 percent). It seems more likely to reflect the importance of there being some women rather than none.

12. This egregiously low percentage has been one of the motivating factors for the recent movement for parity in France, to which I referred earlier in the chapter.

13. In models 6 and 7, I control for the impact of an effective women's policy machinery. The definition and operationalization of this variable is discussed in the next chapter.

Chapter 5

1. Rockman (1994) identifies a third strand: bounded rationality approaches. In this chapter, I follow Atkinson in collapsing the third strand (bounded rationality) into the second (structural theories).

2. Skocpol (1992) does consider the relationship between the women's movement and the state from the 1870s to the 1920s. Although her study is instructive, the historical period with which it is concerned precedes the time in which women enjoyed full civil and political rights. As Skocpol notes, this makes a difference for thinking about the development of gender-group consciousness, as well as for thinking about women's access to the state, and limits the applicability of these findings for the current discussion (which begins with second-wave feminism in countries where women have full civil and political rights).

3. For studies of violence-against-women policy that see the state as inherently inimical to feminist goals, see MacKinnon 1989; Busch 1992; Walker 1990; and Daniels 1997. For feminist state theorists who see the state in general as inimical to feminist concerns, see Brown 1981; Brown 1992; Fraser 1989; MacKinnon 1989; Abramovitz 1988; Borchorst and Siim 1987; and Elshtain 1983. For critiques of this view, see Gordon 1990; Skocpol 1992; and Brush 1994.

4. Brown's examination (1992) of the bureaucratic mode of the state echoes this analysis, although it does not speak directly to the issue of violence against women.

5. Borchorst and Siim (1987) similarly equate the growth of the welfare state with the expansion of social provision and with increasingly generous social policies. Hantrais (1993) examines the attitude of the French welfare state towards women by studying how women are treated in social policy. For further examples, see Misra and Akins 1998; and Gornick, Meyers, and Ross 1997. In these studies, studying the welfare state just means studying policies.

Chapter 6

1. In 1982, the office was renamed the Office of the Status of Women. It was upgraded to a division and returned to the department of the prime minister and cabinet in 1983.

2. This claim is made by an independent scholar, but it appears in a report published by the government of Canada. I was unable to find studies confirming this fact. It does appear that Canada adopted this policy before the United States did (in 1994).

3. Data on policies on violence against women of marginalized subgroups are even harder to come by than data on policies on violence against women in general. Although this problem is not insurmountable in theory, I did not have the resources to undertake a comprehensive review of policies on violence against marginalized groups of women in all thirty-six countries in this study. In addition, we still need theoretical work to determine what sorts of vulnerable subgroups are comparable across countries. For example, can we compare the situation of African American women in the United States with the current situation of immigrant women in Europe? This conceptual work remains to be done (Beckwith 2000).

Chapter 7

1. Taylor-Goodby (1991) argues, similarly, that sustained criticism of state action as a means of solving public problems has resulted in a shift in analytic focus toward the private organization of interests in discussions of the welfare state, an organization

that constitutes a sort of "welfare-pluralism" (97–98).

2. For a succinct review of the literature developing the concept of the iron triangle, as well as a brief account of subsequent critiques, see Walker 1991, 124–25.

3. Walby (1990) follows Giddens in distinguishing between systems and structure, where structures make up systems.

4. Dryzek (1996) calls it a political-economic structure.

5. For a discussion of the relationship between personal identity, social structures, and agency, see Young 2000, 99–102.

6. I do not mean to suggest that feminists and critical theorists have not contributed important accounts of bureaucracy and public administration. Rather, the point is that the relationship between social structures and public administrative structures has been inadequately specified because the effects of variation in both social structures and bureaucratic structures on this relationship have not been adequately explored. In this work I look at the policy impact of the interaction between changing social structures and changes in the structure of public administration. Such an interaction has not been adequately theorized by either feminists or critical theorists, particularly in the literature that focuses on public policy (see chapter 5 for more discussion).

Chapter 8

1. See Williams 1998 for a discussion of institutional mechanisms for improving the representation of marginalized groups.

2. Some have suggested that legislation on violence against women (such as the Violence Against Women Act of 1994 in the United States) does not necessarily challenge prevailing values, because with such legislation "vulnerable women are protected from patriarchal power" (Gelb 1998, 20). But the idea that the state should protect women from men in their homes, workplaces, and personal relationships certainly challenges the traditional model of the male-headed family and male dominance in relationships, so such policies must challenge traditional gender roles to some degree.

3. It might appear that corporatist arrangements to consult workers represent an analogy with class as a social group and/or to the labor movement. However, as I pointed out in chapter 7, the model I am suggesting here is different in important ways from corporatist arrangements, which grant special recognition to both workers and business. As I also noted in chapter 7, corporatist arrangements are well suited for incorporating formal organizations (such as unions) into policy processes but less well suited for including social movements.

References

Note: The U.S. Department of State country reports on human rights for 1994–96 that are listed here were released by the Bureau of Democracy, Human Rights and Labor, U.S. Information Service, U.S. Embassy, Stockholm. The reports can be found at <http://www.usis.usemb.se/human>.

Abramovitz, Mimi. 1988. *Regulating the Lives of Women: Social Welfare Policy from Colonial Times to the Present.* Boston: South End Press.

Abu-Laban, Sharon, Lori Wilkinson, Danielle Juteau, and Patricia Bittar. 1998. "Immigrant and Refugee Women in Canada: A Selective Review of Policy Research Literature, 1987–1996." In Gendering Immigration/Integration, Report from the First National Conference, Responding to Diversity in the Metropolis: Building an Inclusive Research Agenda. Edmonton, Alberta: Research Directorate, Status of Women Canada. <http://www.swc-cfc.gc.ca/>

Agnew, Vijay. 1998. *In Search of a Safe Place: Abused Women and Culturally Sensitive Services.* Toronto: University of Toronto Press.

Aldrich, John H., and Forrest D. Nelson. 1984. *Linear Probability, Logit and Probit Models.* Beverly Hills, Calif.: Sage.

Alford, Robert R., and Roger Friedland. 1985. *Powers of Theory: Capitalism, the State, and Democracy.* Cambridge: Cambridge University Press.

Allison, Paul D. 1984. *Event History Analysis: Regression for Longitudinal Event Data.* Quantitative Applications in the Social Sciences Series, Sage University Paper. Beverly Hills, Calif.: Sage.

Almond, G., and S. Verba. 1963. *Civic Culture.* Series in Comparative Politics and Behavior 23, no. 1. Boston: Little, Brown.

Alter, Karen J., and Jeanette Vargas. 2000. "Explaining Variation in the Use of European Litigation Strategies." *Comparative Political Studies* 33, no. 4:452–82.

Alvarez, Sonia. 1997. "Contradictions of a 'Woman's Space' in a Male-Dominant State: The Political Role of the Commissions on the Status of Women in Post-Authoritarian Brazil." In *Women, International Development and Politics,* edited by Kathleen Staudt. 2nd edition. Philadelphia: Temple University Press.

Andrain, Charles F., and David E. Apter. 1996. *Political Protest and Social Change: Analyzing Politics.* New York: New York University Press.

Andrew, Caroline. 1995. "Getting Women's Issues on the Municipal Agenda: Violence Against Women." In *Gender in Urban Research,* edited by Judith A. Garber and Robyne S. Turner. Thousand Oaks, Calif.: Sage.

Andrew, Caroline, and Sandra Rodgers, eds. 1997. *Women and the Canadian State/Les Femmes et l'état canadien.* Montreal: McGill-Queens University Press.

Archenti, Nélida, and Patricia Laura Gómez. 2000. "Political Representation and Affirmative Actions: Argentina, Before and After the 'Law of Quotas.'" Paper prepared for presentation at the Eighteenth World Congress of the International Political Science Association, Québec, August 1–5.

Arnold, Gretchen. 1995. "Dilemmas of Feminist Coalitions: Collective Identity and Strategic Effectiveness in the Battered Women's Movement." In *Feminist Organizations: Harvest of the New Women's Movement*, edited by Myra Marx Ferree and Patricia Yancey Martin. Philadelphia: Temple University Press.

Arscott, Jane, and Linda Trimble, eds. 1997. *In the Presence of Women: Representation in Canadian Governments*. Toronto: Harcourt Brace Canada.

Ashford, D. 1978. *Comparative Public Policies*. Beverly Hills, Calif.: Sage.

———. 1992. *History and Context in Comparative Public Policy*. Pittsburgh: University of Pittsburgh Press.

Astellara, Judith. 1992. "Women, Political Culture, and Empowerment in Spain." In *Women Transforming Politics*, edited by Jill M. Bystydzienski. Bloomington: Indiana University Press.

Atkinson, Michael M., ed. 1993. *Governing Canada: Institutions and Public Policy*. Toronto: Harcourt Brace Jovanovich Canada.

Atkinson, Michael M., and William D. Coleman. 1992. "Policy Networks, Policy Communities, and Problems of Governance." *Governance* 5:164–80.

Australia. Commonwealth Office of the Status of Women. 1997. Correspondence with author, December 9.

———. 2000a. *Implementation of the Beijing Platform for Action—Australian Government Response*. Department of the Prime Minister and Cabinet. <http://osw.dpmc.gov.au/content/beijing.htm.>

———. 2000b. *Key Findings: Projects with Indigenous Communities*. Partnerships Against Domestic Violence. <http://www.dpmc.gov.au/osw/padv/index.html>

———. 2000c. *Milestones for Australian Women*. <http://osw.dpmc.gov.au/content/resources/milestones.html>

———. Minister for Aboriginal and Torres Strait Islander Affairs. 2000. Law and Justice. <http://www.atsia.gov.au/content/achiev_law1.html>

Austria. Federal Minister for Women's Affairs and Consumer Protection. 1998a. *Austria's National Report on the Implementation of the "Platform for Action."* March. Vienna. <http://www.un.org/womenwatch/followup/national/austria.htm>

———. 1998b. Correspondence with author, February 25.

———. 1998c. *Violence Against Women*. Vienna.

Babb, Cecilia. 1997. "Taking Action Against Violence: A Case Study of Trinidad and Tobago." In *Women Against Violence: Breaking the Silence: Reflecting on Experience in Latin America and the Caribbean*, edited by Ana Maria Brasiliero. New York: UNIFEM.

Bachelor, Lynn W. 1986. "Bureaucratic Responsiveness and Complaint Resolution: The Impact of Fiscal Constraints." *Urban Affairs Quarterly* 22:276–88.

Bachman, R., and L. E. Salzman. 1995. *Violence Against Women: Estimates from the Redesigned Survey*. NCJ-154348. Washington, D.C.: Bureau of Justice Statistics.

Bachrach, Peter, and Morton S. Baratz. 1962. "Two Faces of Power." *American Political Science Review* 5, no. 4 (December): 947–52.

———. 1963. "Decisions and Nondecisions: An Analytical Framework." *American Political Science Review* 57, no. 3 (September): 632–42.

Backhouse, Constance, and David H. Flaherty. *Challenging Times: The Women's Movement in Canada and the United States*. Montreal: McGill-Queens University Press.

Baker, S., M. Kousis, D. Richardson, and S. Young, eds. 1997. *The Politics of Sustain-*

able Development: Theory, Policy, and Practice within the European Union. London: Routledge.

Barbados. Bureau of Women's Affairs. 1998. Correspondence with author, February 18.

Baron, Larry, and Murray A. Straus. 1989. *Four Theories of Rape in American Society: A State-Level Analysis.* New Haven, Conn.: Yale University Press.

Barrett, Jacqueline, ed. 1993. *Encyclopedia of Women's Associations Worldwide.* Farmington Hills, Mich.: Gale Group.

Bart, Pauline B., and Eileen G. Moran. 1993. *Violence Against Women: The Bloody Footprints.* A Gender and Society Reader. Newbury Park, Calif.: Sage.

Bashevkin, Sylvia. 1993. *Toeing the Lines: Women and Party Politics in English Canada.* Toronto: Oxford University Press.

———. 1994. "Building a Political Voice: Women's Participation and Policy Influence in Canada." In *Women and Politics Worldwide,* edited by Barbara J. Nelson and Najma Chowdhury. New Haven, Conn.: Yale University Press.

———. 1996. "Interest Groups and Social Movements." In *Comparing Democracies: Elections and Voting in Global Perspective,* edited by Lawrence LeDuc, Richard G. Niemi, and Pippa Norris. 1996. Thousand Oaks, Calif.: Sage.

———. 1998. *Women on the Defensive.* Chicago: University of Chicago Press.

Basu, A. 1992. *Two Faces of Protest: Contrasting Modes of Women's Activism in India.* Berkeley: University of California Press.

Beckwith, Karen. 1987. "Response to Feminism in the Italian Parliament: Divorce, Abortion, and Sexual Violence Legislation." In *The Women's Movements of the United States and Western Europe,* edited by Mary Katzenstein and Carol Mueller. Philadelphia: Temple University Press.

———. 2000. "Beyond Compare? Women's Movements in Comparative Perspective." *European Journal of Political Research* 37:431–68.

Bégin, Monique. 1997. "The Canadian Government and the Commissions Report." In *Women and the Canadian State/Les Femmes et l'état canadien,* edited by Caroline Andrew and Sandra Rodgers. Montreal: McGill-Queens University Press.

Belanger, Sarah, and Sheila Regehr. 1998. "Engendering Public Policy: The Role of Research, Statistics, and Indicators in the Public Policy Process: Some Examples from Canada." Paper presented to the Fifth Women's Policy Research Conference, Institute for Women's Policy Research, Washington D.C., June 12–13.

Belgium. Belgian Coordinating Committee. 1994. *Fourth World Conference on Women, 1995: Action for Equality, Development, and Peace: Peking, 1995, Belgian Report.* Ministry of Foreign Affairs, External Trade and Development Cooperation. Brussels.

———. Conseil de l'Égalité des Chances entre Hommes et Femmes. 1997. *Rapport d'activités: Septembre 1993–Octobre 1997.* Brussels: Ministère de l'Emploi et du Travail.

———. Ministère de l'Emploi et du Travail. 1997. *Violence physique et sexuelle: Rapport de la journée d'étude.* Brussels: Ministère de l'Emploi et du Travail.

———. Ministère de l'Emploi et du Travail. n.d. *Violence a l'égard des femmes et des enfants . . . Une gifle à la face du monde.* Brussels: Ministère de l'Emploi et du Travail.

———. Ministère de la Justice. 1998. *L'aide financière aux victimes d'actes intentionnels de violence.* Brussels: Ministère de la Justice.

————. Secrétaire d'État à l'Emancipation Sociale. 1987. *Violence voulu? Dossier d'intervention de police: Un dossier sur les circonstances, les causes et les consequences de la violence sexuelle, pour mieux situer l'intervention de police.* Brussels: Secrétaire d'État à l'Emancipation Sociale.

Bell, Diane. 1994. "Representing Aboriginal Women: Who Speaks for Whom?" In *The Rights of Subordinated Peoples,* edited by Oliver Mendelsohn and Upendra Baxi. Delhi: Oxford University Press.

Bergman, Solveig. 1999. "Women in New Social Movements." In *Equal Democracies? Gender and Politics in the Nordic Countries,* edited by Christina Bergqvist. Oslo: Scandinavian University Press.

Bergqvist, Christina, ed. 1999. *Equal Democracies? Gender and Politics in the Nordic Countries.* Oslo: Scandinavian University Press.

Berk, Richard A., Phyllis Y. Newton, and Sarah Fenstermaker Berk. 1986. "What a Difference a Day Makes: An Empirical Study of the Impact of Shelters for Battered Women." *Journal of Marriage and the Family* 48, no. 3:431–90.

Berkman, Michael B., and Robert E. O'Connor. 1993. "Do Women Legislators Matter? Female Legislators and State Abortion Policy." *American Politics Quarterly* 21, no. 1 (January): 102–24.

Berry, William D., and Stanley Feldman. 1985. *Multiple Regression in Practice.* Sage University Paper no. 70, Quantitative Applications in the Social Sciences. Newbury Park, Calif.: Sage.

Beveridge, Fiona, Sue Nott, and Kylie Stephen. 1998. "Predicting the Impact of Policy: Devising a Gender Auditing Model (in the U.K.)." Paper presented to the Fifth Women's Policy Research Conference, Institute for Women's Policy Research, Washington, D.C., June 12–13.

Blee, K. 1998. "Diversity and the Curriculum." Keynote Address, University of Pittsburgh Diversity Seminar. University of Pittsburgh.

Block, Fred. 1987 "State Theory in Context." In *Revising State Theory: Essays in Politics and Postindustrialism,* edited by Fred Block. Philadelphia: Temple University Press.

Blomquist, William. 1999. "The Policy Process and Large-N Comparative Studies." In *Theories of the Policy Process,* edited by Paul A. Sabatier. Boulder, Colo.: Westview Press.

Boardman, Robert, ed. 1992. *Canadian Environmental Policy: Ecosystems, Politics, and Process.* New York: Oxford University Press.

Bobrow, Davis B., and John S. Dryzek. 1987. *Policy Analysis by Design.* Pittsburgh: University of Pittsburgh Press.

Bock, Gisela. 1983. "Racism and Sexism in Nazi Germany: Motherhood, Compulsory Sterilization, and the State." *Signs: Journal of Women and Culture* 8, no. 3:400–421.

Bock, Gisela, and P. Thane, eds. 1991. *Maternity and Gender Policies: Women and the Rise of the European Welfare States , 1880s–1950s.* London: Routledge.

Bolger, Audrey. 1991. *Aboriginal Women and Violence: A Report for the Criminology Research Council and the Northern Territory Commissioner of Police.* Australia National University, North Australia Research Unit, Darwin.

Bonoli, G. 1997. "Classifying Welfare States: A Two-Dimension Approach." *Journal of Social Policy* 26, no. 3 (July): 351–72.

Borchorst, Annette. 1995. "A Political Niche: Denmark's Equal Status Council." In

Comparative State Feminism, edited by Dorothy McBride Stetson and Amy G. Mazur. California: Thousand Oaks, Calif.: Sage.

Borchorst, Annette, and Birte Siim. 1987. "Women and the Advanced Welfare State." In *Women and the State: The Shifting Boundaries of Public and Private,* edited by Anne Showstack Sassoon. New York: Routledge.

Botswana. Women's Affairs Division. 1995. Department of Culture and Social Welfare, Ministry of Labour and Home Affairs. *Botswana: Draft National Plan of Action.* Gaborone.
<gopher://gopher.un.org:70/oo/conf/fwcw/natrep/NatActPlans/botswall.txt%09>

Boyd, Robert L. 1996. "Convergence or Divergence?" *Social Indicators Research,* July, 329–31.

Bradley, Christine. 1994. "Why Male Violence Against Women Is a Development Issue: Reflections from Papua New Guinea." In *Women and Violence: Realities and Responses Worldwide,* edited by Miranda Davies. London: Zed Books.

Bradshaw, Jonathon, John Ditch, Hilary Holmes, and Peter Whiteford. 1993. "A Comparative Study of Child Support in Fifteen Countries." *Journal of European Social Policy* 3, no. 4:255–71.

Brasiliero, Ana Maria, ed. 1997. *Women Against Violence: Breaking the Silence: Reflecting on Experience in Latin America and the Caribbean.* New York: UNIFEM.

Bremer, Stuart A. 1992. "Dangerous Dyads." *Journal of Conflict Resolution* 36, no. 2 (June): 309–41.

Brown, Carol. 1981. "Mothers, Fathers, and Children: From Private to Public Patriarchy." In *Women and Revolution: A Discussion of the Unhappy Marriage of Marxism and Feminism,* edited by Lydia Sargent. Boston: South End Press.

Brown, Wendy. 1992. "Finding the Man in the State." *Feminist Studies* (spring): 7–34.

Brownmiller, Susan. 1975. *Against Our Will: Men, Women, and Rape.* New York: Simon and Schuster.

———. 1999. *In Our Time: Memoir of a Revolution.* New York: Dial Press.

Brush, Lisa D. 1994. "The Curious Courtship of Feminist Jurisprudence and Feminist State Theory: Smart on the Power of Law." *Law and Social Inquiry* 19, no. 4:1059–77.

———. 1996. "Love, Toil and Trouble: Motherhood and Feminist Politics" *Signs: Journal of Women and Culture* 21, no. 2 (winter): 429–54

———. 2000. "Battering, Traumatic Stress, and Welfare-to-Work Transition." *Violence Against Women* 6, no. 10:1039–65.

Bunch, Charlotte, ed. 1992. *Violence Against Women: Addressing a Global Problem.* New York: Ford Foundation's Women's Program Forum.

Burt, Sandra. 1998. "Advisory Councils as Sites of Research, Policy Influence, and Networking." In *Women and Political Representation in Canada,* edited by Manon Tremblay and Caroline Andrew. Ottawa: University of Ottawa Press.

Busch, Diane Mitsch. 1992. "Women's Movements and State Policy Reform Aimed at Domestic Violence Against Women: A Comparison of the Consequences of Movement Mobilization in the United States and India." *Gender and Society* 6, no. 4 (December): 587–608

Butler, Judith. 1990. *Gender Trouble: Feminism and the Subversion of Identity.* New York: Routledge.

Buzawa, Eve S., and Carl G. Buzawa, eds. 1992. *Domestic Violence: The Changing Criminal Justice Response.* Westport, Conn.: Auburn House.

Bystydzienski, Jill M. 1988. "Women in Politics in Norway." *Women and Politics* 8, nos. 3–4:73–95.

———. 1992a. "Influence of Women's Culture on Public Politics in Norway." In *Women Transforming Politics: Worldwide Strategies for Empowerment,* edited by Jill M. Bystydzienski. Bloomington: Indiana University Press.

———, ed. 1992b. *Women Transforming Politics: Worldwide Strategies for Empowerment.* Bloomington: Indiana University Press.

———. 1995. "Women's Equality Structures in Norway: The Equal Status Council." In *Comparative State Feminism,* edited by Dorothy McBride Stetson and Amy G. Mazur. Thousand Oaks, California: Sage.

Bystydzienski, Jill M., and Joti Sekhon. 1999. *Democratization and Women's Grassroots Movements.* Bloomington: Indiana University Press.

Cacoullos, Ann R. 1994. "Women Confronting Party Politics in Greece." In *Women and Politics Worldwide,* edited by Barbara J. Nelson and Najma Chowdhury. New Haven, Conn.: Yale University Press.

CAFRA Bahamas. 1998. Correspondence with author, February 3.

The Crisis Centre, Nassau. 1998. Correspondence with author, February 27.

Caldeira, Teresa P. R. 1998. "Justice and Individual Rights: Challenges for Women's Movements and Democratization in Brazil." In *Women and Democracy—Latin America and Central and Eastern Europe,* edited by Jane S. Jacquette and Sharon L. Wolchik. Baltimore: Johns Hopkins University Press.

Canada. Canadian Advisory Council on the Status of Women (CACSW). 1982. *A Brief on Wife Battering with Proposals for Federal Action.* Ottawa.

———. Canadian Council on Social Development and Native Women's Association of Canada. 1991. *Voices of Aboriginal Women: Aboriginal Women Speak Out About Violence.* Ottawa: Canadian Council on Social Development.

———. Canadian International Development Agency (CIDA). 1999. *Policy on Gender Equality.* Hull: CIDA.

———. Canadian Panel on Violence Against Women. 1993. *Final Report.* Ottawa: Minister of Supply and Services.

———. 1993. *Inuit Women/inuinait angnat: the Final Report of the Canadian Panel on Violence Against Women: Changing the Landscape: Ending Violence—Achieving Equality.* Ottawa: Minister of Supply and Services.

———. Department of Justice Canada. 1995. *Abuse Is Wrong in Any Language.* Ottawa: Minister of Public Works and Government Services Canada.

———. Family Violence Prevention Division, Health Canada. 1996a. *Breaking the Links Between Poverty and Violence Against Women: A Resource Guide.* National Clearinghouse on Family Violence. Ottawa: Minister of Public Works and Government Services Canada.

———. 1996b. *Family Violence in Aboriginal Communities: An Aboriginal Perspective.* National Clearinghouse on Family Violence. Ottawa: Minister of Public Works and Government Services Canada.

———. Family Violence Prevention Unit, Health Canada. 2000. *Two Steps Forward . . . One Step Back: An Overview of Canadian Initiatives and Resources to End Woman Abuse, 1989–1997.* National Clearinghouse on Family Violence. Ottawa: Minister of Public Works and Government Services Canada.

———. Health and Welfare Canada. 1992. *Transition Houses and Shelters for Battered Women in Canada.* Ottawa: Government of Canada.

————. House of Commons. Standing Committee on Health, Welfare, Social Affairs, Seniors and the Status of Women. 1982. *Report on Violence in the Family: Wife Battering.* Ottawa: Minister of Supply and Services.

————. Status of Women Subcommittee of the Standing Committee on Health, Welfare, Social Affairs, Seniors and the Status of Women. 1991. *The War Against Women.* Ottawa: Minister of Supply and Services.

————. Statistics Canada. 1990. *Women in Canada: A Statistical Report.* 2nd edition. February. Ottawa: Statistics Canada.

————. 1993. *National Survey on Violence Against Women: Survey Highlights.* Ottawa: Statistics Canada.

————. Status of Women Canada/Condition féminine Canada. 1991. *Living Without Fear . . . Everyone's Goal, Every Woman's Right.* Federal Government Response to the Report of the Standing Committee on Health and Welfare, Social Affairs, Seniors and the Status of Women. Ottawa: Government of Canada.

————. 1995. *Setting the Stage for the Next Century: The Federal Plan for Gender Equality.* <gopher:gopher.un.org:70/oo/conf/fwcw/natrep/NatActPlans/Canada/>

Carroll, Barbara Waje, and Terrance Carroll. 1999. "Civic Networks, Legitimacy, and the Policy Process." *Governance* 12, no. 1:1–28.

Call, Jack E., David Nice, and Susette M. Talarico. 1991. "An Analysis of State Rape Shield Laws." *Social Science Quarterly* 72, no. 4:774–88.

Castles, Francis G. 1993. *Families of Nations: Patterns of Public Policy in Western Democracies.* Aldershot, England: Dartmouth.

Castles, Francis G., and Christopher Pierson. 1996. "A New Convergence?" *Policy and Politics* 24 (July): 233–45.

Chalk, Rosemary, and Patricia King, eds. 1998. *Violence in Families: Assessing Prevention and Treatment Programs.* Committee on the Assessment of Family Violence Interventions, Board on Children, Youth, and Families, Commission on Behavioral and Social Sciences and Education, National Research Council, and Institute of Medicine. Washington, D.C.: National Academy Press.

Chaney, Carole Kennedy, and Grace Hall Salzstein. 1998. "Democratic Control and Bureaucratic Responsiveness: The Police and Domestic Violence." *American Journal of Political Science* 42:745–68.

Charlton, Sue Ellen M., Jana Everett, and Kathleen Staudt, eds. 1989. *Women, the State, and Development.* Albany: State University of New York Press.

Christensen, Ann-Dorte. 1999. "Women in Political Parties." In *Equal Democracies? Gender and Politics in the Nordic Countries,* edited by Christina Bergqvist. Oslo: Scandinavian University Press.

Chowdhury, Najma, and Barbara J. Nelson with Kathryn A. Carver, Nancy J. Johnson, and Paula L. O'Loughlin. 1994. "Redefining Politics: Patterns of Women's Political Engagement from a Global Perspective." In *Women and Politics Worldwide,* edited by Barbara J. Nelson and Najma Chowdhury. New Haven, Conn.: Yale University Press.

Chowdhury, Najma, Nancy J. Johnson, Barbara J. Nelson, and Paula L. O'Loughlin. 1994. "Global Research on Women's Political Engagement: The History of the Women and Politics Worldwide Project." In *Women and Politics Worldwide,* edited by Barbara J. Nelson and Najma Chowdhury. New Haven, Conn.: Yale University Press.

Clarke, Roberta. 1997. "Combatting Violence in the Caribbean." In *Women Against*

Violence: Breaking the Silence: Reflecting on Experience in Latin America and the Caribbean, edited by Ana Maria Brasiliero. New York: UNIFEM.

Cockburn, Cynthia. 1991. *In the Way of Women: Men's Resistance to Sex Equality in Organizations.* New York: ILR Press.

Cohen, Roger. 1999. "Woman Sets Out to Lead Kohl's Party out of Its Crisis." *New York Times,* April 11.

Coleman, Sally, Jeffrey L. Brudney, and J. Edward Kellough. 1998. "Bureaucracy as a Representative Institution: Toward a Reconciliation of Bureaucratic Government and Democratic Theory." *American Journal of Political Science* 42, no. 3 (July): 717–44.

Coleman, William D., Grace Skogstad, and Michael M. Atkinson. 1997. "Paradigm Shifts and Policy Networks: Cumulative Change in Agriculture." *Journal of Public Policy* 16:273–301.

Collins, Patricia Hill. 1994. "Shifting the Center: Race, Class, and Feminist Theorizing about Motherhood." In *Representations of Motherhood,* edited by Donna Bassin, Margaret Honey, and Merle Mahrer Keplan. New Haven, Conn.: Yale University Press.

Colombia. 1996. *Plan de Action National: Revision Despues de la Conferencia De Beijing.* <gopher://gopher.un.org:70/00/conf/fwcw/natrep/NatActPlans/colombia.txt>

Colombia Bulletin: A Human Rights Quarterly. 1998 (summer). Colombia Support Network, Madison, Wis.

Connors, Jane Frances. 1989. *Violence Against Women in the Family.* ST/CSDHA/2. Vienna: United Nations Centre for Social Development and Humanitarian Affairs.

———. 1994. "Government Measures to Confront Violence Against Women." In *Women and Violence: Realities and Responses Worldwide,* edited by Miranda Davies. London: Zed Books.

Conway, M. Margaret, David Ahern, and Gertrude Steuernagel. 1995. *Women and Public Policy: A Revolution in Progress.* Washington, D.C.: CQ Press.

Conway, M. Margaret, David Ahern, and Gertrude Steuernagel. 1999. *Women and Public Policy: A Revolution in Progress.* 2nd edition. Washington D.C.: CQ Press.

Cook, Elizabeth Adell, Sue Thomas, and Clyde Wilcox. 1994. *The Year of the Woman: Myths and Realities.* Boulder, Colo.: Westview Press.

Cook, Paul, and Colin Kirkpatrick. 1997. "Globalization, Regionalization, and Third World Development." *Regional Studies* 31 (1 February): 55–66.

Costain, Anne N. 1998. "Women Lobby Congress." In *Social Movements and American Political Institutions,* edited by Anne N. Costain and Andrew S. McFarland. Lanham, Md.: Rowman and Littlefield.

Costain, Anne N., and Andrew S. McFarland, eds. 1998. *Social Movements and American Political Institutions.* Lanham, Md.: Rowman and Littlefield.

Curthoys, Ann. 1993. "Feminism, Citizenship, and National Identity." *Feminist Review,* no. 44 (summer): 19–38.

Dahl, Robert. 1956. *A Preface to Democratic Theory.* Toronto: University of Toronto Press.

———. 1971. *Polyarchy.* New Haven, Conn.: Yale University Press.

Dahlerup, Drude. 1987. "Confusing Concepts—Confusing Reality: A Theoretical Discussion of the Patriarchal State." In *Women and the State: The Shifting Boundaries of Public and Private,* edited by Anne Showstack Sassoon. New York: Routledge.

Dalton, Russell J. 1996. "Political Cleavages, Issues, and Electoral Change." In *Com-*

paring Democracies: Elections and Voting in Global Perspective, edited by Lawrence LeDuc, Richard G. Niemi, and Pippa Norris. Thousand Oaks, Calif.: Sage.

Daniels, Cynthia R., ed. 1997. *Feminists Negotiate the State: The Politics of Domestic Violence.* Lanham, Md.: University Press of America.

Darcy, R., Susan Welch, and Janet Clark. 1987. *Women, Elections, and Representation.* New York: Longman.

Darden, Joe T. 1984. "Black Political Underrepresentation in Majority Black Places." *Journal of Black Studies* 15, no. 1:101–6.

Davies, Miranda, ed. 1994. *Women and Violence: Realities and Responses Worldwide.* London: Zed Books.

Davis, Angela. 1990. *Women, Culture, Politics.* New York: Vintage Books.

Davis, Rebecca Howard. 1997. *Women and Power in Parliamentary Democracies: Cabinet Appointments in Western Europe, 1968–1992.* Lincoln, Nebr.: University of Nebraska Press.

Denham, Donna, and Joan Gillespie. 1998. *Two Steps Forward . . . One Step Back: An Overview of Canadian Resources and Initiatives to End Woman Abuse, 1989–1997.* National Clearinghouse on Family Violence, Family Violence Prevention Unit, Health Issues Division, Health Canada. Ottawa: Government of Canada.

Denmark. Danish Equal Status Council. 1995. *The Danish Equal Status Council.* Ligestillingsrädet. Copenhagen: Government of Denmark.

———. Ministry of Foreign Affairs. 1994. *Equality in Denmark: The Danish National Report to the Fourth World Conference on Women, 1995.* Copenhagen: Ministry of Foreign Affairs.

———. 1996. *Statement to the Folketing on Follow-Up at National and International Levels to the United Nations' Fourth World Conference on Women.* April 3. <gopher://gopher.un.org:70/oo/conf/fwcw/natrep/NatActPlans/denmark.txt>

———. Ministry of Foreign Affairs and the Equal Status Council Secretariat. 1996. *Fourth Periodic Report by the Government of Denmark on the Implementation of the Convention on the Elimination of All Forms of Discrimination Against Women.* Copenhagen: Government of Denmark.

———. Ministry of Justice. 1998. Correspondence with author, February.

———. Ministry of Social Affairs. 1998. Correspondence with author, February 16.

Desai, Neera, and Maithreyi Krishnaraj. 1987. *Women and Society in India.* Delhi: Ajanta Publications.

Diamond, Irene, ed. 1983. *Families, Politics, and Public Policy: A Feminist Dialogue on Women and the State.* New York: Longman.

Directory of Third World Women's Publications. 1990. Rome, Italy: ISIS International.

Dobash, R. Emerson, and Russell P. Dobash, eds. 1998. *Rethinking Violence Against Women.* Thousand Oaks, Calif.: Sage.

Dobash, Russell P., and R. Emerson Dobash. 1992. *Women, Violence, and Social Change.* New York: Routledge.

Dobrowolsky, Alexandra. 1998. "Of 'Special Interest': Interest, Identity, and Feminist Constitutional Activism in Canada." *Canadian Journal of Political Science/Revue canadienne de science politique* 31, no. 4 (December): 707–42.

Dodson, Debra L., ed. 1991. *Gender and Policymaking: Studies of Women in Office.* The Impact of Women in Public Office Project. Rutgers, N.J.: Center for American Women and Politics.

Dodson, Debra L., and Susan J. Carroll. 1991. *Reshaping the Agenda: Women in State Legislatures.* The Impact of Women in Public Office Project. Rutgers, N.J.: Center for American Women and Politics.

Dogan, Mattei, and Ali Kazancigil. 1994. *Comparing Nations: Concepts, Strategies, Substance.* Malden, Mass.: Blackwell Publishers.

Dryzek, John S. 1990. *Discursive Democracy: Politics, Policy, and Political Science.* Cambridge: Cambridge University Press.

——. 1996. *Democracy in Capitalist Times: Ideals, Limits, and Struggles.* New York: Oxford University Press.

Duerst-Lahti, Georgia. 1989. "The Government's Role in Building the Women's Movement." *Political Science Quarterly* 104, no. 3:249–68.

Duerst-Lahti, Georgia, and Rita Mae Kelly, eds. 1995. *Gender Power, Leadership, and Governance.* Ann Arbor, Mich.: University of Michigan Press.

Duncan, Simon. 1995. "Theorizing European Gender Systems." *Journal of European Social Policy* 5, no. 4:263–84.

——. 1996. "The Diverse Worlds of European Patriarchy." In *Women of the European Union: The Politics of Work and Daily Life,* edited by Maria Dolors García-Ramon and Janice Monk. New York: Routledge.

Dutton, Donald G. 1984. *The Criminal Justice System Response to Wife Assault.* Vancouver: Solicitor General of Canada.

Dye, Thomas R. 1998. *Understanding Public Policy.* 9th ed. Englewood Cliffs, N.J.: Prentice Hall.

Eckstein, Harry, and David E. Apter. 1963. *Comparative Politics, A Reader.* New York: Free Press of Glencoe.

Edwards, Susan S. M. 1989. *Policing Domestic Violence: Women, the Law, and the State.* Thousand Oaks, Calif.: Sage.

Eisenstein, Hester. 1995. "The Australian Femocratic Experiment: A Feminist Case for Bureaucracy." In *Feminist Organizations: Harvest of the New Women's Movement,* edited by Myra Marx Ferree and Patricia Yancey Martin. Philadelphia: Temple University Press.

Elman, R. Amy. 1993. "Debunking the Social Democrats and the Myth of Equality." *Women's Studies International Forum* 16, no. 5:513–22.

——. 1995. "The State's Equality for Women: Sweden's Equality Ombudsman." In *Comparative State Feminism,* edited by Dorothy McBride Stetson and Amy G. Mazur. Thousand Oaks, Calif.: Sage.

——. 1996a. *Sexual Subordination and State Intervention: Comparing Sweden and the United States.* Providence/Oxford: Berghahn.

——, ed. 1996b. *Sexual Politics and the European Union: The New Feminist Challenge.* Providence/Oxford: Berghahn.

Elman, R. Amy, and Maud L. Eduards. 1991. "Unprotected by the Swedish Welfare State: A Survey of Battered Women and the Assistance They Received." *Women's Studies International Forum* 14, no. 5:413–21.

Elperin, Juliet. 1998. "House Votes Funds to Fight Violence Against Women—Nearly 1 Billion in Anti-pedophile Measure." *Washington Post,* June 14, A-12.

Epstein, Julia, and Kristina Straub, eds. 1995. *Body Guards: The Cultural Politics of Gender Ambiguity.* New York: Routledge.

Erickson, Jan. 1998. "Anti-violence Victories in Congress and More." *NOW Legislative Update* (fall): <http://www.now.org/nnt/fall-98/legupdate.html>

Esping-Andersen, Gøsta. 1990. *The Three Worlds of Welfare Capitalism.* Princeton, N.J.: Princeton University Press.

Etzkowitz, Henry, Carol Kemelgor, Michale Neushatz, Brian Uzzi, and Joseph Alonzo. 1994. "The Paradox of Critical Mass for Women in Science." *Science* 266, no. 5182 (7 October): 51–54

Everett, Jana M. 1979. *Woman and Social Change in India.* New York: St. Martin's Press.

———. 1998. "Indian Feminists Debate the Efficacy of Policy Reform: The Maharashtra Ban on Sex-Determination Tests." *Social Politics* (fall): 314–37.

Ferguson, Ann. 1983. "On Conceiving Motherhood and Sexuality: A Feminist Materialist Approach." In *Mothering: Essays in Feminist Theory,* edited by Joyce Trebilcot. Lanham, Md.: Rowman and Littlefield.

Ferguson, Kathy E. 1984. *The Feminist Case Against Bureaucracy.* Women in Political Economy Series, edited by Ronnie Steinberg. Philadelphia: Temple University Press.

Ferree, Myra Marx. 1995. "Making Equality: The Women's Affairs Offices in the Federal Republic of Germany." In *Comparative State Feminism,* edited by Dorothy McBride Stetson and Amy G. Mazur. Thousand Oaks, Calif.: Sage.

Ferree, Myra Marx, and Patricia Yancey Martin. 1995. *Feminist Organizations: Harvest of the New Women's Movement.* Philadelphia: Temple University Press.

Finland. 1889. *The Penal Code of Finland.* December 19, 1889/39.

———. 1997a. *Equality Programme of the Finnish Government.* February 6.
<http://www.un.org/womenwatch/followup/national/finisnap.htm>

———. 1997b. *Proposals for the Amendment of the Penal Code of Finland.* Government Bill to Parliament no. 6/1997.

———. Ministry of Justice. 1998. Correspondence with author, January 23.

Finnemore, Martha. 1996. "Norms, Culture, and World Politics: Insights from Sociology's Institutionalism." *International Organization* 50, no. 2 (spring): 325–47.

Forbes, Geraldine. 1979. "The Women's Movement in India: Traditional Symbols and New Roles." In *Social Movements in India,* vol. 2, edited by M. Rao. New Delhi: Manohar Publications.

Ford Foundation. 1992. *Violence Against Women: Addressing a Global Problem.* New York: Ford Foundation Women's Program Forum.

Forum Against the Oppression of Women. 1994. "Women's Organizations Against Rape in India." In *Women and Violence: Realities and Responses Worldwide,* edited by Miranda Davies. London: Zed Books.

France. Le Ministre Chargé des Droits des Femmes. 1997. *Programme national d'action en application des recommandations de la Conférence de Pékin.*
<http://www.un.org/womenwatch/followup/national/france.htm>

Fraser, Nancy. 1989. *Unruly Practices: Power, Discourse, and Gender in Contemporary Social Theory.* Minneapolis: University of Minnesota Press.

———. 1992. "The Uses and Abuses of French Discourse Theories for Feminist Politics." In *Revaluing French Feminism: Critical Essays on Difference, Agency, and Culture,* edited by Nancy Fraser and Sandra Lee Bartky. Bloomington: Indiana University Press.

Frederickson, George M. 1999. "Reflections on the Comparative History and Sociology of Racism." In *Racism,* edited by Leonard Harris. Amherst, New York: Humanity Books.

Freedom House. 1991. *Freedom in the World: Political Rights and Civil Liberties: 1990–1991*. Freedom House Survey Team. New York: Freedom House.

———. 1997. *The Comparative Survey of Freedom, 1995–1996: Survey Methodology.* <http://www.freedomhouse.org/Political/method.htm.>

Freeman, J. 1975. *The Politics of Women's Liberation.* New York: David MacKay.

Frieze, Irene. 1983. "Investigating the Causes and Consequences of Marital Rape." *Signs: Journal of Women and Culture* 8, no 3:532–53

Frieze, Irene, and Angela Browne. 1989. "Violence in Marriage." In *Family Violence,* edited by Lloyd Ohlin and Michael Tonry. Crime and Justice Series 11. Chicago: University of Chicago Press.

Fuentes, M., and A. Gunder Frank. 1989. "Ten Theses on Social Movements." *World Development* 17, no. 2:179–91.

Gauthier, Anne Hélène. 1996. *The State and the Family: A Comparative Analysis of Family Policies in Industrialized Countries.* Oxford: Clarendon Press.

Gelb, Joyce. 1989. *Feminism and Politics: A Comparative Perspective.* Berkeley: University of California Press.

———. 1995. "Feminist Organization Success and the Politics of Engagement." In *Feminist Organizations: Harvest of the New Women's Movement,* edited by Myra Marx Ferree and Patricia Yancey Martin. Philadelphia: Temple University Press.

———. 1998. "Legislating Against Violence: The Violence Against Women Act of 1994." Paper presented at the Annual Meeting of the American Political Science Association, Boston, September 3–6.

Gelb, Joyce, and Marian Lief Palley. 1982. *Women and Public Policies.* Princeton, N.J.: Princeton University Press.

Geller-Schwartz, Linda. 1995. "An Array of Agencies: Feminism and State Institutions in Canada." In *Comparative State Feminism,* edited by Dorothy McBride Stetson and Amy G. Mazur. Thousand Oaks, Calif.: Sage.

Gelpi, Barbara C., Nancy C. M. Hartsock, Clare Novak, and Myra H. Strober, eds. 1986. *Women and Poverty.* Chicago: University of Chicago Press.

Genovese, Michael A., ed. 1993. *Women as National Leaders.* Newbury Park, Calif.: Sage.

George, Alexander L., and Timothy J. McKeown. 1985. "Case Studies and Theories of Organizational Decision Making." In *Advances in Information Processing in Organizations,* vol. 2. Greenwich, Conn.: JAI Press.

Gerber, Marjorie. 1995. "The Chic of Araby: Transvestism, Transsexualism, and the Erotics of Cultural Appropriation." In *Body Guards: The Cultural Politics of Gender Ambiguity,* edited by Julia Epstein and Kristina Straub. New York: Routledge.

Germany. 1996. *National Action Plan.* <gopher://gopher.un.org:70/oo/conf/fwcw/natrep/NatActPlans/germany/GERMATOC.TXT>

———. Federal Ministry for Family Affairs, Senior Citizens, Women and Youth. 1995. *Equality, Participation, Partnership: National Strategies for the Implementation of the Platform for Action of the 4th World Conference on Women.*

———. 1998. Permanent Mission of Germany to the United Nations. Correspondence with author, January 30.

Giddens. Anthony. 1982. *Profiles and Critiques in Social Theory.* Berkeley: University of California Press.

Gigendil, Elisabeth. 1996. "Gender and Attitudes Towards Quotas for Women Candidates in Canada." *Women and Politics* 16, no. 4:21–43.

Gigendil, Elisabeth, and Richard Vengroff. 1997. "Representational Gains of Canadian Women or Token Growth? The Case of Quebec's Municipal Politics." *Canadian Journal of Political Science/Revue canadienne de science politique* 30, no. 3:513–37.

Githens, Marianne, Pippa Norris, and Joni Lovenduski. 1994. *Different Roles, Different Voices: Women and Politics in the United States and Europe.* New York: HarperCollinsCollege.

Glendon, Mary Ann. 1987. *Abortion and Divorce in Western Law.* Cambridge, Mass.: Harvard University Press.

Goggin, Malcolm L., ed. 1993. *Understanding the New Politics of Abortion.* Newbury Park, Calif.: Sage.

Gondolf, E. W., and E. R. Fisher. 1988. *Battered Women as Survivors.* Lexington, Mass.: Lexington Books.

Gonzalez-Suarez, Mirta. 1994. "With Patience and Without Blood: The Political Struggles of Costa Rican Women." In *Women and Politics Worldwide,* edited by Barbara J. Nelson and Najma Chowdhury. New Haven, Conn.: Yale University Press.

Gordon, Linda, ed. 1990. *Women, the State, and Welfare.* Madison: University of Wisconsin Press.

Gornick, Janet C., and David S. Meyer. 1996. "Invoking the State: Anti-rape Activism and Public Policy in the United States, 1970–1980." Paper presented at the Annual Meeting of the American Political Science Association, San Francisco.

Gornick, Janet C., Marcia K. Meyers, and Katherin E. Ross. 1997. "Supporting the Employment of Mothers: Policy Variation Across Fourteen Welfare States." *Journal of European Social Policy* 7, no. 1:45–70.

Gotell, Lise. 1998. "A Critical Look at State Discourse on 'Violence Against Women': Some Implications for Feminist Politics and Women's Citizenship." In *Women and Political Representation in Canada,* edited by Manon Tremblay and Caroline Andrew. Ottawa: University of Ottawa Press.

Gough, Ian. 1979. *The Political Economy of the Welfare State.* London: Macmillan.

———. 1997. "Social Assistance in OECD Countries." *Journal of European Social Policy* 7, no. 1:17–43.

Greece. General Secretariat for Equality. Ministry of Interior Public Administration and Decentralization. 1998. Correspondence with author, January 14.

Greenfeld, Lawrence A. 1997. *Sex Offenses and Offenders: An Analysis of Data on Rape and Sexual Assault.* U.S. Department of Justice, Office of Justice Programs, Bureau of Justice Statistics, NCJ-163392. Washington, D.C.: GPO.

Grofman, Bernard, Lisa Handley, and Richard G. Niemi. 1992. *Minority Representation and the Quest for Voting Equality.* New York: Cambridge University Press.

Guadagnini, Marila. 1995. "The Latecomers: Italy's Equal Status and Equal Opportunity Agencies." In *Comparative State Feminism,* edited by Dorothy McBride Stetson and Amy G. Mazur. Thousand Oaks, California: Sage.

Gujarati, Damodar N. 1995. *Basic Econometrics.* 3rd edition. New York: McGraw-Hill.

Haas, Peter M. 1997. *Knowledge, Power, and International Policy Coordination.* Columbia, S.C.: University of South Carolina Press.

Haavio-Mannila, Elina. 1983. "Caregiving in the Welfare State." *Acta Sociologica* 26, no. 1: 61–82

Haavio-Mannila, Elina, ed. 1985. *Unfinished Democracy: Women in Nordic Politics.* Translated by Christine Badcock. Oxford: Pergamon Press.

Habermas, Jurgen. 1987. *The Theory of Communicative Action.* Vol. 2. Translated by Thomas McCarthy. Boston: Beacon Press.

Hague, Gill. 1998. "Interagency Work and Domestic Violence in the UK." *Women's Studies International Forum* 21, no. 4:441–49.

Hall, Peter A. 1986. *Governing the Economy: The Politics of State Intervention in Britain and France.* New York: Oxford University Press.

Halperin, Sandra. 1997. *In the Mirror of the Third World: Capitalist Development in Modern Europe.* Ithaca, N.Y.: Cornell University Press.

Handler, Joel. 1994. *The Poverty of Welfare Reform.* New Haven, Conn.: Yale University Press.

Haney, Lynne. 1996. "Homeboys, Babies, Men in Suits: The State and the Reproduction of Male Dominance." *American Sociological Review* 61 (October): 759–78.

Hanmer, Jalna. 1996. "The Common Market of Violence." In *Sexual Politics and the European Union: The New Feminist Challenge,* edited by R. Amy Elman. Providence/Oxford: Berghahn.

Hansen, Susan Blackall. 1993. "Differences in Public Policies Toward Abortion: Electoral and Policy Context." In *Understanding the New Politics of Abortion,* edited by Malcolm L. Goggin. Newbury Park, Calif.: Sage.

———. 1997. "Talking About Politics: Gender and Contextual Effects on Political Proselytizing." *Journal of Politics* 41:37–56.

Hantrais, Linda. 1993. "Women, Work, and Welfare in France." In *Women and Social Policies in Europe: Work, Family, and the State,* edited by Jane Lewis. Brookfield, Vt.: Edward Elgar.

———. 1999a. *Gendered Policies in Europe: Reconciling Employment and Family Life.* New York: St. Martin's Press.

———. 1999b. "Socio-Demographic Change, Policy Impacts, and Outcomes in Social Europe." *Journal of European Social Policy* 9, no. 4:291–309.

Harder, Sandra. 1996. *Women in Canada: Socio-economic Status and Other Contemporary Issues.* Political and Social Affairs Division, Research Branch Library of Parliament Canada. Ottawa: Government of Canada.

Harding, Sandra. 1987. *Feminism and Methodology: Social Science Issues.* Bloomington: Indiana University Press; Milton Keynes: Open University Press.

Haussman, Melissa A. 1992. "The Personal Is the Constitutional: Feminist Struggles for Equality Rights in the United States and Canada." In *Women Transforming Politics,* edited by Jill M. Bystydzienski. Bloomington: Indiana University Press.

Heclo, Hugh. 1974. *Modern Social Policies in Britain and Sweden: From Relief to Income Maintenance.* New Haven, Conn.: Yale University Press.

———. 1978. "Issue-Networks and the Executive Establishment." In *The New American Political System,* edited by Anthony King. Washington, D.C.: American Enterprise Institute.

Heidenheimer, Arnold J., Hugh Heclo, and Carolyn Teich Adams. 1990. *Comparative Public Policy.* 3rd edition. New York: St. Martin's Press.

Heise, Lori, with Jacqueline Pitanguy and Adrienne Germain. 1994. *Violence Against Women: The Hidden Health Burden.* World Bank Discussion Papers. Washington, D.C.: World Bank.

Heise, Lori, Alanagh Raikes, Charlotte H. Watts, and Anthony B. Zwi. 1994. "Violenc

Against Women: A Neglected Public Health Issue in Less Developed Countries." *Social Science and Medicine* 39:1165–79.

Hellman, Judith Adler. 1996. "Italian Women's Struggle Against Violence: 1976–1996." Paper presented at the Annual Meeting of the American Political Science Association, San Francisco, August 28–September 1.

Hernes, Helga. 1987. *Welfare State and Woman Power: Essays in State Formation.* Oslo: Norwegian University Press.

Hester, Marianne, Liz Kelly, and Jill Radford. 1996. *Women, Violence, and Male Power.* Buckingham, Philadelphia: Open University Press.

Hill, David B. 1981. "Political Culture and Female Representation." *Journal of Politics* 43, no. 1:159–68.

Hill, M. 1997. *The Policy Process in the Modern State.* London: Prentice Hall.

Hoberg, George. 1998. "Distinguishing Learning from Other Sources of Policy Change: The Case of Forestry in the Pacific Northwest." Paper prepared for delivery at the Annual Meeting of the American Political Science Association, Boston, September 3–6.

hooks, bell. 1981. *Ain't I a Woman: Black Women and Feminism.* Boston: South End Press.

———. 2000. *Feminist Theory: From Margin to Center.* Boston: South End Press.

Hoskyns, Catherine. 1996. *Integrating Gender: Women, Law, and Politics in the European Union.* New York: Verso.

Human Rights Watch. 1994. *Second Class Citizens: Discrimination Against Women Under Botswana's Citizenship Act.* A607. New York: 9/94.

———. 1995. *The Human Rights Watch Global Report on Women's Human Rights.* New York: Human Rights Watch Women's Project.

Htun, Mala. 1999. "Electoral Quotas for Women in Latin America" Paper presented to the Annual Meeting of the American Political Science Association, Sept. 2–5, Atlanta.

Immergut, Ellen M. 1992. *Health Politics.* New York: Cambridge University Press.

India. Ministry of Education and Social Welfare, Department of Social Welfare. 1974. *Towards Equality: Report of the Committee on the Status of Women in India.* December. New Delhi: Ministry of Education and Social Welfare, Department of Social Welfare.

Inglehart, Ronald, and Maria Carballo. 1997. "Does Latin America Exist? (And Is There a Confucian Culture?): A Global Analysis of Cross-Cultural Differences." *PS: Political Science and Politics* 30, no. 1:34–47.

International Bank for Reconstruction and Development (IBRD). 1998. *World development indicators.* Washington, D.C.: IBRD.

International Labour Organization. 1994. *Maternity and Work: Conditions of Work Digest* 13. Geneva.

Interparliamentary Union. 1995. *Women in Parliaments, 1945–1995: A World Statistical Survey.* Geneva: Interparliamentary Union.

Ireland. Office of the Tanaiste. 1997a. *Acceptance of Domestic Violence Must End: 1 Million Pounds Extra This Year for Domestic Violence Services.* Statement by Minister of State Eithne Fitzgerald TD Chairperson of Task Force on Violence Against Women at Launch of Task Force Report. Dublin: Government of Ireland.

———. 1997b. *Introductory Remarks by Mr. Dick Spring, T.D. Tanaiste and Minister for Foreign Affairs at the Launch of the Task Force Report on Violence Against Women.* Dublin: Government of Ireland.

———. 1997c. *Report of the Task Force on Violence Against Women.* Dublin: Government of Ireland.

Israel. Prime Minister's Advisor on the Status of Women. 1997. *Continued Progress: National Report on the Status of Women in Israel.* Submitted to the 41st Session of the Commission on the Status of Women of ECOSOC. March.
<gopher://gopher.un.org:70/oo/conf/fwcw/natrep/NatActPlans/israel.txt>

Italy. 1996. *National Plan of Action to Implement the Beijing Platform for Action.*
<gopher://gopher.un.org:70/oo/conf/fwcw/natrep/NatActPlans/italy.txt>

———. Ufficio del Ministro per le Pari Opportunita. Presidenza Consiglio dei Ministri. 1997. Correspondence with author, December 17.

Jacquette, Jane. 1994. *The Women's Movement in Latin America.* Boulder, Colo.: Westview Press.

Jacquette, Jane S., and Sharon L. Wolchik, eds. 1998. *Women and Democracy—Latin America and Central and Eastern Europe.* Baltimore: Johns Hopkins University Press.

Jaffe, P., D. Wolfe, S. K. Wilson, and L. Zak. 1986. "Family Violence and Child Adjustment." *American Journal of Psychiatry* 143, no. 1:74–77.

Jaising, I. 1995. "Violence Against Women: The Indian Perspective." In *Women's Rights, Human Rights: International Feminist Perspectives,* edited by Julie Peters and Andrea Wolper. New York: Routledge.

Jamaica. Bureau of Women's Affairs. 1998. Correspondence with author, February 18.

Jamison, Andrew, Ron Eyerman, Jacqueline Cramer, and Jeppe Laessoe. 1990. *The Making of the New Environmental Consciousness: A Comparative Study of Environmental Movements in Sweden, Denmark, and the Netherlands.* Edinburgh: Edinburgh University Press.

Japan. Office for Gender Equality. 1998a. *Draft National Plan of Action.* Country Report to CEDAW. Tokyo: Government of Japan.

———. 1998b. *Gender Information Site.* <http://www.sorifu.go.jp/danjyo>

———. 1998c. Correspondence with author, January 22.

Jayawardena, Kumari. 1986. *Feminism and Nationalism in the Third World.* London: Zed Books.

Jenkins, J. Craig, and Bert Klandermaans, eds. 1995. *The Politics of Social Protest: Comparative Perspectives on States and Social Movements.* Minneapolis: University of Minnesota Press.

Jenson, Jane, and Mariette Sineau. 1994. "The Same or Different? An Unending Dilemma for French Women." In *Women and Politics Worldwide,* edited by Barbara J. Nelson and Najma Chowdhury. New Haven, Conn.: Yale University Press.

John, Peter, and Alistair Cole. 2000. "When Do Institutions, Policy Sectors, and Cities Matter? Comparing Networks of Local Policymakers in Britain and France." *Comparative Political Studies* 33, no. 2 (March 2000): 248–68.

Johnson, Holly. 1998. "Rethinking Survey Research on Violence Against Women" In *Rethinking Violence Against Women,* edited by R. Emerson Dobash and Russell P. Dobash. Sage Series on Violence Against Women, vol. 9. Thousand Oaks, Calif.: Sage.

Jones, Mark P. 1996. "Increasing Women's Representation via Gender Quotas: The Argentine Ley de Cupos." *Women and Politics* 16, no. 4:75–98.

Kanter, Rosabeth M. 1977. "Some Effects of Proportion on Group Life: Skewed Sex Ratios and Response to Token Women." *American Journal of Sociology* 82:965–90.

Kaplan, Gisela. 1992. *Contemporary Western European Feminism*. New York: New York University Press.

Karvonen, Lauri, and Per Selle. 1995. *Women in Nordic Politics: Closing the Gap*. Aldershot, England: Dartmouth.

Kathlene, Lyn. 1995. "Position Power versus Gender Power: Who Holds the Floor?" In *Gender Power, Leadership, and Governance*, edited by Georgia Duerst-Lahti and Rita Mae Kelly. Ann Arbor: University of Michigan Press.

Katzenstein, Mary Fainsod. 1989. "Organizing Against Violence: Strategies of the Indian Women's Movement." *Pacific Affairs* 62 (spring): 53–71.

———. 1995. "Discursive Politics and Feminist Activism in the Catholic Church." In *Feminist Organizations: Harvest of the New Women's Movement*, edited by Myra Marx Ferree and Patricia Yancey Martin. Philadelphia: Temple University Press.

———. 1998. *Faithful and Fearless*. Ithaca, N.Y.: Cornell University Press.

Katzenstein, Mary, and Carol Mueller, eds. 1987. *The Women's Movements of the United States and Western Europe*. Philadelphia: Temple University Press.

Keck, Margaret, and K. Sikkink. 1998. *Activists Across Borders*. Ithaca, N.Y.: Cornell University Press.

Keeley, James, and Ian Scoones. 1999. "Understanding Environmental Policy Processes: A Review." IDS Working Paper 89, Environment Group, Institute of Development Studies, University of Sussex.

Kelly, L. 1999. "Violence Against Women: A Policy of Neglect or a Neglect of Policy." In *New Agendas for Women*, edited by Sylvia Walby. New York: St. Martin's Press.

King, Gary, Robert Keohane, and Sidney Verba. 1994. *Designing Social Inquiry: Scientific Inference in Qualitative Research*. Princeton, N.J.: Princeton University Press.

Kingdon, John W. 1984. *Agendas, Alternatives, and Public Policies*. Boston: Little, Brown and Co.

———. 1995. *Agendas, Alternatives and Public Policies*. 2nd edition. New York, N.Y.: HarperCollins.

Kishwar, Madhu, and Ruth Vanita, eds. 1984. *In Search of Answers: Women's Voices from Manushi*. London: Zed Books.

Kitschelt, H. 1993. "Social Movements, Political Parties, and Democratic Theory." *Annals of the American Academy of Political and Social Science*, no. 528:13–29.

Knapp, Kiyoko Kamio. 1995. "Still Office Flowers: Japanese Women Betrayed by the Equal Employment Opportunity Law." *Harvard Women's Law Journal* 18 (spring): 83–138.

Knight, Jack. 1992. *Institutions and Social Conflict*. New York: Cambridge University Press.

Korpi, Walter. 1978. *The Working Class in Welfare Capital: Work, Unions, and Politics in Sweden*. London: Routledge and Kegan Paul.

Koss, Mary. 1992. "The Underdetection of Rape: Methodological Choices Influence Incidence Estimates." *Journal of Social Issues* 48, no. 1:61–75.

———. 1993. "Detecting the Scope of Rape: A Review of Prevalence Research Methods." *Journal of Interpersonal Violence* 8, no. 2:198–222.

———. 1996. "The Measurement of Rape Victimization in Crime Surveys." *Criminal Justice Behavior* 23, no. 1 (March): 55–69

Koven, Seth, and Sonya Michel. 1993. "Introduction: Mother Worlds. In *Mothers of a New World: Maternalist Politics and the Origins of Welfare States*, edited by Seth Koven and Sonya Michel. New York and London: Routledge.

Koven, Seth, and Sonya Michel, eds. 1993. *Mothers of a New World: Maternalist Politics and the Origins of Welfare States*. New York and London: Routledge.

Krajewski, Sandra S., Mary-Frann Rybarik, Margaret F. Dosch, and Gary D. Gilmore. "Results of a Curriculum Intervention with Seventh Graders Regarding Violence in Relationships" *Journal of Family Violence* 11, no. 2: 93–112.

Kriesi, Hanspeter, Ruud Koopmans, Jan Willem Duyvendak, and Marco G. Guigni. 1995. *New Social Movements in Western Europe: A Comparative Analysis*. Minneapolis: University of Minnesota Press.

Krishnaraj, Maithreyi, ed. 1991. *Women and Violence: A Country Report*. Sponsored by UNESCO. Bombay, India: Research Center for Women's Studies, SNDT University.

Krugman, Paul. 1993. "The Narrow and Broad Arguments for Free-Trade." *American Economic Review* 83, no. 2 (May): 362–366.

Kugler, Jacek, and William Domke. 1986. "Comparing the Strength of Nations." *Comparative Political Studies* 19, no. 1 (April): 39–69.

Kurian, George Thomas. 1991. *The New Book of World Rankings*. 3rd edition. New York: Facts on File.

Kvindecenterfonden. Dannerhuset (The Danner House, Copenhagen). 1998. Correspondence with author, March 2.

Lake, David. 1988. "The State and American Trade Strategy in the Pre-hegemonic Era." In *The State and American Foreign Economic Policy,* edited by G. John Ikenberry, David Lake, and Michael Mastanduno. Ithaca, N.Y.: Cornell University Press.

Lakeman, Lee. 1991. "New Panel to Study Old Violence." *Kinesis* (Vancouver), September.

Landsorganisation af Kvinderkrisecentre (LOKK) (Danish Organization of Crisis Centers). 1996. *Statistics*. Helsinger, Denmark.

———. 1998. Correspondence with author, March 18.

Lavoie, F., L. Vezina, C. Piche, and M. Boivin. 1995. "Evaluation of a Prevention Program for Violence in Teen Dating Relationships." *Journal of Interpersonal Violence* 10, no. 4: 516–24

LaRoque, Emma D. 1994. *Violence in Aboriginal Communities*. National Clearinghouse on Family Violence, Family Violence Prevention Division, Health Canada. Ottawa.

Le Doeuff, Michèle, 1995. "Problèmes d'investiture (De la parité, etc.)." *Nouvelles Questions Féministes* 16, no. 2:5–80.

LeDuc, Lawrence, Richard G. Niemi, and Pippa Norris. 1996. *Comparing Democracies: Elections and Voting in Global Perspective*. Thousand Oaks, Calif.: Sage.

Leijenaar, Monique, and Kees Niemoller. 1994. "Political Participation of Women: The Netherlands." In *Women and Politics Worldwide,* edited by Barbara J. Nelson and Najma Chowdhury. New Haven, Conn.: Yale University Press.

Leira, Arnlaug. 1993. "The Woman-Friendly Welfare State? The Case of Norway and Sweden." In *Women and Social Policies in Europe: Work, Family, and the State,* edited by Jane Lewis. Brookfield, Vt.: Edward Elgar.

Lehmbruch, Gerhard. 1982. "Introduction: Neo-corporatism in Comparative Perspective." In *Patterns of Corporatist Policymaking,* edited by Gerhard Lehmbruch and Phillippe C. Schmitter. Sage Modern Politics Series, vol. 7. Beverly Hills, Calif.: Sage.

Lemke, Christiane. 1994. "Women and Politics: The New Federal Republic of Germany." In *Women and Politics Worldwide*, edited by Barbara J. Nelson and Najma Chowdhury. New Haven, Conn.: Yale University Press.

Levinson, David. 1989. *Family Violence in Cross-Cultural Perspective*. Newbury Park, Calif.: Sage.

———. 1994. *Aggression and Conflict: A Cross-Cultural Encyclopedia*. Santa Barbara, Calif.: ABC-CLIO.

Lewis, Jane, ed. 1993. *Women and Social Policies in Europe: Work, Family, and the State*. Brookfield, Vt.: Edward Elgar.

———. 1998. *Gender, Social Care, and Welfare State Restructuring in Europe*. Brookfield, USA: Aldershot, England: Ashgate.

Liddle, J., and R. Joshi, 1986. *Daughters of Independence: Gender, Caste, and Class in India*. London: Zed Books.

Ling, Yuriko, and Azusa Matsuno, with Jill M. Bystydzienski. 1992. "Women's Struggle for Empowerment in Japan." In *Women Transforming Politics*, edited by Jill M. Bystydzienski. Bloomington: Indiana University Press.

Lipset, Seymour Martin. 1963. *Political Man*. New York: Anchor Books.

Lipton, Merle. 1988. "Capitalism and Apartheid." In *South Africa in Question*, edited by John Lipton. Portsmouth, N.H.: Heinemann Educational Books.

Lovenduski, Joni. 1986. *Women and European Politics: Contemporary Feminism and Public Policy*. Brighton, England: Wheatsheaf.

———. 1994. "The Rules of the Political Game: Feminism and Politics in Great Britain." In *Women and Politics Worldwide*, edited by Barbara J. Nelson and Najma Chowdhury. New Haven, Conn.: Yale University Press.

———. 1995. "An Emerging Advocate: The Equal Opportunities Commission in Great Britain." In *Comparative State Feminism*, edited by Dorothy McBride Stetson and Amy G. Mazur. Thousand Oaks, Calif.: Sage.

Lovenduski, Joni, and Pippa Norris. 1993. *Gender and Party Politics*. Thousand Oaks, Calif.: Sage.

Lugones, Maria. 1994. "Purity, Impurity, and Separation." *Signs: Journal of Women and Culture* 19, no. 2 (winter): 458–79.

Luxembourg. Ministère de la Promotion Féminine. 1995. *Rapport initial et 2e rapport périodique de Grand Duche de Luxembourg: Convention sur l'Élimination de Toutes les Formes de Discrimation à l'Égard des Femmes*. Luxembourg: Ministère de la Promotion Féminine.

Lycklama à Nijeholt, Geertje, Virginia Vargas, and Sakia Wieringa, eds. 1998. *Women's Movements and Public Policy in Europe, Latin America, and the Caribbean*. New York: Garland.

McAdam, Doug. 1999. "Do Movements Matter? Towards a More Systematic Analysis of Movement Impacts." Paper presented in the Department of Sociology and Anthropology, Purdue University, West Lafayette, Indiana, October 6.

McAdam, Doug, Sidney Tarrow, and Charles Tilly. 1996. "To Map Contentious Politics." *Mobilization* 1:17–34.

MacDonald, Gordon J., Daniel L. Nielson, and Marc A. Stern, eds. 1997. *Latin American Environmental Policy in International Perspective*. Boulder, Colo.: Westview Press.

MacKinnon, Catharine A. 1983. "Feminism, Marxism, Method, and the State: Toward Feminist Jurisprudence." *Signs: Journal of Women and Culture* 8, no. 4:635–58.

————. 1987. "Difference and Dominance: On Sex Discrimination (1984)." In *Feminism Unmodified: Discourses on Life and Law.* Cambridge, Mass.: Harvard University Press.

————. 1989. *Toward a Feminist Theory of the State.* Cambridge, Mass.: Harvard University Press.

MacLeod, Linda, and Maria Shin. 1990. *Isolated, Afraid, and Forgotten: The Service Delivery Needs and Realities of Immigrant and Refugee Women Who Are Battered.* Prepared for the National Clearinghouse on Family Violence, Health and Welfare Canada. Ottawa: Government of Canada.

Maguire, Kathleen, and Ann L. Pastore. 1996. *Sourcebook of Criminal and Justice Statistics, 1995.* U.S. Department of Justice, Bureau of Justice Statistics. Washington, D.C.: GPO.

Mahon, Evelyn. 1995. "Ireland's Policy Machinery: The Ministry of State for Women's Affairs and Joint Oireachtas Committees for Women's Rights." In *Comparative State Feminism,* edited by Dorothy McBride Stetson and Amy G. Mazur. Thousand Oaks: Calif.: Sage.

Majone, Giandomenico. 1989. *Evidence, Argument, and Persuasion in the Policy Process.* New Haven, Conn.: Yale University Press.

Makin, Kirk. 2000. "Rape-Shield Law under Scrutiny Again." *Toronto Globe and Mail,* February 21.

Malloy, Johnathan. 1999. "What Makes a State Advocacy Structure Effective? Conflicts Between Bureaucratic and Social Movement Criteria." *Governance: An International Journal of Policy and Administration* 12, no. 3 (July): 267–88.

Mansbridge, Jane. 1995. "What Is the Feminist Movement?" In *Feminist Organizations: Harvest of the New Women's Movement,* edited by Myra Marx Ferree and Patricia Yancey Martin. Philadelphia: Temple University Press.

————. 1999. "Should Blacks Represent Blacks and Women Represent Women? A Contingent 'Yes.'" *Journal of Politics* 61, no. 3 (August): 628–57.

Maoz, Zeev, and Nasrin Abdollali. 1989. "Regime Type and International Conflict." *Journal of Conflict Resolution* 33, no. 1:3–35.

Maracle, Lee. 1988. *I Am Woman.* North Vancouver, Canada: Write-On.

March, James, and Johan Olsen. 1989. *Rediscovering Institutions: The Organizational Basis of Politics.* New York: Free Press.

Marin, Alexandra Ayala. 1997. "Beyond the Conventions: Violence Prevention in the Andean Region." In *Women Against Violence: Breaking the Silence: Reflecting on Experience in Latin America and the Caribbean,* edited by Ana Maria Brasiliero. New York: UNIFEM.

Martin, Del. 1976. *Battered Wives.* San Francisco: Glide Publications.

Martin, Margaret E. 1997. "Double Your Trouble: Dual Arrest in Family Violence." *Journal of Family Violence* 12 (June): 139–57.

Marx, Anthony. 1998. *Making Race and Nation.* Cambridge: Cambridge University Press.

Massey, Douglas S., and Nancy A. Denton. 1993. *American Apartheid: Segregation and the Making of the Underclass.* Cambridge, Mass.: Harvard University Press.

Matland, Richard E. 1993. "Institutional Variables Affecting Female Representation in National Legislatures: The Case of Norway." *Journal of Politics* 55, no. 3 (August): 737–55.

Matland, Richard, and Donley T. Studlar. 1996. "The Contagion of Women Candidates in Single-Member District and Proportional Representation Electoral Systems: Canada and Norway." *Journal of Politics* 58, no. 3:707–33.

Matthews, Nancy. 1993. "Surmounting a Legacy: The Expansion of Racial Diversity in a Local Anti-rape Movement." In *Violence Against Women: The Bloody Footprints,* edited by Pauline B. Bart and Eileen G. Moran. A Gender and Society Reader. Newbury Park, Calif.: Sage.

———. 1995. "Feminist Clashes with the State: Tactical Choices by State-Funded Rape Crisis Centers." In *Feminist Organizations: Harvest of the New Women's Movement,* edited by Myra Marx Ferree and Patricia Yancey Martin. Philadelphia: Temple University Press.

Mazur, Amy G. 1995a. *Gender Bias and the State: Symbolic Reform at Work in Fifth Republic France.* Pittsburgh: University of Pittsburgh Press.

———. 1995b. "Strong State and Symbolic Reform: The Ministère des Droits de la Femmes in France." In *Comparative State Feminism,* edited by Dorothy McBride Stetson and Amy G. Mazur. Thousand Oaks, Calif.: Sage.

———. 1996. "The Interplay: The Formation of Sexual Harassment Legislation in France and EU Policy Initiatives." In *Sexual Politics and the European Union: The New Feminist Challenge,* edited by R. Amy Elman. Providence/Oxford: Berghahn.

———. 1999. "Feminist Comparative Policy: A New Field of Study." *European Journal of Political Research* 35, no. 4:483–506.

Mazur, Amy G., and Dorothy McBride Stetson. 1995. "Conclusion: The Case for State Feminism." In *Comparative State Feminism,* edited by Dorothy McBride Stetson and Amy G. Mazur. Thousand Oaks, Calif.: Sage.

Meier, Kenneth, Robert D. Wrinkle, and J. L. Polinard. 1999. "Representative Bureaucracy and Distributional Equity: Addressing the Hard Question." *Journal of Politics* 61, no. 4:1025–39.

Mendez, Maria Theresa Gallego. 1994. "Women's Political Engagement in Spain." In *Women and Politics Worldwide,* edited by Barbara J. Nelson and Najma Chowdhury. New Haven, Conn.: Yale University Press.

Meyer, Fred A., and Ralph Baker, eds. 1993. *State Policy Problems.* Chicago: Nelson-Hall.

Mezey, Susan Gluck. 1994. "Increasing the Number of Women in Office: Does It Matter?" In *The Year of the Woman: Myths and Realities,* edited by Elizabeth Adell Cook, Sue Thomas, and Clyde Wilcox. Boulder, Colo.: Westview Press.

Migdal, Joel S., Atul Kohli, and Vivienne Shue. 1994. *State Power and Social Forces: Domination and Transformation in the Third World.* Cambridge Studies in Comparative Politics. Cambridge: Cambridge University Press.

Mills, Linda G. 1998. "Mandatory Arrest and Prosecution Policies for Domestic Violence: A Critical Literature Review and the Case for More Research to Test Victim Empowerment Approaches." *Criminal Justice and Behavior* 25, no. 3 (Sept.): 306–18.

Misra, Joya, and Frances Akins. 1998. "The Welfare State and Women: Structure, Agency, and Diversity." *Social Politics* (fall): 259–85.

Molgat, Anne, with Joan Grant Cummings. 2000. *"An Action That Will Not Be Allowed to Subside": NAC's First Twenty-five Years.* <http://www.nac-cca.ca/about/his_e.htm>

Molyneux, Maxine. 1991. "Marxism, Feminism, and the Demise of the Soviet Model."

In *Gender and International Relations,* edited by Rebecca Grant and Kathleen Newland. Bloomington: Indiana University Press.

———. 1998. "Analyzing Women's Movements." In *Feminist Visions of Development: Gender Analysis and Policy,* edited by Cecile Jackson and Ruth Pearson. London: Routledge.

Morken, Kristin, and Per Selle. 1995. "An Alternative Movement in a 'State-Friendly' Society: The Women's Shelter Movement." In *Women in Nordic Politics: Closing the Gap,* edited by Lauri Karvonen and Per Selle. Aldershot, England: Dartmouth.

Mørkhagen, Pernille Lønne. 1991. *The Position of Women in Norway.* Oslo: Norinform, Ministry of Foreign Affairs.

Morrison, Samuel Eliot, Henry Steele Commager, and William E. Leuchtenberg. 1980. *The Growth of the American Republic.* 7th edition. Vol. 1. New York: Oxford University Press.

Murphy, Patricia. 1997. "Domestic Violence Legislation and the Police: The Role of Socio-economic Indicators, Political Factors, and Women's Political Activism on State Policy Adoption." *Women and Politics* 18, no. 2:27–53.

Naples, Nancy A. 1998. "Toward a Multiracial, Feminist, Social-Democratic Praxis: Lessons from Grassroots Warriors in the U.S. War on Poverty." *Social Politics* (fall): 286–313.

Narayan, Uma. 1997. *Dislocating Cultures: Identities, Traditions, and Third World Feminism.* New York: Routledge.

National Council of Women of the United States. 1963. *International Directory of Women's Organizations.* New York: Research and Action Associates.

National Organization of Women. 1998. *Pressing for a Second Violence Against Women Law.* <http:www.now.org./nnt/01-98/pressin.html>

Neilson, Joyce McCarl. 1990. *Feminist Research Methods: Exemplary Readings in the Social Sciences.* Boulder, Colo.: Westview Press.

Nelson, Barbara J., and Kathryn A. Carver. 1994. "Many Voices but Few Vehicles: The Consequences for Women of Weak Political Infrastructure in the United States." In *Women and Politics Worldwide,* edited by Barbara J. Nelson and Najma Chowdhury. New Haven, Conn.: Yale University Press.

Nelson, Barbara J., and Najma Chowdhury, eds. 1994. *Women and Politics Worldwide.* New Haven, Conn.: Yale University Press.

Nelson, Toni. 1996. "Violence Against Women." *Worldwatch* (July/August): 33–38.

New Zealand. Ministry of Women's Affairs. 1997. Correspondence with author, December 9.

———. 1999. *Briefing for the Incoming Minister: Justice and Safety.* <http://www.mwa.govt.nz./women/brief/justice.html>

———. Non-governmental Organization Coordinating Committee. 1996. *Beyond Beijing: The New Zealand Way: Kei Tua o Beijing Kote Ahua Mahi a aotearoa—New Zealand Women's Response to the Platform for Action from the UN Fourth World Conference on Women.* July. <gopher://gopher.un.org:70/oo/conf/fwcw/natre/NatActPlans/newzeala.txt>

Nicholson, Linda. 1986. *Gender and History.* New York: Columbia University Press.

Nixon, David L., and R. Darcy. 1996. "Special Election and the Growth of Women's Representation in the U.S. House of Representatives." *Women and Politics* 16, no. 4:99–107.

Norris, Pippa. 1987. *Politics and Sexual Equality: The Comparative Position of Women in Western Democracies.* Boulder, Colo.: Lynne Rienner.

Norway. Gender Equality Ombudsman. n.d. *Gender Equality by Law: The Norwegian Model.* QO: 510. Oslo.

———. Gender Equality Ombudsman. 1978. *The Norwegian Act on Gender Equality: Act No. 45 of June 9th, 1978, on Gender Equality.* QO: 0507. Oslo.

———. Permanent Mission of Norway to the United Nations, New York. 1998. Correspondence with author, January 16.

———. Royal Ministry of Foreign Affairs and Royal Ministry of Children and Family Affairs. 1994. *Gender Equality in Norway: The National Report to the Fourth UN Conference on Women in Beijing 1995.* Q 0854. Oslo: Ministry of Children and Family Affairs.

O'Connor, Julia S., Ann Shola Orloff, and Sheila Shaver. 1999. *States, Markets, Families: Gender, Liberalism, and Social Policy in Australia, Canada, Great Britain, and the United States.* New York: Cambridge University Press.

O'Donnell, Guillermo. 1993. "On the State, Democratization, and Some Conceptual Problems: A Latin American View with Glances at Postcommunist Countries." *World Development* 21, no. 8:1355–69.

Offe, Claus. 1984. *Contradictions of the Welfare State.* Edited by John Keane. London: Hutchinson.

Outshoorn, Joyce. 1995. "Administrative Accommodation in the Netherlands: The Department for the Coordination of Equality Policy." In *Comparative State Feminism,* edited by Dorothy McBride Stetson and Amy G. Mazur. Thousand Oaks: Calif.: Sage.

———. 1996. "The Meaning of 'Woman'" in Abortion Policy: A Comparative Approach." Paper presented to the Annual Meeting of the American Political Science Association, San Francisco, August 29–September 1.

———. 1998. Correspondence with author, University of Leiden, Netherlands. April 15.

Organization for Economic Cooperation and Development (OECD). 1995. *Gender-Equality: Moving Towards Sustainable, People-Centred Development.* Development Assistance Committee. Paris: OECD.

Orloff, A. S. 1993."Gender and Social Rights of Citizenship: The Comparative Analysis of Gender Relations and Welfare States." *American Sociological Review* 58 (June): 303–28.

Ortiz, Marcela. 1997. "Violence Against Women: A Regional Crisis." In *Women Against Violence: Breaking the Silence: Reflecting on Experience in Latin America and the Caribbean,* edited by Ana Maria Brasiliero. New York: UNIFEM.

Ostrom, Elinor. 1995. "New Horizons in Institutional Analysis." *American Political Science Review* 89, no. 1 (March): 174–78.

Overbye, Elinar. 1994. "Convergence in Policy Outcomes." *Journal of Public Policy* 14 (April–June): 147–74.

Papageorgiou-Limberes, Yota. 1992. "The Women's Movement and Greek Politics." In *Women Transforming Politics,* edited by Jill M. Bystydzienski. Bloomington: Indiana University Press.

Patel, Vibhuti. 1991. "Women's Action Groups and the State Machinery." In *Women and Violence: A Country Report,* edited by Maithreyi Krishnaraj. Sponsored by UNESCO. Bombay, India: Research Center for Women's Studies, SNDT University.

Pateman, Carole. 1989. "The Patriarchal Welfare State." In *The Disorder of Women: Democracy, Feminism, and Political Theory.* Stanford, Calif.: Stanford University Press.

Paternottre, M.P. 1998. (Advisor, Head of the Equal Opportunities Unit, Belgium.) Correspondence with author, 18 February.

Pauly, Louis W., and Simon Reich. 1997. "National Structures and Multinational Corporate Behavior: Enduring Differences in the Age of Globalization." *International Organization* 51, no. 1:1–31.

Perry, Elizabeth J. 1993. *Shanghai on Strike: The Politics of Chinese Labor.* Stanford, Calif.: Stanford University Press.

Peters, B. Guy. 1991. *European Politics Reconsidered.* New York: Holmes and Meier.

———. 1998. *Comparative Politics: Theory and Methods.* New York: New York University Press.

Peterson, Susan Rae. 1977. "Coercion and Rape: The State as Male Protection Racket." In *Feminism and Philosophy,* edited by Mary Vetterling-Braggin, Frederick A. Elliston, and Jane English. Totowa, N.J.: Littlefield, Adams, and Co.

Pfau-Effinger, Birgit. 1998. "Culture or Structure as Explanations for Differences in Part-Time Work in Germany, Finland, and the Netherlands?" In *Part-Time Prospects: An International Comparison of Part-Time Work in Europe, North America, and the Pacific Rim,* edited by Jacqueline O'Reilly and Colette Fagan. New York: Routledge.

Phillips, Anne. 1995. *The Politics of Presence.* Oxford: Clarendon Press.

Pitkin, Hannah Fenichel. 1967. *The Concept of Representation.* Berkeley: University of California Press.

Piven, Frances Fox. 1990. "Ideology and the State: Women, Power, and the Welfare State." In *Women, the State, and Welfare,* edited by Linda Gordon. Madison: University of Wisconsin Press.

Piven, Frances Fox, and Richard A. Cloward. 1993. *Regulating the Poor: The Functions of Public Welfare.* Updated edition. New York: Vintage Books.

Pollak, Nancy. 1991. "Rape Shield Gone." *Kinesis* [Vancouver] (September): 3.

Portugal. Commission for Equality and Women's Rights. Ministerio do Emprego e da Segurança Social. 1994. *Portugal: Status of Women.* Lisbon: Ministerio do Emprego e da Segurança Social.

———. Council of Ministers. 1997. *National Action Plan: Portugal.* <http://www.un.org/womenwatch/followup/national/portnap.htm>

Powell, G. Bingham. 1982. *Contemporary Democracies: Participation, Stability, and Violence.* Cambridge, Mass.: Harvard University Press.

Pringle, R., and Watson, S. 1992. "Women's Interests and the Post-structuralist State." In *Destabilizing Theory: Contemporary Feminist Debates,* edited by Michelle Barrett and Anne Phillips. Cambridge: Polity Press.

Putnam, Robert. 1993. *Making Democracy Work: Civic Traditions in Modern Italy.* Princeton, N.J.: Princeton University Press.

Randall, Vicki. 1987. *Women and Politics: An International Perspective.* 2nd edition. Chicago: University of Chicago Press.

"Rape Shield Protections Upheld." 2000. *Globe and Mail* (Toronto), October 12.

Raphael, Jody. 1996a. *Domestic Violence: Telling the Untold Welfare-to-Work Story.* A Taylor Institute Report. Chicago: Taylor Institute.

———. 1996b. "Domestic Violence and Welfare Receipt." *Harvard Women's Law Journal* 19:201–27.

———. 1997. "Domestic Violence as a Barrier to Employment." *Poverty and Race* 6, no. 4:11–12.

Reinelt, C. 1995. "Moving onto the Terrain of the State: The Battered Women's Movement and the Politics of Engagement." In *Feminist Organizations: Harvest of the New Women's Movement*, edited by Myra Marx Ferree and Patricia Yancey Martin. Philadelphia: Temple University Press.

Reinharz, Shulamit. 1992. *Feminist Methods in Social Research.* New York: Oxford University Press.

Rhode, Deborah. 1989. *Justice and Gender: Sex Discrimination and the Law.* Cambridge, Mass.: Harvard University Press.

Richardson, Jeremy. 1982. "Convergent Policy Styles in Europe?" In *Policy Styles in Western Europe,* edited by Jeremy Richardson. London: George Allen and Unwin.

Richardson, Jeremy, Gunnel Gustafson, and Grant Jordon. 1982. "The Concept of Policy Style." In *Policy Styles in Western Europe,* edited by Jeremy Richardson. London: George Allen and Unwin.

Riker, William H. 1964. *Federalism: Origin, Operation, Significance.* Boston: Little, Brown.

Rochon, Thomas R., and Daniel A. Mazmanian. 1993. "Social Movements and the Policy Process." *Annals, AAPSS* 528 (July): 75–87.

Rockman, Bert. 1994. "The New Institutionalism and the Old Institutions." In *New Perspectives on American Politics,* edited by Lawrence C. Dodd and Calvin Jillson. Washington, D.C.: CQ Press.

Rodrik, Dani, and Richard Zeckhauser. 1988. "The Dilemma of Government Responsiveness." *Journal of Policy Analysis and Management* 7:601–20.

Rosenau, Pauline Marie. 1992. *Post-modernism and the Social Sciences: Insights, Inroads, and Intrusions.* Princeton, N.J.: Princeton University Press.

Rossi, Peter H., and E. Freeman. 1993. *Evaluation: A Systematic Approach.* 5th edition. Newbury Park, Calif.: Sage.

Ruggie, Mary. 1988. "Gender, Work, and Social Progress: Some Consequences of Interest Aggregation in Sweden." In *The Feminization of the Labor Force,* edited by Jane Jensen, Elizabeth Hagen, and Ceallaigh Reddy. New York: Oxford University Press.

Rule, Wilma, and Joseph S. Zimmerman, eds. 1994. *Electoral Systems in Comparative Perspective: Their Impact on Women and Minorities.* Westport, Conn.: Greenwood Press.

Russett, Bruce, and Harvey Starr. 1989. *World Politics.* 3rd edition. The Menu for Change. New York: W. H. Freeman and Company.

Ryden, Y. 1997. "Policy Networks, Local Discourses, and the Implementation of Sustainable Development." In *The Politics of Sustainable Development: Theory, Policy, and Practice within the European Union,* edited by S. Baker, M. Kousis, D. Richardson, and S. Young. London: Routledge.

Sabatier, Paul A., ed. 1999. *Theories of the Policy Process.* Boulder, Colo.: Westview Press.

Sabatier, Paul A., and Hank C. Jenkins-Smith. 1999. "The Advocacy Coalition Framework: An Assessment." In *Theories of the Policy Process,* edited by Paul A. Sabatier. Boulder, Colo.: Westview Press.

Sachs, Jeffrey. 1989. *Developing Country Debt and the World Economy.* Chicago: University of Chicago Press.

Sagot, Monserrat. 1994. "Women, Political Activism, and the Struggle for Housing: The Case of Costa Rica." In *Women, the Family and Policy: A Global Perspective,*

edited by Esther Ngan-ling Chow and Catherine White Burheide. Albany: State
University of New York Press.

Saint-Germain, Michelle A. 1989. "Does Their Difference Make a Difference? The Impact of Women on Public Policy in the Arizona Legislature." *Social Science Quarterly* 70:956–68.

Sanchez, Patricia Duarte, and Gerardo Gonzalez. 1997. "Unequal Status, Unequal De-
velopment: Gender Violence in Mexico." In *Women Against Violence: Breaking the
Silence: Reflecting on Experience in Latin America and the Caribbean*, edited by
Ana Maria Brasiliero. New York: UNIFEM.

Sanday, Peggy Reeves. 1981. *Female Power and Male Dominance: On the Origins of
Sexual Inequality*. New York: Cambridge University Press.

Sapiro, Virginia. 1981. "When Are Interests Interesting? The Problem of Political Representation of Women." *American Political Science Review* 75, no. 3:701–16.

Saraceno, Chiara. 1987. "Division of Family Labor and Gender Identity." In *Women
and the State: The Shifting Boundaries of Public and Private,* edited by Anne Showstack Sassoon. New York: Routledge.

———. 1994. "The Ambivalent Familism of the Italian Welfare State" *Social Politics* 1:
60–82.

Sartori, Giovanni. 1991. "Comparing and Miscomparing." *Journal of Theoretical Politics* 3, no. 3:243–57.

Saso, Mary. 1990. *Women in the Japanese Workplace*. London: Hilary Shipman.

Sassoon, Anne Showstack, ed. 1987. *Women and the State: The Shifting Boundaries of
Public and Private*. New York: Routledge.

Saunders, Daniel G. 1995. "The Tendency to Arrest Victims of Domestic Violence: A
Preliminary Analysis of Officer Characteristics." *Journal of Interpersonal Violence*
10 (June): 147–58.

Sawer, Marian. 1994. "Locked Out or Locked In? Women and Politics in Australia." In
Women and Politics Worldwide, edited by Barbara J. Nelson and Najma Chowdhury. New Haven, Conn.: Yale University Press.

———. 1995. "'Femocrats in Glass Towers?' The Office of the Status of Women in
Australia." In *Comparative State Feminism,* edited by Dorothy McBride Stetson
and Amy G. Mazur. Thousand Oaks, Calif.: Sage.

Schmitter, Phillippe C. 1982. "Reflections on Neo-corporatism." In *Patterns of Corporatist Policymaking,* edited by Gerhard Lehmbruch and Phillippe C. Schmitter. Sage
Modern Politics Series, vol. 7. Beverly Hills, Calif.: Sage.

———. 1998. "Contemporary Democratization: The Prospects for Women." In
Women and Democracy—Latin America and Central and Eastern Europe, edited
by Jane S. Jacquette and Sharon L. Wolchik. Baltimore: Johns Hopkins University
Press.

Schrier. 1988. *Women's Movements of the World*. A Keesing's Reference Publication.
Phoenix, Ariz.: Oryx Press.

Seager, Joni. 1997. *The State of Women in the World Atlas*. 2nd edition. London: Pen-
guin.

Shaler, Carmel. 1995. "Women in Israel: Fighting Tradition." *Women's Rights, Human
Rights: International Feminist Perspectives,* edited by Julie Peters and Andrea
Wolper. New York: Routledge.

Sharfman, Daphna. 1994. "Women and Politics in Israel." In *Women and Politics*

Worldwide, edited by Barbara J. Nelson and Najma Chowdhury. New Haven, Conn.: Yale University Press.

Shaver, Sheila. 1993. "Body Rights, Social Rights, and the Liberal Welfare State." *Critical Social Policy* 13 (winter): 66–93.

Shugart, Matthew S. 1994. "Minorities Represented and Underrepresented." In *Electoral Systems in Comparative Perspective: Their Impact on Women and Minorities,* edited by Wilma Rule and Joseph S. Zimmerman. Westport, Conn.: Greenwood Press.

Siaroff, Alan. 2000. "Women's Representation in Legislatures and Cabinets in Industrial Democracies." *International Political Science Review,* 21, no. 2:197–215.

Siim, Birte. 1988. "Toward a Feminist Rethinking of the Welfare State." In *The Political Interests of Gender,* edited by Kathleen Jones and Anna Jonasdottir. Newbury Park, Calif.: Sage.

———. 1993. "The Gendered Scandinavian Welfare States." In *Women and Social Policies in Europe: Work, Family, and the State,* edited by Jane Lewis. Brookfield, Vt.: Edward Elgar.

Silver, Brian D., and Kathleen M. Dowley. 2000. "Measuring Political Culture in Multiethnic Societies: Reaggregating the World Values Survey." *Comparative Political Studies* 33, no. 4:517–50.

Singh, Robert. 1998. *The Congressional Black Caucus: Racial Politics in the U.S. Congress.* Thousand Oaks, Calif.: Sage.

Skocpol, Theda. 1979. *States and Social Revolutions: A Comparative Analysis of France, Russia, and China.* Cambridge: Cambridge University Press.

———. 1992. *Protecting Mothers and Soldiers.* Cambridge, Mass.: Harvard University Press.

Smart, Carol. 1992. "Disruptive Bodies and Unruly Sex: The Regulation of Reproduction and Sexuality in the Nineteenth Century." In *Regulating Womanhood: Historical Essays on Marriage, Motherhood, and Sexuality,* edited by Carol Smart. London: Routledge.

Smith, Honor Ford. 1994. "No! to Sexual Violence in Jamaica." In *Women and Violence: Realities and Responses Worldwide,* edited by Miranda Davies. London: Zed Books.

Spain. Instituto de la Mujer. Ministerio de Asuntos Sociales. 1992. *Condigo de conducta para combatir el acoso sexual.* Comision de las Comunidades Europeas, numero 12, serie documentos. Madrid: Instituto de la Mujer.

———. Instituto de la Mujer. Ministerio de Trabajo y Asuntos Sociales. 1996. *Violencia contra las mujeres.* Salud XII. Madrid: Instituto de la Mujer.

———. 1997a. *Mujer, conoce tus derechos.* Madrid: Instituto de la Mujer.

———. 1997b. *III Plan Para la Igualdad de Oportunidades entre Mujeres y Hombres, 1997–2000.* March 7. Madrid.

———. 1998. Correspondence with author, April 22.

Spelman, Elizabeth. 1988. *Inessential Woman.* Boston: Beacon Press.

Sproule, Lynne Dee. 1998. "Between a Rock . . . Finding a New Place." Paper presented to the Fifth Women's Policy Research Conference, Institute for Women's Policy Research, Washington, D.C., June 12–13.

Sproule-Jones, Mark. 1993. *Canadian Parliamentary Federalism and Its Public Policy Effects.* Toronto: University of Toronto Press.

Stake, Robert E. 1995. *The Art of Case Study Research.* Thousand Oaks, Calif.: Sage.

Stämpfli, Regula. 1994. "Direct Democracy and Women's Suffrage: Antagonism in Switzerland." In *Women and Politics Worldwide,* edited by Barbara J. Nelson and Najma Chowdhury. New Haven, Conn.: Yale University Press.

Staudt, Kathleen, ed. 1997. *Women, International Development, and Politics: The Bureaucratic Mire.* Philadelphia: Temple University Press.

Staudt, Kathleen. 1998. *Policy, Politics, and Gender: Women Gaining Ground.* Bloomfield, Conn.: Kumarian Press.

Stetson, Dorothy McBride. 1995. "The Oldest Women's Policy Agency: The Women's Bureau in the United States." In *Comparative State Feminism,* edited by Dorothy McBride Stetson and Amy G. Mazur. Thousand Oaks, Calif.: Sage.

———. 1998. *Women's Rights in the USA.* 2nd edition. New York: Garland.

Stetson, Dorothy, and Amy G. Mazur. 1995. "Introduction." In *Comparative State Feminism,* edited by Dorothy McBride Stetson and Amy G. Mazur. Thousand Oaks, Calif.: Sage.

Stetson, Dorothy McBride, and Amy G. Mazur, eds. 1995. *Comparative State Feminism.* Thousand Oaks, Calif.: Sage.

Steinmo, Sven, Kathleen Thelen, and Frank Longstreth eds. 1992. *Structuring Politics: Historical Institutionalism in Comparative Analysis.* Cambridge: Cambridge University Press.

Stivers, Camilla. 1993. *Gender Images in Public Administration: Legitimacy and the Administrative State.* Newbury Park, Calif.: Sage.

Stone, Deborah. 1997. *Policy Paradox: The Art of Political Decision Making.* New York: Norton.

Sullivan, C. M. 1991. "The Provision of Advocacy Services to Women Leaving Abusive Partners." *Journal of Interpersonal Violence* 6, no. 1:41–54.

Swarup, Hem Lata, Niroj Sinha, Chitra Ghosh, and Pam Rajput. 1994. "Women's Political Engagement in India: Some Critical Issues." In *Women and Politics Worldwide,* edited by Barbara J. Nelson and Najma Chowdhury. New Haven, Conn.: Yale University Press.

Sweden. Equality Affairs Division. Ministry of Labour. 1998. Correspondence with author, February 3.

———. Ministry of Justice, Ministry of Health and Social Affairs, and Ministry of Labour. 1998. *New Measures to Prevent Violence Against Women.* February. N.p.: Government of Sweden.

———. Ministry of Labor. 1997. *Sweden's Follow-Up to the UN Fourth World Conference on Women.* July. <http://www.un.org/womenwatch/followup/national/swedenap.htm>

Switzerland. 1994. *4e Conférence Mondiale de L'ONU sur les Femmes: Lutte pour l'égalité, le développement et la paix, Pékin 1995, Rapport national suisse.* December. N.p.: Government of Sweden.

Tamerius, Karin. 1995. "Sex, Gender, and Leadership in the Representation of Women." In *Gender Power, Leadership, and Governance,* edited by Georgia Duerst-Lahti and Rita Mae Kelly. Ann Arbor: University of Michigan Press.

Tan, Cheribeth, Joanne Basta, Cris Sullivan, and William Davidson. 1995. "The Role of Social Support in the Lives of Women Exiting Domestic Violence Shelters: An Experimental Study." *Journal of Interpersonal Violence* 10, no. 4:437–51.

Tarrow, Sidney. 1996. "Social Movements in Contentious Politics: A Review Article." *American Political Science Review* 90, no. 4:874–83.

———. 1998. *Power in Movement: Social Movements and Contentious Politics.* 2nd edition. Cambridge Studies in Comparative Politics. Cambridge: Cambridge University Press.

Taylor-Goodby, Peter. 1991. "Welfare State Regimes and Welfare Citizenship." *Journal of European Social Policy* 1, no. 2:93–105.

Texas. General Services Commission. 2000. *Historically Underutilized Business.* <http://www.gsc.state.tx.us/hubid/hubindex.html>

Thomas, Sue. 1994. *How Women Legislate.* New York: Oxford University Press.

Tilly, Charles. 1978. *From Mobilization to Revolution.* Reading, Mass.: Addison-Wesley.

———. 1995. *Popular Contention in Great Britain, 1758–1834.* Cambridge, Mass.: Harvard University Press.

Timmerman, Greetje, and Cristien Bajema. "Sexual Harassment in Northwest Europe: A Cross-Cultural Comparison." *European Journal of Women's Studies* 6:419–39.

Tjaden, Patricia, and Nancy Thoennes. 1998. *Prevalence, Incidence, and Consequences of Violence Against Women: Findings from the National Violence Against Women Survey.* Research in Brief. National Institute of Justice, Centers for Disease Control and Prevention. Washington D.C.: U.S. Department of Justice.

Tremblay, Manon. 1998. "Do Female MPs Substantively Represent Women? A Study of Legislative Behaviour in Canada's 35th Parliament." *Canadian Journal of Political Science/Revue canadienne de science politique* 31, no. 3 (September): 435–65.

Tremblay, Manon, and Caroline Andrew, eds. 1998. *Women and Political Representation in Canada.* Ottawa: University of Ottawa Press.

Trotter, Joe William, Jr., and Eric Ledell Smith. 1997. *African Americans in Pennsylvania: Shifting Historical Perspectives.* University Park: Pennsylvania Historial and Museum Commission and The Pennsylvania State University Press.

Truman, David. 1953. *The Governmental Process.* New York: Knopf.

Tuohy, Carolyn. 1992. *Policy and Politics in Canada: Institutionalized Ambivalence.* Philadelphia: Temple University Press.

———. 1993. "Social Policy: Two Worlds." In *Governing Canada: Institutions and Public Policy,* edited by Michael M. Atkinson. Toronto: Harcourt Brace Jovanovich Canada.

United Kingdom. Foreign and Commonwealth Office. 1993. *Women in Britain.* London: Foreign and Commonwealth Office.

———. Women's Unit. n.d. <http://www.womens-unit.gov.uk>

United Nations (UN). 1991. *The World's Women: Trends and Statistics: 1970–1990.* Social Statistics and Indicators, Series K, no. 8. New York: United Nations.

———. 1993. *Declaration on the Elimination of Violence Against Women.* A/Res/48/104. 85th Plenary Meeting. December 20.

———. 1995a. *The Platform for Action: 12 Critical Areas of Concern* and *The Beijing Declaration.* Fourth World Conference on Women, September 4–15, 1995, Beijing. <http:www.un.org.womenwatch/daw/beijing/platform/declar.htm>

———. 1995b. *Report of the Fourth World Conference on Women (Beijing, 4–15 September 1995).* A/CONF.177/20. October 17.

———. 1995c. *The World's Women: Trends and Statistics: Social Statistics and Indicators.* Series K, no. 9. New York: United Nations.

————. Committee on Elimination of Discrimination Against Women (CEDAW). 1988. *Concluding Observations of the Committee on the Elimination of Discrimination Against Women: Jamaica.* 116th Meeting. <http://www.unhcr.ch/tbs/>

————. 1988. *Concluding Observations of the Committee on the Elimination of Discrimination Against Women: New Zealand.* <http://www.unhcr.ch/tbs/doc.nsf/>

————. 1989a. *Concluding Observations of the Committee on the Elimination of Discrimination Against Women: Ireland.* 135th Meeting, February 22.

————. 1989b. *Concluding Observations of the Committee on the Elimination of Discrimination Against Women: Ireland.* 141st Meeting, February 27.

————. 1989c. *Concluding Observations of the Committee on the Elimination of Discrimination Against Women: New Zealand.* <http://www.unhcr.ch/tbs/doc.nsf/>

————. 1994. *Barbados Praised for Efforts to Achieve Gender Equality, at Committee on Elimination of Discrimination Against Women.* Committee on Elimination of Discrimination Against Women, 13th Session, 245th meeting (AM) Press Release Wom.718, January 26.
<gopher://gopher.un.org:70/oo/uncurr/press_releases/WOM/94_01/718>

————. 1994. *Concluding Observations of the Committee on the Elimination of Discrimination Against Women: Barbados.* <http://www.unhcr.ch/tbs/>

————. 1994. *Concluding Observations of the Committee on the Elimination of Discrimination Against Women: Colombia.* <http://www.unhcr.ch/tbs/>

————. 1994. *Concluding Observations of the Committee on the Elimination of Discrimination Against Women: Denmark.* <http://www.unhcr.ch/tbs/>

————. 1994. *Concluding Observations of the Committee on the Elimination of Discrimination Against Women: Japan.* <http://www.unhcr.ch/tbs/>

————. 1994. *Concluding Observations of the Committee on the Elimination of Discrimination Against Women: Netherlands.* <http://www.unhcr.ch/tbs/doc.nsf/>

————. 1994. *Experts at Committee on Elimination of Gender Discrimination Praise Efforts to Advance Women's Status in Colombia.* Committee on Elimination of Discrimination Against Women, 13th Session, 250th Meeting (PM) Press Release Wom.723, January 31.
<gopher://gopher.un.org:70/oo/uncurr/press_releases/WOM/94_01/723>

————. 1994. *Initial Report of the Netherlands.* 234th and 239th Meetings, January 17 and 20, CEDAW/C/SR.234 and 239.CEDAW/C/NET/1 and Add. 1-3.

————. 1995. *Address Given by the Head of the Portuguese Delegation, Her Excellency the Minister for Education, Dr. Manuela Ferreira Leite, to the 4th World Conference on Women.* Beijing, September 5.
<gopher://gopher.un.org:70/oo/conf/fwcw/conf/950905214211 3.txt>

————. 1995. *Concluding Observations of the Committee on the Elimination of Discrimination Against Women: Colombia.* <http://www.unhcr.ch/tbs/>

————. 1995. *Concluding Observations of the Committee on the Elimination of Discrimination Against Women: Mauritius.* <http://www.unhcr.ch/tbs/doc.nsf/>

————. 1995. *Contribution Luxembourgeoise pour la 4e Conférence Mondiale sur les Femmes organisée par l'ONU à Pékin.*
<gopher://gopher.un.org:70/oo/fwcw/conf/gov/950906202748.txt>

————1995. *Examen de los Informes Presentados por los estados partes con arreglo al artí'culo 18 de la Convencio'n sobe la eliminacio'n de todas las formas de discriminacion contra la mujer.* (Terceros informes periodicos de los Estados partes) Venezuela. CEDAW/C/VEN/3 21 de marzo. New York: United Nations.

————. 1995. *Report on Status of Finland's Women Presented to Committee on Elimi-*

nation of Discrimination Against Women. Committee on Elimination of Discrimination Against Women, 14th Session, 272th meeting (PM) Press Release Wom.796, January 24.
<gopher://gopher.un.org:70/oo/uncurr/press_releases/WOM/95_01/796.>

———. 1995. *Statement by Honourable Mrs. Sheilabai Bappoo, Minister of Women's Rights, Child Development and Family Welfare.* Republic of Mauritius. Fourth World Conference on Women, Beijing, September.
<gopher://gopher.un.org:70/oo/conf/fwcw/conf/gov/950912134629.txt>

———. 1995. *Statement by Ms. Felicia Dobunaba, Head of Papua New Guinea Delegation to the Fourth United Nations World Conference on Women, Beijing, China, 11 September, 1995.*
<gopher://gopher.un.org:70/oo/conf/fwcw/conf/gov/950913183413.txt>

———. 1995. *Statement by Ms. Marlene Moses, Head: Republic of Nauru Delegation, Fourth World Conference on Women, Beijing, China, 4–15 September, 1995.*
<gopher://gopher.un.org:70/oo/conf/fwcw/conf/gov/950915030738.txt>

———. 1995. *Swiss Confederation Statement by Federal Councilor Ruth Reifuss, Head of Swiss Delegation to the Fourth World Conference on Women in Beijing, September 4–5, 1995.*
<gopher://gopher.un.org:70/oo/conf/fwcw/conf/gov/950911155038.txt>

———. 1995. *Women's Integration in Mauritius's Development Not Hindered by Structural Adjustment, Women's Committee Is Informed.* Committee on Elimination of Discrimination Against Women, 14th Session, 268th Meeting (PM) Press Release Wom.792, January 20.
<gopher://gopher.un.org:70/oo/uncurr/press_releases/WOM/95_01/792>

———. 1996. *Concluding Observations of the Committee on the Elimination of Discrimination Against Women: Iceland.* <http://www.unhcr.ch/tbs/>

———. 1996. *Iceland's State Treasury to be Responsible for Damages to Victims of Domestic Violence, Anti-discrimination Committee Told.* Committee on Elimination of Discrimination Against Women, 15th Session, 290th Meeting (AM) Press Release Wom.880, January 18.
<gopher://gopher.un.org:70/oo/uncurr/press_releases/WOM/96_01/880>

———. 1997. *Concluding Observations of the Committee on the Elimination of Discrimination Against Women: Luxembourg.* <http://www.unhcr.ch/tbs/doc.nsf/>

———. 1998a. *Forty-Second Meeting of CEDAW: Report.*
<http://www.un.org/womenwatch/daw/csw/42sess.html#official>

———. 1998b. *Report of the Special Rapporteur on Violence Against Women, Its Causes and Consequences.* New York: United Nations.
<http://www.un.org/womenwatch/daw/csw>

———. 1998c. *Thematic Issues Before the Commission on the Status of Women.* E/CN.6/1998/5.

United Nations (UN). Crime and Justice Information Network (UNCJIN). 1996. Fourth United Nations Survey of Crime Trends and Operation of Criminal Justice Systems (1986-1990). Online Dataset.
http://www.uncjin.org/Statistics/WCTS/WCTS4/wcts4.html

——— Development Programme. 1995. *Human Development Report, 1995.* New York: Oxford University Press.

———. Division for the Advancement of Women. 1993. *Directory of National Machinery for Advancement of Women.* Vienna: Division for the Advancement of Women.

———. 1998. *Follow-Up to Beijing: Summary of National Action Plans and Strategies for Implementation of the Platform for Action.* <http://www.un.org/womenwatch/followup/national/>

United Nations. International Criminal Research Institute (UNICRI). 1996. *International Criminal (Victimization) Survey, (IC(V)S).* Rome: UNICRI.

———. Office at Vienna, Center for Social Development and Humanitarian Affairs. 1993. *Strategies for Confronting Domestic Violence: A Resource Manual.* UN/ST/CSDHA/20. New York: United Nations.

———. UNESCO. 1993. *Women in Politics: Australia, India, Malaysia, Philippines, Thailand.* New York: United Nations.

United States. Bureau of Justice Statistics. 1988. *International Crime Rates.* Special Report. Washington, DC: U.S. Department of Justice.

———. 1998. *Violence by Intimates: Analysis of Data on Crimes by Current or Former Spouses, Boyfriends, and Girlfriends.* NCJ-167237. Washington, D.C.: Office of Justice Programs, Bureau of Justice Statistics.

United States. Central Intelligence Agency. 1993. *CIA World Factbook, 1993–1994.* Washington, D.C.: Brassey's.

———. Department of Justice. 1996. *A Community Checklist: Important Steps to End Violence Against Women.* Department of Health and Human Services; Department of Justice. Washington, D.C.

———. n.d. *Domestic Violence Awareness: Stop the Cycle of Violence: What You Can Do.* Department of Health and Human Services; Department of Justice. Washington, D.C.

———. Office of Justice Programs. Bureau of Justice Statistics. 1994. *Criminal Victimization in the United States: 1973–1992 Trends.* A National Crime Victimization Survey Report, NCJ-147006. July. Washington, D.C.

———. Violence Against Women Office. 1998. Telephone interview with author, May 7.

———. n.d. *Violence Against Women Act.* <http://www.usdoj.gov./vawo/vawa/>

United States. Department of Labor, Women's Bureau, and President's Interagency Council on Women. 1996. *Bringing Beijing Home: The Fourth World Conference—A Success for the World's Women.* January. Washington, D.C.

———. Department of State. 1995. *Austria Country Report on Human Rights Practices for 1994.*

———. 1995. *Barbados Country Report on Human Rights Practices for 1994.*

———. 1995. *Belgium Country Report on Human Rights Practices for 1994.*

———. 1995. *Botswana Country Report on Human Rights Practices for 1994.*

———. 1995. *Colombia Country Report on Human Rights Practices for 1994.*

———. 1995. *Denmark Country Report on Human Rights Practices for 1994.*

———. 1995. *Ireland Country Report on Human Rights Practices for 1994.*

———. 1995. *Japan Country Report on Human Rights Practices for 1994.*

———. 1995. *Mauritius Country Report on Human Rights Practices for 1994.*

———. 1995. *Portugal Country Report on Human Rights Practices for 1994.*

———. 1995. *Spain Country Report on Human Rights Practices for 1994.*

———. 1995. *Switzerland Country Report on Human Rights Practices for 1994.*

———. 1995. *Venezuela Country Report on Human Rights Practices for 1994.*

———. 1996. *France Human Rights Practices, 1995.*

———. 1996. *Greece Human Rights Practices, 1995.*

———. 1996. *Iceland Human Rights Practices, 1995.*

————. 1996. *Nauru Human Rights Practices, 1995.*
————. 1996. *Netherlands Human Rights Practices, 1995.*
————. 1997. *1996 Human Rights Report: Australia.*
————. 1997. *1996 Human Rights Report: Italy.*
————. 1997. *1996 Human Rights Report: Jamaica.*
————. 1997. *1996 Human Rights Report: The Netherlands.*
————. 1997. *1996 Human Rights Report: New Zealand.*
————. 1997. *1996 Human Rights Report: Norway.*
————. 1997. *1996 Human Rights Report: Papua New Guinea.*
————. 1997. *1996 Human Rights Report: Switzerland.*
————. 1997. *1996 Human Rights Report: Trinidad and Tobago.*
————. 1997. *1996 Human Rights Report: United Kingdom.*
————. 1997. *1996 Human Rights Report: Bahamas.*
————. 1997. *Barbados Country Report on Human Rights Practices for 1996.*
————. 1997. *Botswana Country Report on Human Rights Practices for 1996.*
————. 1997. *Canada Country Report on Human Rights Practices for 1996.*
————. 1997. *Colombia Country Report on Human Rights Practices for 1996.*
————. 1997. *Costa Rica Country Report on Human Rights Practices for 1996.*
————. 1997. *Denmark Country Report on Human Rights Practices for 1996.*
————. 1997. *Finland Country Report on Human Rights Practices for 1996.*
————. 1997. *Greece Country Report on Human Rights Practices for 1996.*
————. 1997. *Iceland Country Report on Human Rights Practices for 1996.*
————. 1997. *India Country Report on Human Rights Practices for 1996.*
————. 1997. *Ireland Country Report on Human Rights Practices for 1996.*
————. 1997. *Japan Country Report on Human Rights Practices for 1996.*
————. 1997. *Luxembourg Country Report on Human Rights Practices for 1996.*
————. 1997. *Mauritius Country Report on Human Rights Practices for 1996.*
————. 1997. *Spain Country Report on Human Rights Practices for 1996.*
United States. Department of Transportation. 2000. *Disadvantaged Business Enterprise Program.* <http://osdbuweb.dot.gov/business/dbe/dbeqna.html>
————. National Institute of Justice. 1998. Telephone interview with author, May 7.
————. President's Interagency Council on Women. 1996. *U.S. Follow-Up to the U.N. Fourth World Conference on Women.* May.
<gopher://gopher.un.org:70/oo/conf/fwcw/natrep/NatActPlans/usa.txt>
Valenzuela, Maria Elena. 1998. "Women and the Democratization Process in Chile." In *Women and Democracy—Latin America and Central and Eastern Europe,* edited by Jane S. Jacquette and Sharon L. Wolchik. Baltimore: Johns Hopkins University Press.
Valiente, Celia. 1995. "The Power of Persuasion: The Instituto de la Mujer in Spain." In *Comparative State Feminism,* edited by Dorothy McBride Stetson and Amy G. Mazur. Thousand Oaks, Calif.: Sage.
————. 1996. "Gender Equality Policy and Women's Policy Machineries: The Case of Spain." Paper presented at the Annual Meeting of the American Political Science Association, San Francisco, August 29–September 1.
Van der Ros, Janeke. 1994. "The State and Women: A Troubled Relationship." In *Women and Politics Worldwide,* edited by Barbara J. Nelson and Najma Chowdhury. New Haven, Conn.: Yale University Press.
Vargas, Gladys Acosta. 1997. "Women's Human Rights and Latin American Criminal

Law." In *Women Against Violence: Breaking the Silence: Reflecting on Experience in Latin America and the Caribbean,* edited by Ana Maria Brasiliero. New York: UNIFEM.

Vargas, Virginia. 1997. "Introduction." In *Women Against Violence: Breaking the Silence: Reflecting on Experience in Latin America and the Caribbean,* edited by Ana Maria Brasiliero. New York: UNIFEM.

Vargas, Virginia, and Saskia Wierenga. 1998. "The Triangles of Empowerment: Processes and Actors in the Making of Public Policy." In *Women's Movements and Public Policy in Europe, Latin America, and the Caribbean,* edited by Geertje Lycklama à Nijeholt, Virginia Vargas, and Sakia Wieringa. New York: Garland.

Varikas, Eleni. 1995. "Une Représentation en tant que femme? Réflexions critiques sur la demand de la parité des sexes." *Nouvelles questions féministes* 16, no. 2:81–127.

Vickers, Jill, Pauline Rankin, and Christine Appelle. 1993. *Politics as if Women Mattered.* Toronto: University of Toronto Press.

Voet, Rian. 1992. "Political Representation and Quotas: Hannah Pitkin's Concept(s) of Representation in the Context of Feminist Politics." *Acta Politica* 4:191.

Wagar, J. M., and M. R. Rodway. 1995. "An Evaluation of a Group Treatment Approach for Children." *Journal of Family Violence* 10, no. 3:295–307.

Walby, Sylvia. 1990. *Theorizing Patriarchy.* Oxford: Basil Blackwell.

Walby, Sylvia, ed. 1999. *New Agendas for Women.* New York: St. Martin's Press.

Walker, Gillian. 1990. *Family Violence and the Women's Movement: The Conceptual Politics of Struggle.* Toronto: University of Toronto Press.

Walker, Jack L., Jr. 1991. *Mobilizing Interest Groups in America: Patrons, Professions, and Social Movements.* Ann Arbor: University of Michigan Press.

Watson, Sophie, ed. 1990. *Playing the State: Australian Feminist Interventions.* London: Verso.

Weaver, R. Kent, and Bert A. Rockman, eds. 1993. *Do Institutions Matter? Government Capabilities in the United States and Abroad.* Washington, D.C.: Brookings Institution.

Weber, Max. 1992. *The Protestant Ethic and the Spirit of Capitalism.* Translated by Talcott Parsons. New York: Routledge.

Weir, Margaret, Ann Shola Orloff, and Theda Skocpol, eds. 1988. *The Politics of Social Policy in the United States.* Princeton, N.J.: Princeton University Press.

Welch, Susan. 1990. "The Impact of At-Large Elections on the Representation of Blacks and Hispanics." *Journal of Politics* 52, no. 4:1050–76.

Welch, Susan, and Donley T. Studlar. 1990. "Multi-member Districts and the Representation of Women: Evidence from Britain and the United States." *Journal of Politics* 52, no. 2:391–412.

Welch, Susan, and Sue Thomas. 1991. "Do Women in Public Office Make a Difference?" In *Gender and Policymaking: Studies of Women in Office,* edited by Debra L. Dodson. The Impact of Women in Public Office Project. Rutgers, N.J.: Center for the American Woman and Politics.

Weldon, S. Laurel. 1992. "The Shah Bano Controversy: Gender Versus Minority Rights in India." M.A. thesis, Department of Political Science, University of British Columbia, Vancouver.

———. 1999a. "The Committee Model of Representation: The Impact of a Critical Mass." In *Stand! Comparative Politics,* edited by Rebecca Davis. Madison, Wisc.: Coursewise Publishing.

———. 1999b. "Explaining Cross-National Variation in Government Response to Violence Against Women: Women's Movements and Political Institutions in Democratic Policymaking." Ph.D. diss., Graduate School for Public and International Affairs, University of Pittsburgh.

Whyte, John D. 1984. "The Lavell Case and Equality in Canada." *Queen's Quarterly* 81, no. 1 (spring): 28–42.

Wilensky, Harold. 1975. *The Welfare State and Equality.* Berkeley: University of California Press.

Wilensky, Harold, and Charles Lebeaux. 1958. *Industry, Society, and Social Welfare.* New York: Routledge.

Williams, Melissa. 1998. *Voice, Trust, and Memory: Marginalized Groups and the Failings of Liberal Representation.* Princeton, N.J.: Princeton University Press.

Women's Center and Shelter of Greater Pittsburgh. 1998. Correspondence with author.

Women's Electoral Lobby (Australia). 1994. "Submissions Since 1973." <http://wel.org.au/issues/subsidx2.htm>

Women's Research Center (Canada). 1982. *A Study of Protection of Battered Women.* Vancouver: Press Gang Publishers.

World Bank. 1995. *Advancing Gender Equality: From Concept to Action.* Washington, D.C.: World Bank. <http://www.worldbank.org/html/extpb/abshtml/13405.htm>

———. 1998. *Mainstreaming Gender and Development in the World Bank: Progress and Recommendations.* Washington, D.C.: World Bank. <http://www.worldbank.org/html/extpb/abshtml/14262.htm>

Wormald, Eileen. 1994. "Rhetoric, Reality, and a Dilemma: Women and Politics in Papua New Guinea." In *Women and Politics Worldwide,* edited by Barbara J. Nelson and Najma Chowdhury. New Haven, Conn.: Yale University Press.

Yamaguchi, Kazuo. 1991. *Event History Analysis.* Applied Social Research Methods Series, vol. 28. Newbury Park, Calif.: Sage.

Yeatman, Anna. 1990. *Bureaucrats, Technocrats, Femocrats: Essays on the Contemporary Australian State.* Sydney: Allen and Unwin.

Yin, Robert K. 1994. *Case Study Research: Design and Methods.* 2nd edition. Applied Social Research Methods Series, vol. 5. Thousand Oaks, Calif.: Sage.

Yishai, Yael. 1997. *Between the Flag and the Banner: Women in Israeli Politics.* Binghamton, N.Y.: State University of New York Press.

Yoko, Nuita, Yamaguchi Mitsuko, and Kubo Kimiko. 1994. "The U.N. Convention on Eliminating Discrimination Against Women and the Status of Women in Japan." In *Women and Politics Worldwide,* edited by Barbara J. Nelson and Najma Chowdhury. New Haven, Conn.: Yale University Press.

Young, Iris Marion. 1990a. *Justice and the Politics of Difference.* Princeton, N.J.: Princeton University Press.

———. 1990b. "Women and the Welfare State." In her *"Throwing like a Girl" and Other Essays in Feminist Philosophy and Social Theory.* Bloomington: Indiana University Press.

———. 1994. "Gender as Seriality: Thinking About Women as a Social Collective." *Signs: Journal of Women and Culture* 19, no. 3 (spring): 713–38.

———. 1996. "Deferring Group Representation." In *Nomos: Group Rights,* edited by Will Kymlicka and Ian Shapiro. New York: New York University Press.

———. 2000. *Democracy and Inclusion.* Oxford Series in Political Theory. Oxford: Oxford University Press.

Yudelman, Sally. 1997. "The Inter-American Foundation and Gender Issues: A Feminist View." In *Women, International Development and Politics,* edited by Kathleen Staudt. 2nd edition. Philadelphia: Temple University Press.

Zimmerman, Joseph S. 1994. "Equity in Representation for Women and Minorities." In *Electoral Systems in Comparative Perspective: Their Impact on Women and Minorities,* edited by Wilma Rule and Joseph S. Zimmerman. Westport, Conn.: Greenwood Press.

Index

Aboriginal and Torres Strait Islanders Commission (ATSIC), 144–45, 162
aboriginal women, 177, 201, 206, 208–9; Australia and, 144–46; Canada and, 152–53; marginalization and, 159–62
abortion, 55, 73, 207
accountability, 130–33, 199
activism, 65–66, 198; accountability and, 130–33; Canada and, 154–56, 200; conceptualization of, 171–73; effectiveness and, 126–33, 139; global approach and, 206; movements as reactions to structure, 183–89; political institutions and, 113; poverty and, 131. *See also* women's movements
actors, political, 107–8; gender and, 110–11; institutional bias and, 119–22
administrative structure, 107–10; bias and, 119–22; feminist institutionalism and, 122–26; structural approach and, 189–90. *See also* structural approach
advisory councils, 198
Advocacy Coalition Framework (ACF), 170
advocacy structures, 15, 198–99
Africa, 41; institutional bias and, 120; regionalism and, 39–40
African Americans, 21; Confederate flag and, 185–86; economic issues and, 10; representation of interests and, 176; women's agenda and, 71, 73
alcohol, 12, 20
anti-dowry violence movement (ADVM), 64
Arbeitsstab Frauenpolitik (Germany), 125
Asia, 39, 41
Australia, 5, 24, 200; aboriginal women and, 144–45; autonomy and, 102, 142–48; beginning action on violence, 143–44; coordinating authority for violence against women and, 16; effectiveness and, 132; expansion of response, 144, 146–47; federalism and, 118; inclusion

and, 202; institutionalism and, 125, 127, 129–30; labor parties and, 56–58; legal reform and, 20, 30–31; marginalization and, 159, 161–62, 199; maternity leave and, 45–46; police training and, 2–3; policy analysis of, 147–48; targeted programs of, 145–46; WEL and, 97; women's movements and, 65
Austria: labor parties and, 55–56; legal reform and, 31–32; maternity leave and, 45
autonomy: articulation and, 64; Australia and, 102, 142–48; bureaucracy and, 81–82; Canada and, 148–56; coalitions and, 200; cross-national analysis and, 83–84, 140; effectiveness and, 139; future directions for, 208–9; importance of, 84–85; inclusion and, 202–4; independence and, 201; institutional interaction and, 139–41; male dominance and, 82–83; perspective articulation and, 79–83. *See also* women legislators

backlash, 109
Bahamas, 31–32
Bano, Shah, 109
Barbados, 31–32
battered women's movement (BWM), 64
Begin, Monique, 100
Beijing Conference, 19, 74–75, 205–6
Belgium, 9, 45, 132
bias. *See* gender
Biden, Joseph, 100, 142
Botswana, 31–32; institutionalism and, 125; regionalism and, 39–40
Brazil, 16
Britain: centralization and, 115–16; corporatism and, 117; women legislators and, 88
Brundtland, Gro Harlem, 93
Buchanan, John, 55
Buddhism, 42